Hesther

by

S. J. Johnson

Copyright 2024 S. J. Johnson

ISBN: 978-1-917129-55-8

All rights reserved. No part of this publication may be reproduced or transmitted in any form or by any means, electronic or mechanical including photocopying, recording or any information storage or retrieval system, without prior permission in writing from the author.

Prologue

She watches them embrace. Velvet butterfly wings flutter somewhere deep within her belly. Sometimes it feels like a pair of sparring pigeons, but not today. Today it's just a benign reminder of life, a gentle caress from her unborn child. She watches their lips draw together. They kiss with the solemn fervor of youth. Kissing for the sake of kissing, something mystifying to her. She seeks solace from the cool solidity of the lamp post. A mellow August dusk shrouds their bodies, until they appear as one; a two headed creature dwelling in the shadow lands. A sudden beam of light illuminates her lair, but she knows from experience they will not see her. Her advantage lies in teenage infatuation, a world boiled down to two.

Limbs disentangle, until she can make out the figures of a boy and a girl. The boy leaves the girl at the corner of the street. The girl never looks back, walks, hesitantly at first, then with a fierce fortitude down the tree lined Avenue, through imposing iron gates, ready to be swallowed whole by a hulking crimson door. The boy watches until she's out of sight, pushes his hands deep into the pockets of a pair of threadbare jeans, begins to drift home, a two up two down in the oldest part of town. She used to follow him. But it's not the boy who interests her.

She pushes through the hedge at its weakest point, slides down onto a satin smooth lawn. The temperature is falling, she wraps the folds of her cardigan around bare legs, looks up at the closed curtains, behind which she can imagine the girl scribbling frantically with a freshly sharpened pencil. It's Thursday, so the girl's sandals will lie abandoned on top of a pile in the corner of the hallway. Tomorrow she will place each discarded item back to its rightful place.

Tomorrow is the day the girl's life will come crumbling down around her. She made the first call earlier today, from a phone box on the other side of town. It didn't go quite as planned, coins expiring almost as swiftly as her frantic words. Tomorrow for the first time in over two years, she will look into those hazel eyes, smile gently, say the words out loud, words she's dreamt of since it started.

As she walks home, the butterflies mutate into anxious bats. She strokes the unfamiliar roundness of her belly. This life inside her was never part of the plan. But she can see clearly now, the baby is her reward. Finally they are bonded by blood. Finally they are a family.

Chapter 1

Stuart

Sarah's cooking. Something's afoot. When Sarah cooks, I mean really cooks, there's always some hidden meaning behind it. By the look of the kitchen this is a full orchestral symphony, rather than a simple bowl of pasta. Keith Floyd rests knowingly on the burgundy iron book stand her parents gave her last Christmas. When Keith comes out to play, we both know it's serious. She wafts around the kitchen, bathed in a fragrant haze of garlic and herbs.

I long since learned my role in performances such as these. We consume the culmination of her exertions in quiet contemplation, savour each mouthful, without so much as a newspaper for company. Then when sated, engage in a period of constructive criticism, over coffee from beans grown on a small family farm in Kenya, available only from Harrods for the price of a small second hand car. Our analysis of the culinary masterpiece will determine whether the dish will ever grace our table again.

I'm in deperate need of a shower, can still smell her on me. My head's throbbing from beer, heat and repulsion. Sarah hands me a large glass of Rioja, all hope of cleansing Lexie from my skin, then slipping between cool linen sheets fades away.

'I'm going to Chelmney tomorrow. Mummy can't cope ... The time has come ... She's completely worn out, poor thing ... We mustn't judge her Stu, it's not a decision she's come to lightly, you know that don't you. It's my weekend off, I'll stay til Monday, I'm on a late shift, so I'll drive back in the morning. There's tons in the freezer, you can just warm something -'

'I'll come with you.' The words surprise me as much as they appear to surprise her. 'I want to be there for you ... All of you, I mean. Help with the move. You shouldn't have to do this on your own. You know how much I think of your father.'

I really do admire Ron, he's the sort of straight down honest, dependable man who didn't deserve to have a stroke in his sixties. We all hoped that he'd make a stronger recovery, but instead he's become weaker over time, and can only manage to spit out the odd unintelligible word. Mary remained her usual stoical self, but even she has her limits, it would seem. Since the stroke I've tried to avoid visits. Seeing an intelligent, previously robust, paragon of a man, a man who could argue me under the table, but always with tact and humility, reduced to a fading body in a wheelchair is just too much to bear. It's no mystery why I've volunteered to go tomorrow. If Sarah leaves without me, I'll have no option but to call the number scrawled on a bus ticket in my trouser pocket. The prospect of that is far, far worse than a visit to Chelmney, however depressing the circumstances.

My wife looks tired. Adversity looks good on Sarah; grief, a hangover, sickness, stress, exhaustion. Any form of suffering simply accentuates her beauty. My wife is one of the most beautiful women I've ever seen, in real life at least. Not in a beauty from the inside kind of way, but in an objective, non-debatable kind of way. From the way some men look at her, if she'd married anyone but me, the poor sod would probably be serving a life sentence behind bars by now. She's been working extra shifts at the hospital and it looks like it's finally catching up with her.

There's no denying the meal's a roaring success. Lamb melts away from the bone, kissed by a velvety red wine sauce. Golden potatoes when sliced with one of the silver knives we keep for special occasions, have cloud soft innards. A thoughtful selection of vegetables have been steamed to perfection. Lexie's cheap, overly sweet perfume assaults my nostrils, the thought of my hands on her spongy body fills me with disgust. My wife is freshly showered, delicately fragrant, enveloped in a pure silk robe, damp hair falling heavily half way down her slender back.

We eat in silence, which is some sort of blessing. I gulp at my wine for company, Sarah barely touches hers. She's distracted, which is understandable, she dotes on her father. One of the things I admire about her is she sees no need for small talk. It's purposeful debate, or nothing, which from my limited experience of women, is rare. She even spares me the post meal assessment, making her intentions of an early night quite clear.

Under a scorching shower, half a bottle of Sarah's lavender gel removes all traces of Lexie from my skin. Before tossing my work trousers into the basket, I remember to salvage the bus ticket and entomb it deep inside the bin. Between crisp linen sheets, Sarah slips in lightly beside me. The familiar smell of mint and cucumber is a comfort balm after a trying day. Tonight for the first time in weeks, she turns away, rather than reaching for me. Within minutes her breath comes deep and even.

Five months ago over bowls of spaghetti with lobster and clams at our local Italian, she made the devastating announcement that she wanted a baby. Our baby. It felt like an extinct volcano erupting and burying me alive in molten lava. We'd always operated under the implicit agreement that babies were not part of us, babies were for other people. Sarah nurses children every day, but she leaves them behind at the end of each shift. Her home is her sanctuary. She point blank refuses to speak to me for a week, if I eat a packet of crisps on her crushed velvet sofa.

Her decision was non-negotiable. All Sarah's decisions are non-negotiable. Not realising the futility of her actions, virtually every night since, she's insisted on trying. I thought she'd tire of the idea, it's by no means her favourite way to pastime, in fact before the baby thing we'd practically given up on the whole thing. But she's been dogmatic in her endeavours, perhaps this Ron thing will distract her, give her time to think, to change her mind. As I drift off to sleep, I cling tightly to that thin thread of hope.

Chapter 2

Marnie

There was a trial at Brimfield crown court. It was a couple of years ago now. A group of girls from our home were the so called victims. It was all over the bloody Gazette, like they were famous or something, the seedy reporters couldn't get enough. Nothing like that ever happened in Brimfield, in fact nothing at all really happened in Brimfield. Six men were tried, all old, ugly as you like. Except for one, he was younger, maybe seventeen or eighteen, ok looking I suppose, for a boy. They said the men made friends with the girls, just to make it easier to do the things they wanted to do, which turned out to be not very friendly at all. That made me and Charlie howl. We knew that girls like Rose-May, Louise and Charmaine were dumb as pig swill, but anyone with even half a brain cell would have been able to see men like that were not friend material, even if you were desperate as fuck like Louise.

They got twelve years, the men. I felt a bit sorry for them, at the time. To my reckoning, the brain dead girls got exactly what they deserved, especially that cow Charmaine. After what they said happened to her before she came to the home, you'd have thought she'd have known better. After the trial Rose-May turned really weird, even weirder than normal. She kept moping about with this stupid dreamy look on her face, refused to eat at meal times, even though she was already skinny as a stray cat on a building site.

One day I was in the toilets, when I overheard her talking to a girl called Suzy. Rose-May was actually crying, said she was going to wait for the younger one called Craig to get out of prison. They were going to get married, live in a house with kids. I would've pissed myself laughing, if I hadn't already just pissed. There was no way someone that good looking was ever going to marry someone like Rose-May, even if he was a convicted sex offender.

A few days later the silly cow went missing. Eventually the police found her body in the canal, I don't think they were looking very hard because it took them ages to find her, even though the canal was only round the corner from the home. No one really missed her anyway, but she was all over the Gazette. She would've loved that, being the centre of attention, classic narcissistic personality disorder, if I ever saw it. It was the only way someone as ugly as her would ever get their picture all over the front pages, and at least she never had to wait for Craig not to marry her, so it all worked out for the best in the end, I suppose.

When me and Charlie were kids, eleven or twelve, I met this guy called Simon. It was nothing like the dumb girls and trial men, I never really saw him as a friend, just felt sorry for him under the circumstances. He told me I reminded him of his daughter, who was with his wife somewhere abroad. It was something about not having the right papers, which seemed crazy to me at the time, splitting up a perfectly good family who wanted to be together, all because of some bloody stupid papers, when we girls were left to rot in a manky home because our families didn't want us, it just didn't make sense.

He liked to buy me things, sweets, pop, magazines, said it made him feel less guilty about his daughter. After a bit, he started taking me to the wimpy bar in town, just for the company, I suppose. I didn't tell Charlie, he'd have had a hissy fit, been jealous as hell. Charlie used to stay in the home while I went to school. Education just isn't his thing, but this one day, he came to meet me, which was lucky because my bag was crammed full of science books, and he's stronger than me. He can be thoughtful like that, but only when it suits him.

We walked home, Charlie mucking around like a mad thing as usual. Simon pulled over, offered me a lift home, burger and chips on the way. The food at the home was rank, so the burger did it for Charlie and he jumped in before I could stop him. He was good as gold, filling his face in the Wimpy. When we got back in the car, Simon started driving in the wrong direction. I thought his mind must be on his family, all those miles away, and for a second wished he was my dad instead. I told him to turn round, but he just kept on driving, as if he was in a dream or something. Charlie was getting well spooked by that point, which of course made me panic.

Eventually we pulled into a car park in front of some old factory. There were no other cars, just tons of rubbish, a pile of old tyres and a broken down ice cream van. Charlie was seething and there was nothing on earth I could've done to calm him down. Then Simon grinned at me, said he was going to treat me to something way better than a burger, something just for grown-ups. I couldn't see it, not there on a tip in the middle of bloody nowhere.

After that it was all a blur, which it always is when Charlie takes over. Simon slid his hand high up my school skirt. I thought he must be having some sort of episode, due to the grief of losing his family. Then I heard this howl, like a wounded wolf. Charlie grabbed me, pulled me from the car, as I looked back blood was soaking through Simon's jeans. I didn't want to leave him, it didn't seem fair, but Charlie dragged me and we ran like a pair of hyenas, until the car park was out of sight.

When we stopped, Charlie opened his hand, my maths compass was covered in something sticky and red. At the time, I convinced myself it was ink, but of course it was really blood. I could still kill Charlie for doing it. It took us ages to get home, we missed dinner, but at least we'd had the burgers. I never saw Simon again, but often thought about his daughter, having a dad who missed her so much, he literally lost his mind with grief. I locked Charlie in the hole for three days as a punishment, then forgave him like I always do.

My mother just didn't want me. It's as simple as that. I'm only here in Chelmney-On-Sea because of her, I wish I'd never bothered.

These days you can get out of prison in a couple of years, they obviously haven't got enough, you don't see a prison on every corner, do you. Charmaine and Louise better watch their backs, after what they said at the trial. The stupid cows didn't even think to leave Brimfield when they were released from the home. I'm never stepping foot within a hundred miles of the shitty place ever again.

She lived here when she was a kid, but she's not here now.

When you turn sixteen you have to leave the home, they virtually pack your bags for you. She left here before I was born, her and my grandparents. When I came here I had no feelings for her, just curiosity. Now I hate her.

We used to make up stories about our mothers, stories which changed from day to day. Some of the girls could remember their real mothers, remember being taken or given away. But even those girls made up stories, it was easier that way. I found the house where she used to live. It's the wrong sort of house for a girl who gave away her baby. It's like the Miss Havisham mansion, without the decay and an old woman in a wedding dress. A man was sweeping the drive next door, he said they left in the early nineteen seventies, just went one day, the house put up for sale.

When I finish college, I'm going to study at Oxford University. Just two more years in this dump. I haven't told Charlie about college yet, never mind university. Charlie thinks education is for losers. Sometimes I just stand in front of her house. A family live there now, mother and father, three young boys. It's hard to imagine her inside those walls, doing ordinary stuff like cleaning her teeth, brushing her hair. All that space just for three people.

Charlie's wrong about education. You can never have enough. Someone once said knowledge is power, it's more than that, it shows you're not stupid and lazy like Charmaine and Louise, like the nuns who only became nuns because it was the easy thing to do. Knowledge gives you freedom, which is way better than power, and one day I'll prove to Charlie that I freed us through hard work and determination from all the crap in the world. If he had his way we'd sit at home all day eating crisps and drinking lager.

Boys stare at me all the time, think I don't notice, boys are brainless idiots. Soon after we arrived here, a lad called Ray asked us to join him and some mates who were hanging out by the toilets on the harbour. Her handed me a can of lager, which Charlie polished off. We had quite an interesting conversation about the Pygmalion effect, with particular emphasis on research by Rosenthal, turned out Ray had been in prison for aggravated burglary, got himself an 'A' level in psychology, grade B, which was quite an achievement, considering the circumstances. Charlie didn't like it, was jealous as fuck, he hates it when people like me. Especially smart people like Ray. He sulked all the way home, when it should've been me who was pissed at him after what he did when Ray put his arm round me. I let him punish me, then we watched a stupid game show and ate crisps until bed time.

This morning Charlie was sleepy, so he didn't kick up too much of a fuss when I left him at home. It's warm and sunny for once, not the sort of day to be lounging around in the flat with the curtains closed. Charlie can be a paranoid sod, when he wants to be. The three boys are out playing in the garden, they don't notice me, but the mother comes out, looks at me like I'm trash. It's a public road, I hate her almost as much as I hate my own mother.

Time for an adventure. Time to get out of this cesspit of a town for a few hours. Charlie can rot in the flat if he wants to, but I'm taking the train to somewhere.

Chapter 3

Stuart

'It's awful Mummy, far too small, there's a funny smell ... Musty ... Surely there must be somewhere better than this.'

'Look Darling I've searched, rooms in Chelmney are difficult to find. All the blasted Londoners send their loved ones here for a peaceful retirement by the sea. To assuage the guilt, I suppose ... Of abandoning them in their time of need ... That bit too far for regular visits. Most of the poor souls never catch so much as a glimpse of the sea, they could be anywhere. Most places want a small fortune, take advantage of the situation. I know we're not badly off, but I don't want to sell the house. We've been there so long, I couldn't bear the thought of leaving ... This is hard enough, without the disruption of moving ... Daddy wouldn't want it, you know that, don't you.'

'What about that place on Burnham Hill, the Victorian building with the turrets?'

'Darling, it's more than two thousand a week, a waiting list longer than the Nile.' Mary wipes away an invisible tear. 'You know that this is the last thing I want to do, don't you. I don't like to worry you ... You both work so hard ... Stuart said you've been doing extra shifts. There's no need Darling, you look peaky, you know you can ask me if -'

'I'm fine, we've been short staffed, that's all. If this really is the only option, let's take it for now. You've been amazing ... Since the stroke ... Hasn't she Stu ... But you need to look after yourself now, daddy will be well cared for here, even if it is a little rough around the edges. What do you think Stu?'

The question I was dreading. It's grim. They've done their best to make it homely, but it's not a home anyone would choose to live in.

'Well ... I mean he'll be properly cared for here ... Not that you didn't, Mary ... Care for him properly, but we're all getting older, it's a full time job ... A job for the professionals.'

Mary looks as immaculate as ever. I've never seen her without a full face of make-up. Her hair hints at a full morning in the salon, her outfit carefully curated. She's never once appeared at the breakfast table in her dressing down and slippers. She's up with the lark, fragrant, polished, fully attired, right down to a pair of polished court shoes. When Ron had the stroke, her standards never slipped an inch.

My mother died before I met Sarah. If she and my father had still been alive, I would never have been welcomed into the Parker-Forest family. In contrast to Mary, mum would think nothing of spending a full week in the same nightdress, a constant stream of Sherry blurring the boundaries between night and day, until in a moment of clarity she'd experience a sudden urge to slop a generous dollop of antiseptic into the bath, fill it to the brim and attempt to expunge her frail body of stale alcohol and cigarette smoke.

Ron's at home under the watchful eye of an obliging neighbour. Mary didn't see the need to give him a choice as to his future living arrangements. He's gone downhill since I last saw him at Christmas, so thin his belt wraps double round his waist. Mary puts almost as much effort into her husband's appearance as her own. No comfy track suits for Ron. He appears each morning dressed in a suit and tie, as if he's about to grab his briefcase and drive off to the office.

Bluebell Wood, Rest Home for Retired Gentlefolk is displayed proudly on a wooden sign on the freshly cut front lawn. It comes as a relief that neither of my parents could have been described as gentlefolk, and they both drank themselves to death, long before any prospect of retirement.

After making our escape, in an attempt to lighten the mood, I suggest a quick lunch. To my surprise they both agree to the idea. We stroll down to the harbour, the sun high in the sky. It's one of the rare days in Chelmney you could accurately describe as summer. The water, usually a matte grey, sparkles like dancing diamonds. We choose a table outside Sarah's favourite seafood restaurant, where diners can watch boats laden with crab and lobster being unloaded.

One summer during the school holidays, I worked on a

fishing boat. For the first week I was convinced death was imminent. My guts extracted every nutrient from my body. Ropes threatened to trip or throttle me. High seas almost had me overboard on more than one occasion. By the second week I found my sea legs, fell in love with the open waters. Terror became a thrill ride, so I decided school was a waste of time, I had a trade, I was earning money, and more importantly I had muscles for the first time in my life.

When the truancy officer called, my mother was far from sober. I returned home later that afternoon, a little worse for wear myself, after consuming the obligatory four pints in the Old Grapes Inn. Her eyes were more bloodshot than usual, she'd been crying. I never bothered telling my parents about my new career, assuming they wouldn't give a flying gin bottle whether I was staring through a classroom window, or risking life and limb at sea.

She told me to sit down, opened her purse. I thought she'd ask me to go to the corner shop for booze and fags. Instead she put her hand on mine, said if I went back to school, she'd promise to give up the drink, get a job, pay me double the amount I was earning at sea.

I went back to school, not for the money, but because of the look of terror in her misty eyes when she said I was going to turn out just like my father. I never took a penny from her, something which fills me with guilt to this day. Somewhere deep down, I didn't want her sober, leaving the house, mixing with other people. I knew she'd meet someone, leave us, get a brand new shiny family. Drunk, she was mine, so I watched on silently as she slowly and deliberately drowned herself in the sticky amber liquid.

'Shall we have some wine, I know it's lunch time, but it -'

'Oh yes Stuart, I think we all deserve it. We don't get to see you both together very often these days … You work too hard, but that's London for you, everyone rushing round like mad things. Ron could have earned more in London, but he refused to leave Chelmney, he wasn't … I mean isn't, a London sort of man.'

The waiter pours chilled Sancerre, lingering a little longer than necessary by Sarah's chair. Over plates of pearly fish, fresh from this morning's catch, we attempt to distract ourselves from the Ron situation, seek comfort in the banal. Mary takes centre stage, regaling us with tales of the ineptitude of Chelmney parish council, the rudeness of the young cashiers at the new supermarket in town.

'You've hardly touched your wine Sarah, I ordered Sancerre because it's your favourite.'

'Oh, don't fuss Stu, I'm not in the mood that's all, I -'

'You know you really do look tired Darling, I hope you're looking after her Stuart. You really should go for that management position, she can reduce her hours.'

'I'm fine ... Really Mummy. Just upset about daddy, that's all, we are doing the right thing ... Aren't we?'

'Look, I'll go for a stroll after lunch give you a couple of hours to break the news to Ron.'

They don't try to persuade me otherwise. It was always just the three of them, before I came along. They treat me like a bit player, someone who comes and goes, adds little to the plot, which makes it easier for me to get out of difficult family discussions.

They leave arm in arm, Mary flushed from two glasses of wine. I drift in the soft afternoon sunshine, arrive where I always do, at our bench. Bertie and Ethel are still resting peacefully with an eternal ocean view, so I rub the brass plaque with my handkerchief until it gleams, in honour of them, more importantly in honour of you.

The route to the park is so familiar, I hardly notice the journey. It's all different now. The iron monstrosities we used to love; gigantic slide, roundabout which took great delight in tossing tender limbs onto unforgiving concrete, ancient seesaw which planted many a splinter into your bare legs, are all long gone. Plastic imitations stand in their place, smaller, kinder, designed not for fun, but for the risk free demands of modern life. We would wait until the little kids dragged themselves home for tea. Then it was our turn to play. We dressed like teenagers, talked like teenagers, but we were children, both reluctant to dive into the perilous waters of adolescence.

Each summer the field behind the playground was a medley of wild flowers. A glorious carpet of colour, laid out just for us.

We used to bask for hours, framed by fragrant blooms, picnic on penny sweets and lollies which stained our mouths deep red, then kiss diligently, until every last trace of sugar melted away. It's a sports facility now, complete with rubber running track.

On a slow walk back to Mary's I let the memories flood my head. The Princess Cinema, now a bingo hall. The soft weight of your head on my shoulder as we watched *Antony And Cleopatra,* waking as the curtains closed, my shirt dripping with your tears. Your arm around my neck, as we watched the horror films we both hated, but pretended to love.

Mary will be planning supper by now. Meals are never missed in Mary's house, whatever the circumstances. The temptation's too strong to resist. I need to see your house. Sometimes I imagine you'll walk out of the door, run to me, that smile on your face that could bring a tear to my eye. Today is different, today I know I'll never see that smile again. Long gone are the neat rows of roses, the perfectly cut emerald lawn. Now a field of concrete lies littered with abandoned toys, a plastic slide set and a trampoline.

It took me three days in order to summon up the courage to come here, after you failed to show up at our meeting spot. The stillness was almost deathly, curtains neither fully open or closed, as if the person who pulled them couldn't choose between eternal day or eternal night. It was a house left in limbo, just like me. A month later a for sale sign appeared in the middle of the overgrown lawn. A few weeks later it disappeared, the curtains and windows opened to the world, a pile of boxes piled high on the driveway.

As I head back to Mary's, the town's all but vanished. A cumbrous sea fret hangs over Chelmney, like a damp grey sheet. The chill reaches through my summer clothes, right down to the bone. This is a regular occurrence here, comes from nowhere, even on the warmest of days. The only discernible outline is St Bart's steeple, hanging churchless in the sky. A coach regurgitates its load of tourists, they hover like a herd of bewildered cattle, straining their eyes for the promised view, dressed for summer, totally ill prepared for our town's little foible.

We eat a simple supper of homemade quiche with a leafy

salad. Ron attempts to maneuver his fork in the vague direction of his mouth, Mary takes over, feeding him tiny mouthfuls, leaving enough time between each one for the painstaking process of chewing. Her own meal remains untouched.

'I do wish you'd consider a private hospital, Sarah, they wouldn't expect you to work such ridiculously long hours. The NHS is on its knees as usual, Margaret's doing her best, but James and Harold all but brought it to a state of collapse. You could work part time, look after yourself, let Stuart take the reins.'

Mary's never worked a day in her life for anything so vulgar as money. Although she's never said quite as much, in her opnion I'm failing as a husband, by not earning enough to keep my wife at home in her rightful place, even though the woman she considers to be a living saint is running the country. She met Ron at the age of sixteen, waited like a well trained dog until he graduated from law school, secured his hand in marriage on her nineteenth birthday. In their wedding photo they look like statues with porcelain faces which would crack with the merest hint of a smile. Perhaps it was the prospect of marriage without parole. At least we can afford a smirk now, if it all goes horribly wrong, we have a simple get out clause. I'm pretty certain Mary would have stayed with Peter Sutcliffe, even Dr. Crippen, rather than face the public humiliation of divorce. Luckily she got the long straw with Ron.

Sarah sighs deeply, then blesses us with one of her beatific smiles.

'I was going to wait … But I think now's the time to tell you all. It's still early days.' Her gaze rests on her father, she reaches across the table, takes his withered hand in hers, then turns to me. 'It's happened Stu … We're pregnant … I'm going to have a baby.'

Mary's out of her seat in a flash, pats me on the back, kisses her daughter on the cheek.

'Oh Darling, that's such wonderful news. I'm going to be a grandmother, at last.' Ron makes a grunting sound, like he's got something stuck in his throat. Mary strokes his wisps of hair, and he shuts his eyes. 'Of course you'll give up work now, won't you.'

To my amazement, Sarah nods serenely, places a protective hand over the flatness of her belly.

'Yes of course Mummy. Nothing will happen to this baby ... I promise you, I'll protect her with my life.'

'You know the sex already, how far -'

'No Mummy, but she's a girl, I can just feel it.'

The shock renders me almost speechless, like I've been swallowed whole by an avalanche.

'Are you sure ... I mean have you been to a doctor, you must -'

Mary looks at me like I've just admitted to murder.

'Of course she's been to a doctor, Stuart, she's not stupid, she works in a hospital for God's sake.'

'I did three tests, and went to the doctors. You are thrilled, aren't you Stu?'

'Of course I'm thrilled ... It was a shock ... That's all, I never thought we'd -'

'I'll come to London, when daddy's settled. Help with the nursery, take you to Bond Street for baby clothes.'

Mary opens a bottle of port left over from Christmas. They talk baby; names, nurseries, even bloody schools. It's too much for me, so I take a tumbler of port out into the garden. The air is cool and fragrant. Since the stroke Mary employs a gardener for a few hours twice a week. Ron was the gardener of the family, Mary more the general manager. She would like a cleaner, but doesn't trust anyone to keep their home up to her own exacting standards. On the stone bench I try to arrange my thoughts. Sarah would never tell her parents she was having a baby if it wasn't true, especially on Ron's last night at home. If she is pregnant, she's made it clear she wants me to play the role of father. The question is can I do it.

Chapter 4

Sarah

The funny thing about Stu, is that he honestly believes he has secrets from me. He had a vasectomy, about a year after we married, came home from work pale as a waxwork dummy, swallowed three paracetamol with his wine. Stu never takes pills if he can help it. I found an appointment card for a private clinic in his jacket pocket, wrongly assumed he'd caught something nasty from one of his floozies. A quick call the next day, claiming to be the practice nurse from our GP surgery informed me of the fact that he'd rendered us infertile for life. At the time I was pleased he'd taken the initiative. Initiative is something Stuart rarely shows. I didn't want a baby after what happened last time, plus it meant there was no risk of a knock at the door in sixteen years time from the offspring of one of his tarts.

It was an unexpected tsunami of longing. Came from nowhere, knocked me senseless. A baby, my baby, my own flesh and blood resting in my arms. My daughter was ready to come back. My husband being inoperative in that department, meant I had to find another way. Stuart is lazy. More than that he hates a scene. We never argue, because giving in takes less effort than putting up a fight. It was meant to be. My husband is far from ideal father material, biologically at least. He will stand by me as I raise my daughter, no questions asked, rather than admit to the snip.

'If it's a boy, you could name him Winston. We were going to call you Winston, if you'd been a boy, have I told you that before ... I don't believe I have, we could -'

Daddy stirs in his sleep. I wish he could tell me that he understands, that he knows she's coming back.

'No, I've told you, she's a girl. A mother can feel these things, you should know that. I think we'll move house, somewhere with more room … The country perhaps. Stu can commute.'

He made his escape into the garden. This must have been one hell of a shock for him. When mummy runs out of steam, she goes upstairs to put daddy to bed for the last time. I wonder if she'll have the chair lift removed when he's gone. He comes in smelling of fresh air and alcohol, slumps like a sack of coal on daddy's leather armchair. This the moment of reckoning. If he's going to say anything about the baby, it's now when we're alone.

'I think I'll go home tomorrow. It'll be easier for Ron … Just the three of you. You can drive him. I'll take the train back to London. You need to look after yourself now, so no heavy lifting tomorrow.'

It's over. He's going to be her dad.

He goes up to bed. I never intended to break the news like this, in front of my parents, but it turned out to be perfect, he would never cause a scene here, and now it's too late. He was hollow when I met him, in desperate need of something to give him substance, that could've been anything, because the one thing he really wanted, he couldn't have. He belongs to me now, we're going to be a family, and finally that might just be enough.

Chapter 5

Stuart

It's only five-thirty. If I'm quick I can get away before Mary emerges from her room. I throw on yesterday's clothes, Sarah doesn't stir. Her dark hair lies in a silky cascade across the pillow, her face is flushed with sleep. I feel the urge to kiss her flawless cheek, but don't want to wake her, so leave quietly.

The early morning air is cool, but the sky predicts a dazzler of a day. The street's empty except for the milk float rattling along. Ron and Mary have been waking up to two fresh pints of Jersey milk, faithfully delivered by George for years. I expect Mary will reduce her order to one now. Mary rewards George diligently each Christmas, with a good bottle of Claret, and a whole Stilton. He doesn't look like a Claret sort of man, and he owns a bloody dairy. A gift of anything so vulgar as cold hard cash would be too much for Mary to bear.

Strolling towards the station, my mind drifts back to old Chelmney. Our Chelmney. The real Chelmney, rather than this imposter that somehow managed to wheedle its way in during the last decade. Real Chelmney was built for fun, for recreation, for entertainment, somewhere to escape to from the rigours of industrial life. We used to joke that it was our town, designed for the two of us alone. Now our Xanadu is a mecca for retirees flocking from London and the home counties to end their days by the sea. Long gone are the funfairs, football pitch sized ice rink, the numerous moth bitten cinemas, a mile long pier hosting all manner of wondrous amusements.

At the end of the pier stood a ramshackle wooden theatre. We used to sneak in when no one was watching, listen to bawdy comedians tell jokes we could only pretend to understand. One night the porter forgot to lock the stage door, one of the young actresses hanging on his arm as he left. We played out half learned scenes from Romeo and Juliet on the stage in front of an imaginary audience of brown bears. You said bears truly appreciate the arts, unlike humans who only tolerate them in order to impress other people. I swear that I could make out a hulking mass of matted brown fur in the dress circle, hear thunderous applause from hefty paws, wild roars for an encore.

Our town has been redesigned for the elderly. Cinemas have turned into bingo halls, the ice rink an indoor bowling club, on the land where creaking roller coasters used to thrill stands an oversized supermarket. The pier burned down a few years ago, reported as a freak accident, a wooden relic remains stranded out at sea, like one rotten tooth in a gaping mouth. You never watched our town lie down and die. For that at least, I'm grateful.

The sun confirms its intentions. It's going to be the sort of day which drives Londoners in droves to the seaside, the sort of cloudless day that etches itself into the memory, like a dull day never can. It seems wrong to be taking the early morning train to London, when half of London will be taking advantage of a sun soaked Sunday by the sea.

I follow the scent of bacon, like a half starved dog. Pick up one of the red top papers Sarah won't allow at home. In a corner booth, I devour a bacon sandwich and swill down a mug of coffee which could easily pass as dirty dish water. In Sarah's opinion, the only civilized thing to have for breakfast is muesli served with skimmed milk. I spend half my day in the office picking bits of sawdust from my teeth.

A walk before the crowds descend seems the sensible thing to do. The sea's in a playful mood today, erratic waves forming abstract patterns in the slate coloured water. Three doctors can't be wrong, can they. After the procedure, I needed to be sure. You hear stories, babies defying the logic of science. Two doctors later, after countless tests, I was suitably reassured that my lower regions were as barren as the Sahara.

I try to imagine a baby in our house. Sarah treats sick kids, so she knows her way around a child, but having one at home, leaving trails of vomit on her mohair jumpers, sticky finger prints on her meticulously emulsioned walls. It just doesn't seem feasible, somehow.

When she said she wanted to be a nurse, it came as a shock

to us all. She didn't even have a job when we met. Women were up in arms about being called the weaker sex, burning their bras in protest at being treated as second class citizens, and Sarah was living off her parents like some character in a Regency novel. Her parents were convinced the notion would pass. In Mary's opinion the caring professions equate to menial work for the masses, entirely honourable, but not a suitable career choice for a solicitor's daughter.

They offered to buy her a florist shop in Chelmney. Ron found me a post as a junior clerk in a firm of insurance brokers, in order to turn my blue collar a stainless white. Bricklaying was apparently far from a suitable occupation for a solicitor's son in law. She refused point blank to sell flowers, took a position as a student nurse at Chelmney General, and there was nothing Mary could do about it. She astounded us with her tenacity, galloped through the training period like a blinkered horse.

When she qualified, Mary believed that would be the end of the whole thing. She had proved herself, now she could admit that nursing was not for her. A month later she accepted a job on the children's cancer ward at Royal St Barnaby's Hospital, London. House prices in the capital were laughable. A newly qualified nurse and an insurance clerk stood little chance of securing even a tatty bedsit. Mary was forced to accept that Sarah was serious, so insisted on gifting us a more than generous deposit for a house. The thought of leaving Chelmney filled me with a dark dread. But I'd married Sarah, so was forced to go along with her wishes.

At first, I was consumed with guilt. What if you came back, couldn't find me. The thought of it almost broke me. But then it became easier, no memories round every corner waiting to ambush me. I found some degree of solace in an indifferent city of strangers.

A gang of fishermen are hauling crates of shellfish from a boat which looks far from sea worthy. If we hadn't met that summer, I'd have gone back to sea. These men are strong, vital, weatherbeaten, living each day as if it were their last. My soulless office is pretty much risk free, unless you count the stapler. Their days are made of minor miracles, each catch, each safe return to land, each crate sold at market, each meal put on the table. Myself and Sarah wait a whole month for our salaries, only to blow the lot on fancy cushions and Persian rugs we're not allowed to walk on. My wife likes buying nice things. The strange thing is, she takes little pleasure in the things she buys. She'll want nice things for the baby. She'll want to move. If there is a baby, that is. It's time to go home, give myself time to think clearly before Sarah gets home tomorrow.

The train expels an unsightly group of lads clutching cans of lager. I can almost smell testosterone swirling in the air. They gradually disperse and a girl appears from their midst. She's standing alone. A heavy curtain of mahogany hair speckled with amber highlights hangs half way down her back. She's wearing a heavy looking leather jacket, black tights and boots, obviously not prepared for the weather. One of the lads lingers, tries to swing an arm over her shoulder, drag her along with him. She pushes him away, turns and I see her face. My skin turns to nettles, despite the heat, a cold sweat drenches every inch of my body. For a second or two it seems like one of those dreams. They start well, but always leave my eyes wet with tears when I wake. An elderly man proves this is real by pushing roughly past me, almost impaling my foot with his walking stick. I take two steps closer, look into familiar chestnut eyes. She sees me, I reach out a hand, but she turns away, walks slowly towards the ticket office.

Chapter 6

Marnie

There was this bloke. Basically, he found a group of so called 'ordinary' folk. Regular people off the street, with jobs, houses and all that. Not even convicted criminals, or the certified insane. Anyway, he told these 'ordinary' people to dole out electric shocks, like they were sweets or something, to a group of other 'ordinary' people. But the thing was, the thing that blew my mind, they willingly did it to people they didn't know, people they'd never even met before. It could have been Ghandi or Mother Theresa in that other room, but they did it, no questions asked. I told Charlie, he pissed himself laughing, said it would be no fun whatsoever, not with a stranger anyhow.

This girl called Heather moved into the home, a few months before I left. All the girls were dumb, but Heather took the proverbial garibaldi for being just about as dense as they come. Dumb people deserve everything they get. There's no excuse on earth for choosing to remain an uneducated airhead. That's why I chose her. I suppose you could call it an experiment, just like Mr Milgram did. You can get away with anything, if you call it an experiment. Anyway, it was too late with the other girls, thay all hated me, pure jealousy, I suppose.

I was severely lacking in the art of friend making. For research purposes, I watched some of those imbecilic American TV shows, the ones most of the girls loved. As my opening gambit, I asked her for a game of chess one evening after tea. She looked at me like I'd asked her to paint the fucking Mona Lisa. I'd patently way underestimated just how much of a blockhead she really was.

For my next move, I dumbed right down to her level, a simple trip to the cinema, chose a horror, just to be on the safe side. Everyone loves a horror don't they, the plots are so pathetic, anyone can understand them. I didn't want Charlie spoiling everything, so told him it was a romance, he hates anything like that.

The film was so funny, it could've passed for a comedy. This man with a cleaver was trying to chop this other man's leg off and making a right bloody hash of it. They could at least have given him a chainsaw, something with a bit of clout. I looked over and I couldn't believe it, the silly bitch was sobbing her heart out, like it was one of those sad films about animals, rather than a farcical horror. After the film, I took her to the burger bar across the road, She looked a right mess, mascara running down her spotty face. I said I was sorry the film had been so tame, which it really was, except for the scene with a mincer, Charlie would have loved that. The ungrateful cow hardly touched her burger. The friend thing was proving to be far more difficult than I'd anticipated. There was no way I was giving up.

She was only in hospital for two weeks, a couple of minor fractures, but she made a right bloody song and dance about it. In the end it was Charlie who did it, knocked the chair from under Heather's feet, so I could get the keys out of matron's pocket without anyone noticing. The experiment had been a success. They kept our papers in a locked cabinet in Matron's office. Details of why we were there, where we'd come from. We were denied access to our own past, like stray dogs with no pedigree certificates to show where we'd come from.

When a girl got to leave the home, or was evicted as close to her sixteenth birthday as possible, she was invited back a few weeks later, for what matron liked to call a cosy chat over coffee. It was really to check that the girl hadn't turned to prostitution or become a drug addict, because that would reflect badly on the home and matron in particular. The bait they used to get you back was that if you were doing well you could have a copy of your papers, if there were any papers to copy, that was. One girl discovered she was found in a public toilet as a two hour old baby. She left matron's office empty handed, threw herself off the bridge at junction seven of the motorway two weeks later.

I always knew that the minute I walked out of those doors, suitcase in hand, I was never going back. But I needed to know if I had papers, it was my right, wasn't it. The only thing I got for wasting all those hours with Heather, was one piece of paper, crumpled and stained, like it meant nothing to the person who wrote it. Just a name and address; *Hesther Brompton, 6 Highbury Ave, Chelmney-On-Sea.* So for all my effort, all I have is a house. A house full of strangers. I wish I'd just walked away, like the girls who didn't want to know.

Even worse than the electrocuting thing, was this other experiment by a bloke in America. He snatched these baby monkeys away from their mothers. Mothers who loved them dearly, wanted to keep them forever, mothers who most probably died from broken hearts, but no one knows, because the creep was only interested in the babies. Monkey mothers don't give up babies out of choice, like human mothers. It kills me to think of those tiny monkeys, all alone, crying for mothers who loved them so much, they couldn't live without them.

The bastard thought he'd torment the little things a bit more, by making pretend mothers, using coat hangers, like something out of Blue Peter. For a laugh, he made two types of mother, wire ones with food and soft padded ones without food. The mind numbing thing was, he went to all that trouble, ruined who knows how many monkey family lives, all for nothing. Even the dumbest person could tell you which type of mother the babies would prefer. Anyone can give you food, cooks in a school canteen, fosterers, chefs in restaurants, even Charlie shares the odd bag of crisps. You can even steal food, if needs must. A mother is something else altogether. Warm. Soft. Always there to cling onto, to offer comfort. And that's just what those poor little fuckers did, they clung on for dear life, because what they wanted more than anything else in the world, even if they had to starve to death, was their mother. I swear I'd have killed the bastard, if I got the chance.

Sometimes I feel like one of those babies. One that was given a wire mother with food. The difference is my own mother gave me up voluntarily, I wasn't dragged away by some maniac scientist for experimental reasons. I'd never tell Charle, about the monkey thing, there's no way he'd understand, he'd probably choose food over a mother, any day.

A group of scruffy lads get off the train, all get a good eyeful of me, don't even bother to hide it. One of the uglier specimens shouts out a rude remark, one of them even has the cheek to try and drag me along with him. He's lucky Charlie's not here, he'd be waiting for an ambulance by now.

When they go, I see him. He's staring at me, like he's seen a ghost. He's old, middle-aged, at least, dressed like Mr Horton, our geography teacher at school. There's something about the way he's looking at me that makes me want to know more, almost like he can't believe what he's seeing.

There's a train up the coast to Crowton in ten minutes. I've always wanted to visit, but Charlie says it sounds like a bore. I buy the ticket, then, I get it. He wasn't just some aging pervert, like the others, he knows her, Hesther, my mother. I've just seen my father for the first time in my life.

I run, scour the station. He's standing on the London platform. Something about him makes me want to cry, like he's an abandoned puppy, or something.

'Hi, I'm Marnie, do you want to -'

'I'm sorry Marnie, it was rude of me to stare, you just … You just reminded me of -'

'It's alright, come with me, we can talk.'

Chapter 7

Stuart

The London train leaves without me. Her make-up is far too heavy for her delicate features, for your face. Mascara's smeared down her left cheek, her hair's far more tousled than it ought to be.

'Look, you were staring at me ... Before, we can -'

'The resemblance is uncanny. Someone I used to know ... It just took me back, that's all, I'm sorry.'

Her accent isn't Chelmney, it's northern, somewhere in the Manchester region. She pats me gently on the arm, like she's comforting a distressed child.

'She's not dead or anything ... Is she ... The girl who looks like me.'

The next London train fills quickly.

'No ... I don't know, I haven't seen her for a long time. This is my train, you should -'

'You don't have to tell me your name or anything, not if you don't want to, but I'd like to hear about your friend ... The girl.' The train pulls out. 'I'm getting the train to Crowton ... For the day ... You could come with me, we could -'

'I don't know ... Marnie ... It just doesn't seem right, you're so -'

'I think we may be related, me and your friend ... That's why I'm here ... In Chelmney.'

Without waiting for an answer, she links her arm through mine, as if it's the most natural thing in the world, then leads me over the passenger bridge to a waiting train.

Chapter 8

Marnie

His name is Stuart. I'm not ready to call him Dad yet, so call him Stuey. He's not married to my mother, but a nurse called Sarah. He doesn't seem like the sort of man who'd abandon his baby, so I'm guessing she never told him about me. He's nice, kind of vulnerable, not the brightest tack in the box, so I must have inherited my intellect from a great uncle, or something.

We've been walking for an age, it's so bloody hot, I don't want to upset him by taking my jacket off, not yet anyway. It's Charlie's fault, if I get heatstroke.

'I'm going to study at Oxford … After college.' He looks impressed. 'I've just finished reading this book. Two boys went to Oxford, in the olden days, when they didn't allow girls, I mean how crazy was that, everyone knows girls are way smarter than boys.' He doesn't seem to take offence, laughs, which I take as a positive sign. 'One of them, the rich one, went and ruined it all, by drinking too much. You could tell he was nutter, he had this teddy called Aloysius, a grown man with a teddy, can you imagine, Stuey. I've never even owned a teddy bear, not even when I was a kid.'

'I'm parched, Marnie, let's get a drink.'

'When I graduate, I'm going to be a famous psychologist, like Freud or Piaget.'

My dad's not even a teacher, he just looks like one. He sells insurance, which says it all really, didn't even go to college, nevermind university. We order two cokes.

'What's your wife like, how long have you been married, what about my mother … Hesther.'

'How old are you, Marnie?'

'Sixteen.'

'Hesther's not your mother, why did you think that -'

'She never told you, did she … About me. It's alright Stuey, I don't blame you. How could you have looked after me, if you didn't even know I existed.'

'Stop ... No ... You've got it all wrong ... It's my fault, I should never have come here with you.'

'Hesther was your girlfriend ... Right ... And her name was in my file ... It doesn't take a brain surgeon to work it out, does it.'

He looks confused, not as joyful as I'd hoped, after finding his long lost daughter. It's probably best if I rein it in a bit, discuss living arrangements and all that later. He doesn't know where my mother is. Apparently she left Chelmney when she was fifteen, four months before I was born. But it's clear by the way he talks about her that he's still in love with her, I feel sorry for his wife. I suppose it's harder for men, the baby thing, they only get to know if the woman tells them. I wonder what happened to all the monkey fathers, nobody ever mentions them, maybe they didn't know about their babies either. Some women don't get fat, do they, when they're pregnant, I'm not sure about monkeys though. It's weird, because the baby has to be somewhere, doesn't it.

'She used to spend weekends with her father ... Hesther, I mean. Her mother drank ... Was an alcoholic, never sober enough for dinners or parties. He took Hesther instead. She hated it, but she had no choice in the matter.'

We don't look alike, me and Stuey. What if he's not my father. What if I come from a wealthy London family, what if I'm descended from aristocracy. We leave the cafe, walk round some botanical gardens, he doesn't seem in any rush to head back to London. Charlie hates gardens of any description. The flower beds are perfectly manicured, just like the pictures in my history book at school of the Palace of Versailles. I want to go there one day, but this will have to do for now. A fountain throws dancing crystals high into the air, the roses smell sublime. There are tons of places I want to visit; Rome, Buenos Aires, Cambodia, but Charlies wants to go to Spain, get drunk on cheap vodka and swim in a pool full of chemicals and sunburnt bodies. Charlie has no concept of culture, a true heathen, if ever you saw one.

I should leave now, just walk away. He was only looking at

me because of her. Even if he is my dad, you can tell he doesn't want to be. He just wants to talk about her, I guess he doesn't get the chance very often, I mean you can't go on and on about your ex girlfriend to your wife, can you. She loved writing, was an excellent student, which I find hard to believe. My grandfather was a barrister, which explains a lot, my grandmother a dancer, which explains very little. Dancing is a completely pointless activity, in my opinion.

'Do you fancy a stroll around the fun fair, Marnie ... It's been years since I've been.'

This is entering into classic serial killer behaviour, what if I'm just as dumb as Rose-May, after all, but he looks so excited, like a little boy, it would be rude to say no, so I follow him. We ride the roller coaster, big wheel, horses that go round so fast, they make you gag. There's nothing like this in Chelmney, but he says there used to be, years ago, until they pulled it down. I can hardly believe he works in an office, has responsibilities, he laughs like a child at my jokes, buys us sticks of candyfloss bigger than our heads. Later after a bag of sugary doughnuts, I leave the ladies, after a full ten minutes hanging over the toilet bowl. He'll have taken the opportunity to go, no further questions asked.

'I thought you could call him Aloysius ... After the bear in that book you mentioned.'

I can't believe my eyes, he's sitting on a bench, the biggest fucking teddy I've ever seen, sitting right next to him. Now I know for sure I'm in serial killer territory. Tears which have been threatening all day come in torrent and there's nothing I can do to stop them. He fishes in his holdall, pulls out a freshly ironed snow white handkerchief. I deface it with snot and black mascara. The last time I cried, I was six years old. One of the foster daddies hit me so hard, his signet ring sliced into my thigh. My crime, daring to ask why he never took the bag of clubs in the garage, when he went to play golf. After that he started calling me Mardy Marnie. A few weeks later he had a little accident with a live electrical wire. We were unceremoniously deposited back at the home.

Instead of laughing at the prospect of owning a child's toy, I bury my face in his soft fur, wrap my arms tightly round his plump body. I should've been home ages ago, Charlie will be insane with worry by now. We leave the fair, he doesn't mention the crying thing. I'm still not convinced he doesn't want to murder me, but figure that after all the effort he's put in, he's not going to let me go now, so I might as well enjoy my final hours.

'Do you fancy some dinner, Marnie ... Before we get the train. I don't know about you, but I'm ravenous, all the fresh air, I suppose. My treat of course.'

After spewing the entire contents of my guts into the toilet bowl, I'm starving as well. Another hour won't make any difference now, I'm in for it with Charlie anyway, that's if I don't get strangled first. If I'm going to die, it may as well be with a full stomach.

He picks a fancy looking Italian restaurant. A man dressed in a grey suit greets us at the door, asks if we need a table for two. He leads us to a table for four, takes the bear from my arms, sits him in one of the chairs. I should be seething with embarrassment, but no one seems to notice, so I just smile, as if this happens to me every day. A waiter in a dark red waistcoat lights the candle, hands us both a menu.

'What can I get for you and your charming daughter to drink, Sir.'

This is the first time ever I've been in a proper restaurant, the first time someone's handed me a menu, the first time I've been called someone's daughter. Whatever happens next, it's very nearly all been worth it.

Chapter 9

Stuart

She studies the menu like it's War and Peace. It gives me time to think. Are you really her mother. Is that why your father took you away. Weekends in London, anything could have happened. A handsome boy from a well to do family, even worse some older man, it makes my skin crawl just thinking about it. Of course I wanted it, what teenage boy wouldn't, but I loved you far too much to let something so animalistic get in the way. I watch her turn the pages of the menu, her face a study in wonderment. There were no signs, no change in behaviour, no weight gain. We could always read each other's minds. There has to be another explanation. I just have to find it.

'There's so much to choose from. Do you know what you're having yet, Stuey?'

She looks a mess. She looked a mess when I met her, but now her eyes are raw from crying, her make-up greasy streaks down her face, hair more bird's nest than artfully tousled. The bear was a rather clumsy attempt to give her back a piece of her childhood. From what she's told me it was bordering on something out of a Dickens novel. You would never have given her away, however you came by her, of that I'm certain.

'What can I get you Senor, I can recommend the sea bass, it was freshly caught in Chelmney this morning.'

'I'll have the steak, and a bottle of your best Chianti … Marnie, what would you like?'

She orders pizza and a coke. The velvet wine slips smoothly down my throat, soothing away the raw edges of the day. I pour her an inch, she sips it gingerly, then pushes it to one side in disgust. Sarah will have called by now. I'll call her when I get home, tell her I couldn't sleep so went for an evening stroll.

'This is amazing, I've never seen such a big pizza.'

I know I've got to let her go. But I know when I do, we'll

never see each other again, and she's my only link to you.

'Thanks Marnie … For today. You were right, it was a massive shock, just seeing you like that. I know the evidence points to Hesther being your mother, but I think there's some other explanation for all this … Look, what I'm trying to say, is that I want … I mean I'm willing to help you … Find her … Find out the truth.'

'I don't think I want to, not really. I mean she obviously didn't want me … Still doesn't want me, so what's the point, I'm better off without -'

'Do you want dessert? '

'Yes please, but it's really late, won't your wife be -'

'It's fine, she's with her parents right now, I'll call her when I get home.'

We order ice cream sundaes. It's dark now, even by my standards, this is bang out of order. A man out with a girl young enough to be his daughter, some stranger he met at a railway station. She takes her time, licking every spoonful like a Persian cat. We eat in silence, as if for now at least, ice cream is the only thing that matters. I remember our last day together. Galloping along the beach, laughing at some shared secret, two kids with not a care in the world, or so I thought.

'This is amazing, I don't want it to end, do you Stuey. I wasn't going to tell you, but I've never been in a restaurant before, a proper one, like this. You never got over her … Hesther … Did you, even though you married Sarah?'

Her candour knocks me off kilter.

'I never went in a restaurant either, not until I met Sarah. I knocked a glass of red wine over her … It was the nerves, she was wearing a silk dress … A sort of cream colour. She told me a few days later that the stain refused to come out. I offered to buy her a new one, it seemed the right thing to do. She told me how much it cost, more than I earned in a month. She still hasn't got her replacement to this day. The next time we dined out she wore black and ordered a bottle of Sancerre.'

She laughs and finally lays her spoon to rest. She refused to give her jacket to the waiter, it's been glued to her back all day, despite the heat.

'You came here with me today because of her … Didn't you

... Because I remind you of her ... It's all right, I don't mind. What happened when she left, did you look for her?'

'For a while, I asked around, outside her school, that sort of thing, after a while I just gave up.'

Time to leave. It's nearly ten, far later than I thought. Sarah will be anxious by now. We're normally in bed by this time on a Sunday. Marnie's just a child, I should have made sure she was home hours ago.

The streets change at night in a seaside town. A group of drunken revellers stumble out of a pub. A girl not much older than Marnie is slumped on the pavement, shoeless, a pile of vomit and a half eaten kebab lying next to her. A skinny lad hovers round her like a vulture. A benevolent place of recreation has been transformed into a jungle, a palpable thread of danger hanging in the cool night air. I lead her towards the station, eager to seek refuge on the train.

It's deserted, save for one man sleeping on a bench, snoring loudly under newspaper. The timetable tells me the last Chelmney train left half an hour ago.

'I'm so sorry, I should've checked, I'm so used to London transport running into the early hours. I'll get us a taxi, see you home safely, I promise, I'd never -'

'I don't want to go home. Not now. It's too late. He'll be ... I mean, it'll be easier in the morning.'

'You mean stay here all night, in the station, there's not even a cafe open, or -'

'No ... We could find a guest house. It's hard to explain, but I just can't face ... It's just too late, that's all.'

She must have a boyfriend, he'll be mad with worry by now. This has gone way too far. A taxi slows, she takes my arm, leads me back to the row of seedy looking guest houses we passed earlier.

Chapter 10

Sarah

One of the worst days of my life, and Stu refuses to pick up the phone. He never goes out on a Sunday evening, takes a ridiculously long bath, pretends to be enthralled by some tedious antique show, then goes up with one of his war novels from the library.

Daddy didn't make a fuss. There were no tears, not in public, anyway. Mummy acted like we were dropping him at the lodge for a meeting, would be returning to collect him in a couple of hours. We stayed for a while, she unpacked his things, requested morning coffee from a sour looking cleaner. Then we simply kissed him on the cheek and walked away. She intends to visit daily. I told her no one would judge her if she missed the odd visit, but I know she'll perform the role of doting wife to perfection, however long it takes.

It's nearly eleven, mummy never stays up after eleven. I try him again, listen as the phone rings out into a void. He's not there. My husband is never unpredictable, one of his more desirable traits. We say our goodnights, failing to mention the gravity of the occasion. I check out my stomach in the bedroom mirror, it's still flat, what if he didn't believe me, what if he did believe me, refuses to raise another man's child.

It wasn't easy, getting pregnant. I could have opted for the donor route. That would have been quicker, cleaner, but sperm donation is a gamble, and there was no way I was going to gamble with my child. Sperm is merely a bodily secretion, that's all there is to it. There's no way you can tell where it's come from by the look of it. Of course they're going to tell you the donor is a six foot professor of nuclear science who competes at international level athletics as a sideline. In reality it's probably been donated by a balding five foot three waster with the intellect of a fruit fly, someone with nothing better to do than hang around clinics looking at free pornography. It makes sense that all the intellectual Adonis's out there will be far too busy injecting sperm into a real human being in some luxury hotel room, to think about wasting their time with a plastic tube and a smutty magazine for company.

Finding a man was never going to be a problem. Finding the right man was something else altogether. It's still early when I wake, too early for him to have left for work. He still doesn't pick up. He never stays out all night. Stuart sticks to routine like glue. It's time to go home, and quickly.

'Good morning Dear. Did you sleep well. I'm afraid yoghurt and fruit salad will have to suffice this morning, I don't feel like cooking, you can understand why. As you're not at work until this evening, I thought we could visit daddy this morning, then have a look in that dear little baby shop on King Street. I would appreciate the company, it will take my mind off the -'

'Of course, but I have to get off before -'

'You could call in work, explain the situation. Spend a couple of days with me. You look too pale, and you've lost weight. It would give me a chance to look after you, I know Stuart tries, but he's really rather -'

'I'm so sorry Mummy, but I have to get back today. We're short staffed as usual. Of course I'll come and see daddy, but then I really do have to go.'

He looks awful, like a deflating balloon, five years older than yesterday, slumped in the chair, his outfit falling way below mummy's standards. She kisses his cheek, helps him to an upright position, contorts his arms so she can pull a jacket over his shoulders, knots his tie with the precision of an expert. I force the window open, let in some much needed fresh air.

'Sarah's leaving us today, Darling ... Work ... But she'll be handing in her notice.'

He shuffles in the chair, face collapsing into a collage of creases, he tries to say something, it sounds like hymns, perhaps he's already thinking of the christening. He tries to lift his hand, but it's too heavy and falls back to his lap.

'I'll be back soon Daddy, in a week or two, they'll take good -'

'I've told them what to feed you, what time you eat, the need for a two 'o' clock nap. Nothing will go unnoticed, so you needn't worry about that Darling.'

I found him purely by chance. A colleague at work had recommended a garden centre on the outskirts of Slough. I was searching for a small ornamental fountain. It was a Saturday morning. Stu was catching up on work at the office. I watched him touch the leaves, as if he was handling some rare gemstone, all the while deep in conversation with an elderly couple. I could see he was a man of passion, strength, vitality. He looked a few years younger than me, similar enough in skin tone and hair colour to Stu, to make it work. Ten minutes later he swung two fruit trees and a spiky shrub onto a trolley as if they were made of cotton wool.

An hour later, I left with my fountain, six dahlias, and a promising looking pear tree, all stacked by Dave in the boot of my car. But much more importantly a number scribbled on a seed catalogue, stashed at the bottom of my handbag.

We met the following week, by which time I'd managed to compile a list of the necessary criteria for fatherhood. Items such as fertility, clean bill of health, no history of congenital conditions, a wife, or at least a serious girlfriend, so no risk of serious attachment, no drug or alcohol misuse, no criminal record, for anything serious, at least. It was one of those dreadful Mexican themed places, where they try to force you to wear a sombrero to eat your food. He was married, virgins when they met, no children as yet, co-owner of the garden centre, gained a degree in horticulture at university, displayed no discernible mental or physical defects. He said he'd never done this type of thing before, and I believed him from the tear in his eye when he mentioned the guilt. He spouted the usual rubbish, told me I was beautiful, that we shared some kind of spititual connection, the type of stuff Stuart has never said, to me, at least. We parted with a brief, but promising kiss.

On our third date, he made the first deposit, both of us brandishing certificates proving a clean bill of sexual health like badges of honour. He wanted to use protection, so I waited until the point of no return, told him I was on the pill and had a severe allergy to rubber. We met weekly after that, cheap hotels on the wrong side of town, rooms designed for business rather than pleasure. It was a chore, but to be honest, he was slightly more inventive in the bedroom department than my husband. With Stu, it's like a race, he can't wait to get over the finishing line and retire from the circuit. When he finally gave me what I wanted, I failed to show up for our next meeting, secure in the knowledge I'd never visit Slough again.

She insists on buying half the shop; romper suits in muted tones of amber, teal and grey, impossibly tiny hats, cloud soft cot covers. I know what she's doing. She's making up for last time, for tempting fate, for not being prepared for my little girl. But I know this time will be different, my body's ready now, and my baby knows it.

We get home at lunch time. He should be at work, but I try the house phone anyway. Stu and I rigidly adhere to certain protocols in our relationship. Rules and regulations leave no room for error. A cardinal rule is we never call each other at work, unless it concerns the matter of death or dying. It makes sense with me. A call from my husband saying he'll be late home for supper could in theory drag me away from a life or death situation. But he sells insurance, so an unwanted interruption is unlikely to end in disaster.

I find the number in the back of my address book.

'Good afternoon, Blackwell Insurance, Eva speaking.'

'Stuart Horncasle please.'

'Could I ask who's calling.'

'His wife ... Sarah ... Horncastle.'

She adopts a somewhat hostile tone.

'Stuart didn't come in this morning, failed to phone in sick, didn't even have the -'

I drop the receiver. He could be lying dead in a ditch somewhere, and the bitch has the audacity to speak to me like that. It was daddy who got him the job in the first place, and as far as I know he's never missed a day in the office. This is far worse than I imagined. Stu tows the line, hates fuss, is far too lazy to handle chaos. If he wanted a day off, he'd have phoned in with some excuse. The baby thumps out in anger and I vomit breakfast onto the shag pile carpet.

Chapter 11

Stuart

Bleached light floods the room. A pair of threadbare curtains offer little protection from the rising sun. It's ten past seven, I should be eating breakfast by now, ready to catch the seven forty-five tube to work. A swirl of dread chases its tail through my stomach. If I leave now I can be at the office by lunch time. Dressed, I listen at the adjoining door. Silence. She's left already, seen through the madness of yesterday. I can get home before Sarah starts her shift, tell her there was a fault with the phone line or something.

As I'm putting on my shoes, the door swings wide open. Discarded clothes litter the carpet, the bear lies on the bed. She's clearly naked under the sheet draped around her body.

'Stuey, I'm bloody starving, aren't you. That bacon smells amazing, I could've slept all morning, it's great here, I wish we could stay forever, don't you.'

She springs into my room like a kitten, the thin sheet disentangling itself from her slender body. My skin fires up with shame. She tears the curtains apart, daylight illuminates the gentle curves of her body, an expanse of youthful skin. She turns, my eyes are drawn to her arms, a mass of scars, blood crusting at the edge of a deep incision. Who did this to her, no wonder she refused to take off her leather jacket yesterday.

'I'll wait for you downstairs ... In the dining room.'

I leave before she can answer.

The space is too small for five tables. A grease smog hangs in the air. The wallpaper looks at least four decades old. A girl about the same age as Marnie arrives to serve me, her face an abstract study of pimples, crusty beige foundation and thick grey braces clinging to crooked teeth.

'Coffee please and the full breakfast ... Two breakfasts ... I'm waiting for my daughter, to -'

'Stuey, sorry I took so long, I had a bath … We've …. I mean I've only got a shower at home.'

The woman at the next table almost chokes on a charred piece of toast.

'Marnie darling, please don't call me that, I know you're an adult now, but dad will do.'

She's made no attempt to tame her hair, her tights have so many holes she may as well not be wearing them. The jacket is back, even though it feels like we're sitting in in a bacon scented sauna. The food perches precariously on an oil slick, as the waitress slams down my plate, an anemic sausage slides into my lap.

'Sorry, Sir, Mrs Campbell's always telling me I'm clumsy.'

She stares at Marnie as if royalty's dropped in for breakfast. We devour every last morsel, swilling down the grease with milky coffee.

The station's quiet, the Chelmney train half empty. I can get home before Sarah, phone the office, make up some excuse for today.

'Can you remember who sold the house … Her house Hesther's.'

I'd become brave, a courage born out of desperation. I knocked on your neighbours doors, lingered outside your school gates, no one knew where you were. I walked past the agency a hundred times, stopping to look at the pictures of grand houses with even grander price tags. Your sitting room looked like it belonged in a manor house, complete with grand piano.

I borrowed a scratchy tweed jacket from my father's wardrobe, bought a pair of ill-fitting leather shoes for a few pence from a junk shop. I told him I was looking for a house for my parents, was a pupil at the boarding school in a nearby village. He appeared to listen, to take my request to view 6 Highbury Ave seriously, so I pressed on, told him if my parents could speak to the owner, they would probably offer the full asking price, were desperate to move out of London. After letting me sweat for a while, he opened the desk drawer and I honestly thought he was about to pull out the key. Instead he handed me a boiled sweet, said he didn't conduct business with children, especially bare faced liars, as his own son attended that school he knew every pupil by name and derivation. That was the day I finally gave up.

'Yes it was Chiswell and Son ... It's still there actually. I tried, but no one wanted to talk ... I don't blame them, I was a pretty dubious looking lad in those days.'

She's pulling gum out of her mouth in strings.

'Look Stuey ... I know you have to get back and everything ... But, would you come with me ... To the estate agent ... They might have old records, or something.'

As we leave the station, I hear the London train which could have saved me from this mess go without me.

Behind the the same mahogany desk I remember from all those years ago, sits a boy not much older than I was at the time. I glance across at Marnie, she's still chewing gum, clutching the bear tightly to her chest. His suit looks three sizes too big, as if he's been dressed by a mother expecting a sudden spurt of growth.

'How can I help you Sir. Have you seen something you'd like to view, or are you selling. You'll find we're extremely competitive in our rates of commission.' He's trying not to look at Marnie. She's fidgeting in the chair like a toddler. 'You're welcome to browse our properties ... Perhaps you're looking for something in particular.'

'Look, this is a bit of a long shot ... Connor.' His name is proudly displayed on a gold lapel badge. 'But you look like the type of person who would be happy to help ... In a difficult situation, that is. The thing is we ... Me and my daughter ... We're trying to find some distant relations. They lived in Chelmney, until nineteen seventy-three. We've been told your office handled the sale of their property.' His eyes full of hope when we sat down, now shine with confusion. He has a script to follow; buying or selling, isn't trained to deal with family dilemas. 'In any other circumstances, I wouldn't dream of asking. I'm a solicitor myself, so understand the importance of confidentiality.' I lower my voice in an attempt to inject some gravitas into the situation. 'The thing is ... Connor ... My daughter, Mary ... Well she has an incurable condition, we need a donor. So far no one has proved to be compatible.' Marnie makes a little snorting sound, slowly pulls the gum out of her mouth. Connor turns the colour of a beetroot. 'Without a donor ... Connor ... She's going to die.'

'My boss ... I mean the manager ... He's out on a viewing. I really can't help you without -'

'Look, I'll be straight with you Connor. We don't have much time ... More tests later today ... In a hospital ... London. I'm pretty sure that under these extreme circumstances, your boss would reward you for acting quickly and decisively. I can see you're a man well able to use his own initiative.'

We don't speak, don't look at each other, he leaves the door ajar. I hear him unlock a filing cabinet, the rustle of papers. After what seems like an age he hands me a jaundiced piece of paper. Marnie grabs my arm and we're out of the door before he can say a word.

There's a cafe on the next street, we order drinks, the paper remains folded in my pocket.

'There was this girl ... At the home, Rita. She was desperate to find her real family ... Obsessed with it, to be honest. Anyway she came back to have her little chat with Matron ... That's when she could see her papers. They were in the office for bloody ages, we were all dying to know why. When she came out, you could tell the silly cow had been crying. She spent half her life crying ... Pathetic. Anyway this other girl, Helen, said Rita was going nowhere until she spilled the beans. You know what Stuey. Listen to this ... It only turned out her mother wasn't one of the ones who got knocked up with a kid they didn't want. No, she was attacked down an alleyway on her way home from school. But this is the best part ... She was talking to her mother, right there on the phone in matron's office. She wanted to keep Rita, even after what happened, was going to call her Evie after her favourite doll. But her parents wouldn't let her. She held Rita once, then a nurse took her, and that was that.'

'That's a nice story, Marnie ... Well not exactly nice, but -'

'No that's not the end. Get this, her mother wasn't at home talking on the phone ... Do you know where she was, Stuey, you'll never guess ... She was talking from the public phone, in a real life prison. And do you know what she was in for ... Wait for it, not shoplifting or drugs, anything boring like that ... No, she only went and stabbed her husband to death with a kitchen knife. No wonder Rita was a head case. Anyway her mother wanted Rita to visit her, in prison. So it could have been a happy ending. The trouble was, Rita thought she was some sort of princess ... One day her mother would come, whisk her away to some fairytale bloody castle and they'd both live happily ever after.'

'What happened ... Did she go ... To the prison?'

'She jumped under a train. I felt sorry for whoever had to scrape her skinny body from the tracks. Her mother lost her daughter not once, but twice, pure selfishness on Rita's part. The reason I'm telling you all this, is for your own benefit ... I like you Stuey, you're funny. You need to get over Hesther ... She's not like you thought ... You can surely see that by now. She gave me away. She didn't want me and still doesn't. Rita's mother wanted her, even though she'd been raped ... Even though she was in prison. She wanted to be with her daughter ... To be found, whatever the circumstances. Rita was one of the lucky ones ... She just couldn't see it. Face it Stuey, Hesther was a rich bich, who cheated on you, got herself pregnant with me, then ran away so she never had to face up to what she'd done.'

It takes all my self control not to slap her in the face. I carefully unfold the piece of paper, pass it to her.

'I want to help you Marnie ... To find her, we could -'

'It's over Stuey ... They moved to France. There's no telephone number, just an address ... That was years ago, she's probably somewhere else by now. I don't need her. I'm going home now, you should too.

She's wrong. I have an address. But it's worthless without Marnie. I can't just turn up at your doorstep missing out the facts of how I got there.

'You're right. We should both go home ... But as a way of saying sorry for putting you through all this ... Please let me buy you lunch ... It's the least I can do.'

Chapter 12

Marnie

Stuey's house is seriously cool. Way more cool than any of the foster homes. It's like one of those houses you see in the magazines at the doctor's surgery. One day, I'll have a house like this, but I don't know about Charlie. Charlie doesn't do clean and tidy. Stuey told me to stay in the van while he packed a bag. This is far more fun.

I must be mad. We're actually going to France. Things like this never happen to me. We tried to get a phone number, but the operator couldn't find the address. He said we could call at my flat, pick up some things. He doesn't know Charlie, does he. I don't even have a passport, but he says we'll get round that, somehow. If I was Sarah, I'd change the locks and never speak to him again.

In the living room, nothing is out of place, there are no piles of dirty clothes, crisps on the carpet, old kebab wrappers on the sideboard. The thought of Charlie somewhere like this makes me shudder. In their wedding picture, she looks like a film star, so glamorous it's hard to imagine her with someone like Stuey. Her dress clings to her slim body, it looks like silk, not disgusting like those frilly monstrosities. He's grinning like a loony, his hair's longer, he's much skinnier than he is now. The sofa's massive, I throw myself down, it feels like a cloud. Our sofa's sticky as fuck and full of stains. Charlie never washes his hands. If I was Stuey, with this house, a wife like Sarah, I'd have forgotten about Hesther ages ago.

From the state of the kitchen, you'd swear no one lives here. The sink is empty, gleaming, there's no rubbish to be seen, no dirty pans on the stove. I help myself to a swig of apple juice from the biggest fridge ever, take a yoghurt for later. They say people eat snails and frogs in France, but I'm pretty sure that's not true, no one would be that desperate, would they.

'I told you to stay in the van … Sarah could come home any minute.'

He looks like someone out of a Freemans catalogue. He's old, so I suppose it's not his fault.

'I need to use the bathroom.'

'Be quick … Don't touch anything.'

It's just as pristine as the kitchen. Her lotions smell so good, like crushed rose petals. Just in case I take a bar of soap from the top of a pile of fluffy towels. You never know if they'll have soap in France. One of the towels wraps twice round my body, I'd love to take one, but have nowhere to put it.

An hour later we're approaching the port. I've never left Charlie for this long before. This is wrong. This is Stuey's fault. I thought it would be an adventure, but it's not, it's insanity.

'I've changed my mind … About France. Idon't want to go, I don't want to see her. Just turn round and take me home.'

'Look, Marnie, it's ok … I understand you're nervous, but we can't -'

'I mean it Stuey. People get sent to prison for this sort of thing … Don't they. Smuggling people into a foreign country in the back of a bloody van.'

When he said we'd get round the passport thing, I thought he meant lie to the officials, say I lost it or something. But no, he wants me to hide for the whole crossing in the back of the van. The word kidnap springs to mind.

'Look, I'll look after you … I promise … As if you were my own daughter.'

There's a bundle of old rags. He told the man at the hire centre we're collecting some antique furniture from a dealer in France. He piles them on top of me, until I can barely breathe. Charlie would be laughing his head off, saying I'm just as dumb as the other girls. Something shifts in my stomach, then a strange feeling washes over me, it takes a while, but then I realise it's fear.

Chapter 13

Sarah

Mummy insisted we eat lunch, then study the baby section of her catalogue for nearly an hour. To top it all off, there was an accident on the motorway. I'm due on shift in an hour, there's no way I'll make it. The curtains are exactly as I left them. The receptionist at the hospital says she hopes I get well soon, and for some reason that makes me cry.

His dirty clothes are in the wash basket. He's been home. His toothbrush, holdall, and a selection of clean clothes are missing. I open his bedside cabinet, his credit card, passport, and the expensive watch I gave him for Christmas are gone. A pot of peppermint tea calms the baby. There will be clues. My husband always leaves clues. It's just a matter of finding them. In the sitting room, it's clear he sat on the sofa, the cushions have been disturbed. As I rearrange them, I find a half eaten packet of sweets. Stuart never eats sweets. The hairs on the back of my neck bristle. The bed hasn't been slept in. He didn't stay here last night.

The thing with Stu is, although he doesn't actually like me, he respects me, which is far more important in a relationship. He would never bring one of his cheap tarts within a ten mile radius of our home. He never spends the night with them, always uses a condom. Sometimes I truly believe he honestly thinks I don't know what he gets up to, even though he always provides evidence. If it isn't physical proof, it's the guilt written in capital letters all over his face.

Inside the wardrobe his suits hang in a neat row, underneath he keeps his shoes in the boxes they came in. One particular box doesn't contain shoes. Nothing is missing, the contents undisturbed; a faded black and white photo, old cinema stubs, bus tickets, scraps of paper filled with her familiar scrawl, a lock of soft dark hair stuffed inside a sweet wrapper. So he intends to come back. There's no way he'd have left this behind, if he didn't.

After a long soak, I see it. Someone other than my husband has been in my house. The lavender soap mummy brought me back from Cornwall, before daddy had the stroke is gone and whatsmore one of my towels has been unfolded. Stuart would never touch my towels, he has his own, wouldn't dream of taking a bar of soap, preferring that dreadful sticky stuff from a plastic dispenser.

Night settles in, the phone remains silent. Who to call? He has no family, no friends that I know of. I try to remember every detail of Friday evening, Saturday at Chelmney. He'd been with a woman on Friday, I could smell her on him. But there's nothing unusual about that. I was a little shocked that he offered to come to Chelmney, he hates seeing daddy, after the stroke. A wave of nausea washes over me, what if she was in Chelmney. The only woman he'd leave me for. Then the shoe box thing would make perfect sense. He wouldn't need it would he, not if he had the real thing.

In the early hours, it all becomes clear. He'll lead me to her. She's a part of my daughter, after all. Stuart was just driftwood, something to cling onto, to stop me drowning. We'll watch him float away, then it will just be the three of us, like it was always meant to be. Daddy was right, things work out, if you only give them time to.

Chapter 14

Ron

I missed my time to die. Ever since I've been waiting for the final phase of punishment. Now it's here. Strangers touch me, poke fingers into places only my wife should know. They feed me. I eat, though the food chokes me. I don't deserve not to. She will come every day. This is her punishment too.

The ghosts roam freely here. She's not here to protect me. The staff can't see them because they're mine. They dwell where I dwell. They loiter in the shadows, good as gold in daylight hours. At night they prank. Two little girls, so similar in looks, so different in nature. They're playing a game, ask me to join them. It's impossible, I can't move, however much I try. They run in circles, so fast it hurts my eyes, run in ever decreasing circles, until they meet in the centre, mutate into a two-headed, eight limbed Medusa, hair a mass of serpent's tails.

I've heard the screams before, too many times for comfort. Bore witness to a place that bound its inmates with ribbons of barbed wire to the very things they were desperate to escape from. Medusa fades into the darkness. Then the demons come. Two babies with fiery halos floating above moon like heads. I try to wake, make my escape, but sleep holds me in its vice like grip.

Awake, memories are all I have left. One day, high summer, a gentle philanthropic breeze drifting through my study window, my daydreams free as the sparrow singing in the apple tree. Sweet honeyed laughter floating through petal infused air from the orchard we destroyed when Sarah left home. Trees are not easily replaced, take years of dedication. They didn't deserve their fate, at least I deserve mine.

One spring day, about two years earlier, I returned from the office to find two dark heads bent over our kitchen table, instead of the usual one. Hesther arrived in our lives. Before

Hesther, Sarah had no friends, was a born loner, or so the teachers told us. To the delight of my wife, little Hesther was the daughter of an esteemed London barrister. From that day on they were inseparable, Mary often complimented in public for having adorable twin girls, something she never bothered to challenge. Instead she nurtured the friendship, like one of her prize dahlias. But flowers die. We were woefully unprepared for those halcyon years to come to an end.

Sarah is spoilt. We denied her nothing from the day she was born. We were old parents, never bothered trying too hard at procreation. One glass of wine too many at the law society ball, a plush hotel room in London, and at the age of almost forty, Mary was pregnant. So it was clear from the start, Sarah would always be an only child. By that point I was senior partner in a firm of solicitors, so money was not something we had to unduly consider.

In the early months, Mary attempted to befriend Hesther's mother. The wife of a barrister, would have been a peacock feather in her hat at the Rotary club. Auriel was a drinker. Not a social drinker, but a bona fide inebriate. When she married Hesther's father, she exchanged the discipline of ballet, for the tightrope skills of a consumate sot. Charles, her husband was a veritable volcano of a man. Powerful in build, a study in calm composure, until he stood up in the courtroom, where he never lost a single case. Although both trained in the law, his world was a planet away from mine. On the rare occasion we met, I conceded without question to his superiority.

With a mother consumed by gin and a father living largely in London, Hesther was very nearly an orphan. We enveloped her in our small family, then each weekend Charles claimed her for himself, and Sarah became a loner again. If she'd had her way, we would have adopted Hesther, passed her off as our own. Of course we grew to love her. She was the sort of child it was impossible not to love. Anyone could see Hesther didn't need us. Hesther didn't need anybody. Hesther was full to the brim with Hesther. But without realising it, the three of us had forgotten how to live without her sunshine.

Chapter 15

Stuart

I've never given Sarah much cause for concern. Never stayed out too late, missed work, embarrassed myself in front of her parents. I should have called last night, made up something. I'll think of something on the ferry, call her when we get to France.

'Good evening Sir, ticket and passport please.'

My hand shakes as I hand him the documents. Can I trust her. There's silence as he glances into the void behind me.

'Are you travelling alone today, Sir.'

'I'm collecting a fireplace ... From France ... Antique ... For a friend, that's why I rented the van, so that -'

'Very well, Sir.'

He waves his hand in a nonchalant manner, and very slowly we move from the security of land into unchartered waters.

I hate sailing. As I slam the door of the van, there's not a sound from the back. Two large whiskeys help calm my shattered nerves, but the swell is deep and my stomach takes over. I reach the gents just in time to throw the amber liquid into the toilet bowl.

'This is a passenger announcement ... I repeat a passenger announcement. Will a Mr S. Horncastle please proceed immediately to the main desk on deck one.'

The entire contents of my gut evacuated, I venture out, expecting a hand to land squarely on my shoulder. I couldn't trust her, after all. I wonder what she's told them, whatever version of events she chose, I'm not going to come out of this smelling of roses. Dark water swirls in devilish circles below us, a brutish wind cuts through my shirt sleeves. Would it be better down there, prove a softer option than what's waiting for me up there. I imagine Sarah's face, a study in piteous disdain, Mary maintaining a cool composure, but crumbling inside from the shame.

'Mr Horncastle, thank you for coming. So sorry to interrupt your passage.' My hands are shaking, I bury them in my pockets. 'You appear to have left something behind, I wanted to return it to you, before you began to panic.' I can see it in his face, he's toying with me, taking pleasure in my obvious discomfort. She must be in the room behind him. They'll drag me away in handcuffs, I'll never see her again, never see you again. 'I take it you haven't missed it yet.' He's trying to force a confession, perhaps that would make easier.

'Look ... I'm sorry ... It was a supid thing to do, well more than stupid, but I -'

'You left it on the bar ... An easy mistake to make.' He reaches under the desk, produces my wallet with a flourish. 'Be more careful Sir, we get all types on board ... If you know what I mean. Not everyone's as honest as you and me.'

For the rest of the journey, I count the seconds, each one longer than the one before. Back in the van, my mind goes blank, the art of driving evades me, until an emphatic horn shocks my brain into gear.

'Bonsoir Monsieur, your passport, if you please. You are the only passenger, oui?' I knew it was too good to be true, they found her on the ferry, let me reach dry land, so the police could take over. I remove my hands from the steering wheel, ready to raise them at the first sight of a gun. 'Are you alright Monsieur, where are you heading, perhaps I can be of assistance.' I hand him my passport and the piece of paper with your address on it. 'Oh yes, the most beautiful region of my country. Most of the English head to Paris, or the coast ... But you, Monsieur have taste. I spent time as a boy with my grandparents in the next village. I wish you bon voyage. How you say in English ... Drive careful ... Drive smart.'

We clear the environs of the port and I pull into a layby. There's not been a sound from the back of the van.

'You can come out now ... We've done it ... We're in France.' I unlock the door and climb in, the rags are just as I left them. She comes at me like a fiend, nails clawing at my face, fists flailing at my chest, her boots cutting into my shin bones. I let her vent her rage, she's here, she's alive, that's all that matters right now. When she runs out of steam, I hold her in my arms like a child, her sobs come thick and fast. 'I'm so sorry Marnie. It was all my fault. I should never have forced you to do it. Please forgive me, I'll -'

'I hate you ... I was so scared ... I thought you'd told them, thought they were going to lock me up forever.' There's an acrid stench. 'I couldn't help it, I wet myself. You've got the address now, haven't you ... You don't need me anymore ... Not really ... You said you'd treat me like your own daughter ... That's why I came ... It's a bloody good job you never had kids.' Her sobs start to subside. 'The least you can do is buy me dinner, I'm bloody starving.'

Chapter 16

Marnie

I tried to pretend I was Charlie. He'd have screamed and screamed, banged his fists on the side of the van. I just lay there like a dummy. I am a dumb dummy after all. I thought Stuey didn't need me. But now I see it. I'm his way to her. I hold the power, and I intend to use it.

'Look Marnie it's late ... I'm too tired to drive. We can get something to eat, sleep in the van, set off early tomorrow morning.'

Is he joking. There's no way I'm sleeping in the fucking van.

'Find us a hotel. And I need some new clothes. These are filthy. You can buy me some tomorrow ... On the way there.'

We stop at what looks like a service station, there's a hotel and a cafe. We eat burgers and chips, I knew the snail thing must have been wrong. They only have a twin room, but even sharing with him is better than the van. Under a hot shower, I use Sarah's soap. He's gone straight to bed, even though he smells nearly as bad as me. I climb into bed naked, eat the yoghurt from Sarah's fridge with my fingers. The room's small, there's barely a gap between our beds, it's almost as bad as being in the van.

'Marnie ... It's time to go.' It's not even light. He's dressed in yesterday's clothes. It's way too early, me and Charlie always sleep until at least nine. 'Use the bathroom and get dressed, I'll wait outside.'

I have no choice but to put on my stinky clothes. I wrap the soap in a tissue, for later. As we drive, daylight comes, it turns out France looks just like England, except the road signs are in French. I can't help feeling a bit excited though. I never go anywhere, and now I'm in a foreign country. It must be different, in the towns, when you get off the motorway.

'I want to stop ... In a town. She doesn't know we're coming, does she, so it's not as if she'll be waiting for us.'

'I don't know Marnie, we should probably just -'

'Take me to a town Stuey, otherwise I want to go home.'

This is way better than anywhere I've ever been. Not that I've been to many places. One of the fosterers took us to a holiday camp in Wales. I liked it, the swimming pool, the horses, the little wooden house on stilts where we stayed. But Charlie hated it, poured a whole bottle of cooking oil into the pool, tried to set light to it with a match, said it was educational, like a chemistry experiment. We went home three days early. I got the flu, they sent us back to the home. I feel guilty thinking it, but I'm glad Charlie's not here to ruin this for me.

The buildings are made out of sand coloured stone rather than red bricks. There are wooden shutters painted blue round the windows, rather than net curtains and purple flowers growing up the walls. It smells of coffee and bread, rather than chip shop grease. People sit on chairs outside cafes drinking out of tiny cups and smoking cigarettes. We pass by a man selling the biggest peaches ever from a wooden barrow, he hands me one saying it's a gift for a beautiful girl. No one gives you anything in England or calls you beautiful, this is way better, this is where I should be living, and it's her fault I'm not.

I drag him over to a table, order us both coffees, even though I hate coffee, it just seems the right thing to drink here. Madame Gillet used to say that Sharon was top of our class in French. I wish Madame Gillet could see me now. When the waitress brings our drinks, I ask her if there's a chemist nearby and for good measure, where the nearest post box is. Stuey looks suitably impressed, I'm guessing his French is way worse than mine, he hasn't said a word yet. She tells me there's a chemist round the corner and a post box at the end of the street. Instead of just disappearing with a sulky face like the waitress in our local cafe, she's happy to stop and chat, asks me where we're from, what we're doing here. I tell her me and my dad are touring round France, my mother is too weak to travel, wanted us to come, so she could hear of our adventures in the country she was born. Stuey looks in another world, obsessing about her, probably.

Usually I hate small talk. But it's different in French, I could chat to this girl for hours. I suppose the challenge of using another language makes it worthwhile, somehow. She's about my age, pretty in a French way, not like those bimbos you see hanging around the shopping centre at home. Her hair is cut in a bob, I'm going to get mine cut exactly the same when I get home. She tells me about college, I tell her about Oxford. Madame Gillet would take back the 'must try harder' on my school report if she could see me now. The bitch wasn't even French, she just pretended.

'Time to go Marnie … Get back on the road.'

I want to spit at him, for spoiling my fun, but smile, like he's the best dad in the world. The waitress shows me to the ladies. Then to my amazement, as we leave, she kisses me on both cheeks, wishes us bon voyage, and I swear there's a tear in her eye when she wishes my mother a speedy recovery. I can't remember anyone ever kissing me before. I've never had a friend, well not a real friend anyway. It's clear as fuck. This is where I'm meant to be. I've been living in the wrong country all this time. I hate Hesther more than ever, she ruined my life not once but twice.

As we drive, he won't talk, says he needs to concentrate on the road. So to pass the time, I shut my eyes and play out my favourite story. Long dark hair flowing over the pillow, a pale face, blood, bucket loads of blood, pouring like lava onto a white sheet. Two doctors who look like the Ewing brothers from Dallas. The father pacing up and down, a famous film star who looks a lot like Marlon Brando. The Bobby Ewing doctor telling him to sit down. Good news, he has a baby girl, the most beautiful baby girl they've ever seen. The bad news, his wife was too delicate for childbirth. The mother, eyes closed like Sleeping Beauty, but with bucket loads of blood. The father driving three days later to collect his daughter, eyes blinded by tears. The crash. Instant death. A funeral, two ebony coffins, a single red rose on each one. The orphan, stolen by bandits, abused, then left to a life of poverty in a home for delinquent girls. A girl who thrives against all odds, graduates from Oxford, becomes a famous psychologist, buys a mansion in the hills.

That's the last time I'm going to tell it. It's just a dumb

childish story. I hope Hesther is dead, can't wait to see Stuey's face when he finds out he's done all this for nothing.

'Wake up ... Marnie, wake up. We're nearly there.'

I feel awful, it's too hot. I need a cold drink, something to eat. There are too many trees, tiny fields, houses scattered like seeds instead of proper streets. There are goats, enormous white cows, we almost run over a chicken in the road. We reach the village, park next to a church in a small square. I need to pee, have no choice but to go behind a tree. I should've asked the waitress to help me, told her he's not really my dad, that he kidnapped me. Then I'd be with her now, instead of here in the middle of bloody nowhere. The place is deserted, it's nothing like the town we went to earlier. I can't believe they chose to live here.

'Look Stuey, she won't be here. It's the back of beyond. Let's just give up and go -'

'Look ... Over there. It's some sort of bar ... Come on, we can ask there.'

I have two choices. Escape into the wilderness, starve to death or get eaten by a wolf, or go with him. It looks shut, like it closed down years ago. He pulls at the heavy wooden door, it opens. We fight our way through a thick velvet curtain, into a dimly lit room. My eyes struggle to focus after the brightness of the sun. A cloud of cigarette smoke stings my eyes, makes my lungs burn, until I start to choke. Charlie would love it. Three ancient looking men sit at a table next to a narrow bar. They drag their eyes away from the cards in their hands to focus on us. I feel like a species of animal they've never seen before.

One of the speaks, his accent is so strong, I can't understand him. Then one of the others mutters under his breath,

'Mon Dieu ... C'est petite Hesther ... Mon Dieu.'

Her name spurs him in to action.

'Bonjour, do any of you gentlemen speak English. We're looking for -'

From a low door behind the bar, a woman appears. Her hair is tangerine coloured, she's wearing a shapeless purple smock. It's impossible to tell her age, her skin is crinkled as an orange, but there's something bright, almost youthful in her eyes. I'm about to ask for a drink, she sees me, grabs onto the bar to

steady herself.
'Ce n'est pas possible. Non … Ce n'est pas possible.'

Chapter 17

Stuart

I hand her the piece of paper Connor gave me yesterday. She sighs deeply, pushes it back in my hand.

'It is gone ... The house is no longer there.'

'What do you mean .... Gone.'

'It was, how you say ... Too damaged ... After the fire ... She stayed for a while, Hesther's mother, but when she went, they pulled it down.'

'Fire ... What about Hesther ... Her father, what -'

'So tragic, such a beautiful child.' Her eyes rest on Marnie. 'You are so like her, it was a shock, when I saw you ... Standing right here in my bar, like a ghost.'

I can't believe what I'm hearing, a cold sweat drenches me, despite the heat.

'Ghost ... You mean Hesther ... She -'

'She was burned in the fire. They say she was trying to save her father, but I don't know. They took her to the big hospital ... In Lyon. When they let her out, her mother left. Petite Hesther never came back. Such a dear girl, such a kind girl. We rarely saw her father ... He stayed away ... Most of the time. Her mother had her groceries delivered, hardly ever left the house ... But petite Hesther used to sit here in the square ... Always writing ... Toujours a crayon in her hand ... I used to give her food, such a skinny little thing. She loved my tarte aux pommes. It used to make me sad, to see her all alone. Our enfants ... They leave the village ... Go to Paris, Lyon ... And who can blame them, there is nothing here for them. What was here for Hesther, she should have been at college, so bright, but left here all alone, just to sit and write ... It was wrong, but what could we -'

'Her father, what happened to -'

'He died right there in the house. Some people said he

deserved it ... After what happened, but not me, I'

'When they let her out of hospital ... Where did they go, Hesther and her mother.'

'I don't know.'Bile rises in my throat, this can't be the end. Marnie hasn't uttered a word. She never knew you. This is just a story to her. 'Then a year later ... I got a card ... In the post. There was no address, so I could not reply, just a charming letter, so typical of Hesther. After spending all that time in hospital ... She was caring for sick enfants ... Somewhere in Nice, she said ... A children's hospital by the ocean ... It made me happy to think of her there, in the sunshine, she -'

'You said something happened ... With her father, what -'

'It was right here in the square, for all to see. He was with a girl ... Not Hesther, but another girl. A girl who looked like Hesther, about the same age. She was English, screaming at him, crying ... She was not a good girl, like Hesther. He should have known better ... Shouting ... Making a display of them both, it was not good to see. After a while, I went out, and you will not believe it ... The girl, she spat at me like a cat. He dragged her away, then there was the fire. We never saw her again ... The bad girl. But they told us she did not die. She brought evil to our village, then left. But what have you come here for, we have nothing to -'

'She's my mother ... Hesther.' Claudette shakes her head. 'They came here because she was pregnant.' Her voice trembles. 'She sent me back to England, so I couldn't find her.'

'Mais non, Mademoiselle. Hesther was a good girl. She was not with child ... She was only a girl herself.'

'I knew it. You didn't betray me. You're not her mother. The relief is so intense, I feel dizzy and have to sit down.

'Are you quite sure ... We were lead to believe that -'

'Quite sure Monsieur. There was no baby in that little girl, you can trust me on that.'

'Hesther is my mother ... She must have hidden it. Her name was in my file ... In the children's home ... I look like her, there's no other explanation.'

Claudette sighs, shakes her head. We have a lead, it's time to go. I need to call Sarah, before she reports me missing, this is going to take longer than I thought. Marnie is silent as we drive, her eyes closed. When we reach the main road, I turn south. A children's hospital in Nice. A broken thread to cling onto.

Chapter 18

Ron

She was thirteen when the cracks began to show. They'd been there all along, but we chose to ignore them. As they matured into adolescence, Sarah and Hesther became more alike than ever. Or rather, on reflection, Sarah became a paler version of Hesther. Hesther was simply Hesther, it would have been impossible for her to be anything else.

The time came for secondary school. Hesther was enrolled by her father at Grosmont Private Academy For Girls, one of the top ten schools in the country, with a price tag to match. We chose Greenacres, a perfectly respectable private girl's school, just outside Chelmney. Although financially stable, we were nowhere near the Grosmont league. Sarah was an adequate rather than exceptional student, so a scholarship was out of the question. We informed her of our decision over supper. The following day she refused to eat. Then one afternoon a few days later, Mary received a call from the school secretary informing her that Sarah had fainted in class, was everything alright at home.

We remortgaged the house. They both started at Grosmont the following September. The uniform alone cost me a month's salary. Life seemed seamless for Hesther, despite her mother's condition. Her father was wealthy beyond our comprehension, she made top grades at school with little effort, brought the sunshine into a room with her. I sometimes wondered, why just the two of them. Hesther could have taken her pick of friends. But it was rare we saw them with anyone but each other.

Sarah thrived during her first year at Grosmont. We congratulated ourselves for choosing wisely, convinced ourselves it was worth every penny. I can see now that Sarah began to resent the fact I was not as successful as Hesther's father. Most of the girls in her school came from families of a different nature to hers. We were middle class. Charles came from old money, employed a full-time gardener. Hesther said she loved our family home, hated the dark formality of her own. On a rare occasion, when Charles was home, the girls spent time at Hesther's house. Mary was on edge, claimed it was because Sarah was in the company of a drunkard. But we both knew the real reason. We were lost without them, our two little girls. Or rather lost without Hesther shining her light into our shadows.

I dreamt about her last night. She was all alone, her hair hanging in rat's tails, eyes too big for her face. At first I didn't recognise her. She called out 'Daddy'. I tried to reach her, scoop her up in my arms, like I used to when she was a little girl. She was too heavy. Heavy as a sack of lead. He came from nowhere, the man with a clawed hand, picked her up as if she was made of cotton wool. He hissed at me like a serpent. She was his now. I didn't deserve her. I tried to chase him, but my legs turned to stone. My little girl was gone forever.

Chapter 19

Marnie

Everyone has a gun in America. A real gun in your handbag, like it's a comb or a tampon, or something. Charlie says it sounds awesome, guns are so much better than knives. If we were American, I'd be dead by now, for sure. But the weird thing is, even though having a gun is no more illegal than having a ham sandwich, you're not supposed to use it, not in public, anyway. You can shoot a bottle in a wood, but not someone who bugs you on the street. Charlie says it's like giving candy to a baby and telling it not to lick. Weirder still, if you do shoot someone, they can actually kill you for doing it. So murder is ok for them, but not for the ordinary man or woman on the street.

If I had a gun now, I'd seriously consider using it, whatever the consequences. We're going to Nice. I had no choice in the matter. He's lost his mind. I swear if he thought she was on the bloody moon, he'd hire a spaceship and drag me up there with him. He's a psycho, you can't reason with a psycho, can you.

The old woman said my mother wasn't pregnant. There was this girl at the home. She didn't even get really fat, or anything, didn't have a clue, then one day they took her into hospital and a baby popped out. Just because she looked skinny, doesn't mean she didn't have me in her belly. It's hard to believe that after giving me up, she went to nurse other peoples babies in some hospital. If we find her, I'm going to let them know just what sort of a person she really is. She'll get the shock of her life, and in a way, I wish Charlie was here to see it.

'Look Stuey ... Before we get to Nice, I need some clothes ... You promised me. I can't turn up looking like this, and you could do with a wash, as well.'

Aix-en-Provence is even better than the town we stopped in this morning. Stuey's been here with Sarah, so he knows his way around. So many people, even though it's getting late. Everything shuts early in Chelmney. I love the trees, the fountains, restaurants with waiters dressed like penguins. I'm glad Charlie's not here after all, he'd find a way to ruin everything, he always does. Stuey's walking way too fast for me to take it all in. I want to be like a regular tourist for a while, he owes me that. We hurry past shops selling wine, olives, bars of nougat. I needn't have worried on the soap front, there's loads of it. I want to taste an olive. I bet she gorges herself on olives every day. They weren't the sort of food they fed us in the home.

I stop. He doesn't even notice, keeps on walking. I go into the nearest shop. White wooden tables are stacked with soaps, lotions, perfume, sweet smelling candles. A tall skinny woman with a mass of ginger hair piled high on her head, looks up from a newspaper. I know I look a mess, but she doesn't have to glare at me like that. I'm a paying customer, aren't I, she doesn't know I have no money. Everyone here looks so stylish, like they've just stepped out of a magazine. No one would give me a second glance in Chelmney, but here I stick out like a rat in a goldfish bowl. She watches me spray some perfume, smell the soaps and candles. It costs as much as a pair of shoes for a bar of bloody soap, I'm glad I've brought my own, after all. If Charlie was here, he'd really wind the snooty cow up.

I watch him through the window, pacing up and down, peering into doorways, down side streets. I could've been murdered by a charming psychopath in a berret, and it would all be his fault. He has this gormless look on his face, like Columbo, but not pretending. He'd never make a detective, it's a good job he only sells insurance for a living.

'Marnie, thank goodness.' He's panting like a sheep dog, a stream of sweat running down his forehead. Rather than angry, he looks close to tears. 'I turned round, you were gone, why did you -'

I decide to have a bit of fun, Charlie would be proud of me.

'Papa ... I was so scared. You were walking so fast ... A man ... He tried to grab me ... I escaped, came in here for safety ... It brought it all back, the last time, the ransom, the cellar, the knife ... I'm ok Papa, I'm safe.' Miss snooty's eyes are on matchsticks. For good effect I take off my jacket. She sees my arms, gasps out loud. 'I couldn't bear to go through all that again. That last deal you did, the Texan oil baron, I'm scared.'

The shock subsides, she remembers her manners.

'Bonsoir Monsieur, Mademoiselle, if there's anything I can show you, please just ask. There are samples, if you want to try our -'

'You said I could pick out something for my birthday ... Before we go back to the yacht ... In Nice.'

She smiles, waves her hand around the shop. I pile items into a basket, mentally clocking up the price. As she enters the figures into the cash register, I imagine Charlie wiping that self satisfied grin right off her cherry red lips. You could put a deposit on a flat in Chelmney for less, but he doesn't seem to notice, just hands over his credit card, as if he really is a millionaire with a yacht in Nice. We leave the shop with three paper bags of stuff I don't really want. You can only use one bar of soap at a time, can't you. I wish I'd just asked him for the cash. Me and Charlie could have a real holiday with that sort of money.

'Come on Marnie, we need to eat ... We've both had a shock.'

He picks a table outside one of the restaurants. Polished silver cutlery lies on top of napkins, so big you could dry yourself on one of them.

'Thanks for the gifts ... Your face when -'

'Look ... We need to talk, I was out of my mind with worry ... When I lost you. I'm the adult, you're only a child ... Really ... I should never have forced you into coming ... It was wrong, I can see that now.' He looks genuinely sorry, this is turning out way better than I thought. 'I'm giving you the choice, right now. If you want to go home, we'll eat then I'll take you.'

A penguin thrusts a leather bound menu at me. He's good looking, but in a fake film star kind of way. The sort of handsome you never see in England. He even speaks as if he's reading from a script, not like the waitress from this morning. When he walks away, I stick out my tongue and Stuey laughs as if it's the funniest thing he's ever seen. A group of people at the next table are picking fish from shells piled high on a silver platter. I hope they have normal food, maybe the snail thing is true after all. He orders steak and chips for us both, a coke for me, and a bottle of wine. When the penguin brings the wine, he pours a bit into Stuey's glass and Stuey pretends he knows what he's doing, swirling it round his mouth like those nutters on the telly. The penguin pours a glass for us both.

The funny thing about wine is, the more of it you drink, the better it tastes. By my second glass, I love it more than coke. The steak is delicious. It's all been worth it, even the ferry. I never want to go home, not ever. When the bottle's empty, he orders another, asks for the dessert menu. I feel like I'm in heaven, but without the dying bit.

'Look, I can't drive tonight ... After all this wine. I'll find us somewhere to stay, and if you want to, I'll take you home tomorrow.'

'Have you thought about the fire ... We haven't talked about it ... But she'll have scars ... Won't she. Do you really want to see her ... After all those years ... She'll have changed. It's different for me. I just want her to see that you can't just have a baby, throw it away like trash and get away with it forever.'

'You don't know her ... She could never change, no matter how many scars she might have.'

I top up my glass, wine is awesome.

'I saw your wedding photo ... At your house ... You looked happy, Sarah's gorgeous ... I really don't understand why you're doing this ... I know you're using me, to get to her ... But why. I love France ... Do you know that, Stuey. I'm going to stay. This is where I belong. You can just drop me at that town we went to this morning ... Tomorrow ... Then you can do what you want.'

'Sarah say she's pregnant. She told me on Saturday night. I can't have kids, Marnie. She's having a baby, and I've no idea where it came from ... The thing with me and Hesther, is well, we never split up, ended things. We were in love and one day her family just went ... Disappeared. So she's still mine, really. It was easy ... Marrying Sarah, easier than not marrying her. It's hard to explain, but -'

'That must be hard ... Both of them cheating on you, you're just too nice Stuey.'

The bottle's empty. The chocolate mousse bowls licked clean. My head spins when I get up, like it does when Charlie makes us drink vodka and coke. I try to imagine him, all alone in our flat, crazy out of his mind with worry, but I can't, my head feels too woozy.

We walk slowly, the streets are still full of people, it's warm, it feels like home.

'I know a small hotel ... Me and Sarah stayed there once, we were on our way to -'

'I've changed my mind. I want to carry on ... With you ... Tomorrow ... To Nice.'

He runs his hand down my back.

'You won't regret it ... I promise you.'

I don't believe him, but it doesn't matter anymore. I know he doesn't believe it either.

Chapter 20

Sarah

Unlike Stuart I refused to give up. If he'd tried hard enough, he could have found her. He just didn't want it enough. I watched him drift around town, loiter outside her house, as if his very presence would bring her back.

I dressed smartly, careful to hide any sign of my condition. At Chiswell and Son estate agency, I asked to speak to the manager. Mr Chiswell offered me the position on the proviso he could take me for a ride in his brand new Jaguar the following Sunday. I started at nine 'o' clock sharp the following day, by ten-thirty my work was done.

It took far more planning than anticipated. I'd been abroad before, Portugal with my parents, so was equipped with a passport. From a careful examination of a map in the library, it was clear they were living miles away from any airport.

A baby was never part of the plan. He lied and I believed him. When I realised, I was in shock. But then I understood. My baby was evidence, proof I was telling the truth.

When they released me from the so called clinic, I never returned to school. The so called doctors said it was not advisable, and my parents believed them. My world boiled down to walks and books which I never read. They were still together. I used to trail them, pitied them for having nother better to do than go to the cinema or hang around aimlessly. I felt sorry for him then. She was doing it out of spite, to hurt me, he was just a pawn in our game, but the end was near, and we both knew who the winner would be. Sometimes he took her to his house. Somewhere I couldn't follow, made me wait for hours in the rain, only to watch them come out, giggling like children.

Mummy called what happened my teenage stumble. When I got out, my parents hated being left alone with me, I could see the terror in their eyes. One wrong word, one chance encounter, could be enough to tip me back into the abyss, the deep pit where they couldn't reach me.

I invented a new friend called Ellie. The concern on their faces was clear to see, but they never asked to meet her. No one could replace Hesther in their affections, not even me. A weekend away with Ellie and her parents in the Cornish countryside would do me the world of good, they both agreed.

It wasn't until I arrived at Lyon airport that I began to panic. Fortunately my savings account had blossomed over the last few years, due to my confinement. The taxi driver looked like I'd asked him to take me to Mars, but soon changed his mind when he saw the bundle of notes in my purse. Two hours later, I was there.

I was dreaming about her. I always know, because my pillow is damp with tears when I wake up. Two strong coffees make my baby tetchy. Something milky will help to soothe her. I must have missed it yesterday, one of my cherry yoghurts is missing. Stuart would never voluntarily eat a yoghurt. She's been in my fridge. The thought of it makes me want to vomit.

At lunch time, it hits me. The credit card. We have a joint account. Mummy pays it most of the time, anyway, so it's easier that way. He rarely uses it, but it's close to his pay day, he's likely to use it in the interim. A phone call later and I know he's in France. He paid for a ferry crossing, and a hotel near Calais. I need to be sure they're heading south.

Mummy seems satisfied with the story, we're having a few days in Paris to celebrate the baby. To take my mind off things, I deep clean the house, wipe every fingerprint from every surface, change the bed linen, just in case. I need to change the locks, but it will have to wait until I get home. My daughter flutters, so I rest. Tolerating Stuart for all these years has proved worthwhile in the end. Two hours later a fill up at a petrol station proves they're heading south. It's time to pack.

After a last check of the house, I grab the rubbish, set the alarm and leave. There's something unfamiliar in the bin. Stuart never does the rubbish. It looks like a mass of light brown fur. I hesitate to touch it, but curiosity takes over. It's a cheap teddy bear, like the ones you win at the fair. Vomit fills my mouth, I push it head first back into the bin. Cover it with the rubbish bag. The sweets, the bear, it's like they're acting out some childhood fantasy, like time stood still for them. Or even worse, they're playing out some sick game at my expense, just like last time. The ground spins, a fresh wave of nausea forces me to my knees. I was wrong, she doesn't deserve to live in the same world as my daughter. It's just the two of us. This time I'm going to finish what I started.

Chapter 21

Stuart

Aix is beautiful. I loved it from the first time I saw it with Sarah. It's still buzzing with life, at an hour when even London would be slowing down. She says she's changed her mind, it's probably the wine talking. I should never have let her drink so much. There would be dire consequences if I plied a sixteen year old with alcohol in a pub in London. It just seemed different here. We stop outside a brightly lit boutique, the sort of place where price is never displayed or mentioned.

'You need something to wear ... Don't you, for tomorrow.' I expect her to laugh, the clothes in the window really don't look like her sort of thing at all. 'Or we can go somewhere else ... In the morning.'

She takes my hand, leads me through the door. We leave with two bags, my credit card dangerously close to its limit. Mary's unlikely to settle it for me, under the circumstances. Marnie thinks I've done it for her. I wish I had. But I've done it for you. I can't present you with a girl who looks and smells like she's been living on the streets for weeks. Gifts should be gift wrapped, and whoever she is, she's my gift to you.

The cost of two rooms in a small hotel swallows my remaining credit. When I've stowed her safely in her room, I go back to the pay phone in the lobby. The phone rings out, Sarah doesn't pick up. At the bar, I take two large brandys, then stagger up to bed.

A light tap at the door, sounds like a lion's roar in my throbbing head. It comes again, a little louder. I find I'm fully dressed, right down to my shoes. She's almost unrecognisable, yet so achingly familiar. Without the protection of her black armour, she could easily pass for you. The simple linen dress in a duck egg blue is so perfectly cut, it skims her slender body. Her skin is paler than yours. You loved the sunshine, being outdoors. She looks like she's lived in a cave. Her scars are healing nicely, some French sun will do her good. The scuffed black boots have been replaced by a pair of cream patent leather sandals. Her face is scrubbed clean of the heavy make up, her hair hanging in a glossy curtain half way down her back. It's six-thirty in the morning.

'Come on sleepy head. Today's the day … Isn't it.' She twirls round the room, like a little girl in a party dress. 'You need a shower, some clean clothes. We should both look our best … Don't you think, Stuey.'

I splash my face, clean my teeth, don't feel up to showering or shaving. The miles pass by too quickly. I'm not ready, prepared. Whoever she is, she's sixteen. I've smuggled her in the back of a van, shared a hotel room with her, seen her naked, got her drunk on red wine. The past belongs in the past, doesn't it. That's why it's called the bloody past. What if I've turned us into something wrong, something squalid. When you left our love was set in stone forever, just like the couple on our bench in Chelmney. What if I'm about to take a pickaxe to that stone, shatter it into tiny pieces.

It's one of those hangovers that gets worse as the day goes on. The wine appears to have left Marnie unscathed, one of the benefits of youth, I suppose. Sarah adores Nice. I hate it, find it far too picture postcard perfect, a pastiche of a millionaire's playground. Holidays with my wife are to be endured, rather than enjoyed. I found that out quickly. Of course I never had a holiday before we met, so had little to compare it with, except for the beaming faces of the people on those holiday programmes, who to all intents and purposes looked to be having a bloody good time.

On our last trip to Nice, a couple of years ago, I lost her for a while. We visted the Matisse museum. I was honouring a particular painting with a good five minutes of my time. One minute she was right there, then when I glanced over, she'd gone. I searched the whole building, gave up and went for a drink. We met later at the hotel. She was in the bar with a Campari and soda. It seemed rude to ask about her absence, so I simply ordered a glass of wine, and we never spoke of what happened in our three hours apart.

'We're nearly there … Nice … Do you know where it is … The hospital?'

'I've been here before … With Sarah. There's one by the sea, we'll try there first.'

Chapter 22

Marnie

If Charlie could see me dressed like this, he'd piss himself. I never wear dresses, always wear black. We don't do much washing, don't even have a machine, so black is safer. He says wearing black makes us look like we can handle ourselves. But everyone dresses like this here and I want to fit in. When she sees me, I want her to see how well I've done without her.

When we were seven, we were fostered my Mr and Mrs Beech. They had a son of their own called Toby. He was older, maybe twelve or thirteen. His hair was the colour of the beef stew they fed us in the home and he was skinny as a railing, even though the greedy pig never stopped eating. Mr and Mrs Beech looked like a couple from a knitting pattern, all blond hair and glowing skin, they even wore matching jumpers. Toby despised me. One night I went downstairs for a glass of milk. Mr and Mrs Beech were talking in the front room, so I listened at the door. They wanted to adopt me. The thing was, Charlie hated Toby, as much as Toby hated me.

I came up with a plan. If I could make Toby like me, then maybe Charlie would like Toby. It was way better living there than in the home, we had our own room and there was a garden with a swing set and a tree house. Finally it was happening, finally I was going to get a set of parents. The next day I asked Mrs Beech if we could bake a cake, offered to take a piece up to Toby, who was doing homework in his room. Instead of his science book, he was looking at pictures of naked women in a magazine. I went in, gave him the cake, was so desperate for my plan to work, I tried to ignore that his trousers were round his ankles. He invited me to sit next to him, actually smiled at me for the first time. After that it was all a blur. Charlie took over. It was only a bit of blood, but from Toby's reaction, you'd have thought he was being attacked by a mad axeman in a horror film.

Mrs Beech came running in, Charlie scarpered like he always does, dropped his penknife on the way out of the room. The following day, we were back at the home. I didn't speak to him for two weeks. I don't expect I'd be here now, if I hadn't left him at home on Sunday morning. The hospital is awesome. The windows are made of ocean and sunshine coloured glass. It's right by the sea, which is nothing like the sea in Chelmney, it's pure blue like one of those pictures in a travel brochure. I hate hospitals, but this looks more like a posh hotel. We watch people come and go, he doesn't seem in a rush to go inside. Is she here in this building, caring for other people's kids, when she couldn't even be bothered to care for me. The rage comes like hot embers through my veins. I don't think she'll be impressed when she sees Stuey, he looks awful and doesn't smell much better.

'Come on … We might as well get on with it … We're here now aren't we Stuey. You don't have to be nervous … I'll do all the talking.'

The door looks like it belongs to a cathedral, rather than a hospital. Inside the fear comes as quickly as the rage. We wait our turn at the reception desk. Eventually a man asks if he can help us. Then I see him. He's found me. I should've known. Charlie always knows how to find me. He's trying to hide behind a pillar, pokes out his head, sticks out his tongue. Words turn to straw in my throat. He's going to ruin everything. He always does.

Chapter 23

Ron

Guilt is a challenging concept. It's rarely a case of right or wrong, black or white. It comes in shades of grey, in rough brush strokes that leave you wondering what the picture really means. I learned this long ago as a student of the law. The difference was, back then my knowledge was purely theoretical.

The pain of guilt is a different creature altogether. It is hard as stone, black as jet, the most pernicious of punishments. It segregates the good from the bad. To shoulder guilt is a death sentence, without the release of death. Once guilt settles, it spreads like cancer, takes over a body, until all that remains are flaming embers of guilt.

Last night I wet the bed. Death is too good for those constructed out of guilt. I hear the others crying out for mercy in the night. But in the morning we guilty are still here.

We were never reaching for the moon, myself and my wife. Sarah and Stuart, always striving for something better, foreign holidays to places illsuited to the word holiday, meals in exotic restaurants, theatre productions which Einstein would struggle to follow. We were happy in our own way, in a gentle rhythm of hours and days. A rhythm we felt no desire to alter.

When Sarah came, she made few ripples in our world. Babies were easy in those days. For thirteen years we maintained an equilibrium. She was a good girl, and as thus, we believed ourselves to be good parents. Hesther simply made our rhythm sweeter. They were two girls who never strayed too far from the path, showed little interest in the mysteries of the forest on either side.

It was purely by chance that Hesther met a boy. We were no prudes. We knew that in good time our blossoming girls would start to notice boys, or more pertinently, boys would start to notice them. I often wonder, if Sarah hadn't contracted measles, would things have turned out differently. To Sarah's consternation, Hester remained steadfastly spot free, even though most of their class was afflicted.

When Sarah's confinement finally came to an end, Hesther made a joyous return to our home, equipped with flowers and chocolates for the invalid. She made us all sit around the kitchen table, said she had some news to share. I remember the shock of just how much I'd missed her. As the story unfolded, I expected Sarah to squeal in delight, drag her friend upstairs for a postmortem. Instead she listened silent as a stone, as Hesther, face flushed as a rose, regaled us with a story of the start of a teenage romance, declaring herself truly and madly in love.

When Hesther ran out of steam, there was a blankness in Sarah's eyes I'd never seen before. Only one girl reached the top of the stairs, turning to push her friend away as she tried to follow. That was the day the storm arrived. That was the day we came to realise that for thirteen years we'd simply been soaring on a thermal breeze, completely unprepared for what to do when the wind changed direction.

Chapter 24

Stuart

He has the smallest, whitest teeth I've ever seen.
'Bonjour Monsieur, do you speak English?'
'Of course, how can I be of assistance to you?'
Marnie was so excited in the van. Now she looks nervous, picks at one of her scars, a bead of blood drips onto her dress.
'We're looking for someone ... We were told she might still work here ... Or used to, anyway ... A nurse.'
'I'm sorry Monsieur, but we cannot give out that sort of -'
'Hesther Brompton.' He tries to hide it, but I can see it in his eyes. He knows you. His gaze falls on Marnie. 'As you can see by my daughter, we have family connections. We wouldn't take up your time, but -'
'This is not normal procedure ... But I will try to help you ... Please take a seat ... You have come a long way I presume.'
Ten minutes later he leads us down a gleaming corridor. This is nothing like Sarah's hopital, one of the most depressing places I've ever seen. Marnie refuses to look at me, hasn't said a single word since we arrived. He invites us to sit opposite him across an imposing mahogany desk.
'She's my half-sister ... Hesther. We share the same mother ... I was adopted before she was born. We lost my wife ... My daughter Marnie's mother recently. It was such a shock ... Came out of the blue.' For good effect I show him the photo of Sarah from my wallet. He examines it carefully. 'Anyway, Marnie ... She's desperate to meet her aunt, so we -'
'Firstly, let me say how sorry I am for your wasted journey. Perhaps you should have telephoned first. I think that under the circumstances, I do not speak out of the line.' His teeth gleam like tiny pearls, his tongue darts across them as he thinks. 'It was a great honour ... Having your sister here with us, for a time. She was so gentle with les enfants, a great favourite with

the parents ... An angel floating through our wards. We were so very sorry ... When she left us, in fact I-'

'Left you, you mean -'

'It was many years ago. Such a waste. Hesther was blessed with a true vocation for nursing. She was special. We were lucky to have her ... Even for a short time.' It's blindingly obvious, he was in love with you. That's why he agreed to talk. 'Mademoiselle ... You've been blessed with her beauty ... She would want to meet with you ... Of that I'm sure.'

Is she going to open her mouth, ruin everything. Her eyes are fixed on the door, like she's expecting someone to come in at any moment.

'Where did she go?'

'That Monsieur, I don't know. She said she would stay in touch ... But I never heard from her again ... Look, I should not really say ... But, her mother ... Your mother ... She lives near to here ... It was only a few days ago, when I saw her in the street. She says she does not know where our dear Hesther is ... But I don't believe her.'

We sit in silence, a gold fountain pen twirling in his fingers.

'Any information would be much appreciated, we really -'

'I will give you her address ... Your mother ... But you must not say it came from me. I hope it will not come as too much of a shock for her ... She is weak. All I ask of you in return ... If you find Hesther, will you remember me to her ... Tell her it is never to late ... To get in touch ... To come back to us.' He writes from memory, slides the paper across the desk. 'But before you go ... You knew, oui, that she was here ... Your wife ... Some years ago. She was upset ... Confused ... I could not tell her anything, not in that condition ... I'm very sorry for the loss of her.'

We escape down the corridor, into the heat of the rising sun. For the first time in my life, I'm going to meet your mother. Pierre was right, she must know where you are.

'We need to go home ... I'm not joking Stuey. Something bad's going to happen if we don't. It's over ... Take me home please, now.'

Chapter 25

Marnie

He's done it again. Ruined everything. The thing with Charlie is, he's way smarter than I give him credit for. Because of him, I sat there while Stuey told the weasel man a pack of lies. Let them talk about her like she was some sort of saint, rather than a common whore.

I feel sorry for Sarah. Lies drip off his tongue like melted butter. You wouldn't want a husband that can lie like that, would you. If Charlie gets his hands on Stuey, he'll kill him for sure, but I won't be taking the blame, not this time.

'Look Marnie … You're bound to be a bit apprehensive … I am, too. Let's just speak to her mother … It's only a couple of miles away, then you can tell me what you want to do.'

What sort of grandmother gives her granddaughter away, anyway. My stomach's a cement mixer of nerves. He drives, there's nothing I can do to stop him. It's small but pretty. A little white house, with pale blue shutters. In stories, grandmothers tend to be nice. Soft and cuddly, with food thrown in for good measure. Little Red Riding Hood walks through a perilous forest to see her grandmother. The thing is, she's so bloody dumb, when she gets there, she can't even see it's a wolf in the bed posing as her grandmother. At least I know my grandmother is a wolf posing as an old woman.

'Ok, Marnie … We need to think of a story.'

Here we go again, another pack of lies. What's wrong with the truth. Unlike them, I'm about to study at Oxford, one of the best universities in the world. All they could do was get pissed and have teenage sex. He knocks. There's no sign of Charlie, we must have lost him at the hospital. A car parks up down the street, nobody gets out. A few seconds later, the lock turns and I nearly piss myself. She's old, much older than I expected. Her hair's the colour of chalk, her eyes like sour milk. She's all skin and bone. I wonder if she ever met my father. She spots me trying to hide behind Stuey, lets out a high pitched scream. It curdles my blood, brings tears to my eyes, cuts like a scalpel through the silence of the street. Could this monster really be my grandmother. No, it's the wolf, for sure. She raises a fist in my direction, spits out a mixture of French and English, words a grandmother should not be using in the company of her long lost granddaughter. The cottage turns into a witch's hovel. She finishes her rant with the hiss of a cat, then slams the door behind her. I drag Stuey back to the van. Then I see him, hiding behind a bush, he waves at me and winks.

'Just drive will you ... This was all a big mistake ... Take me home now, or I'll tell the police you kidnapped me ... About the ferry and everything.'

He gets out. I watch him knock over and over. After a few minutes she opens the door, sees he's alone and ushers him into her lair. Charlie pokes his head through the window, says it's time to go. I've no choice but to get out and follow him.

Chapter 26

Sarah

I hate France. Nice in particular. It's a dreadful place, full of vulgar yachts and ridiculous tans. I can understand why she left, I would have done the same. Auriel thinks I destroyed her life. The stupid bitch can't see she destroyed it all by herself, long before I met her. She's brought him here to meet her mother before she dies, I'm pretty certain of it.

When my daughter came back to me, I decided enough was enough. I could leave Hesther in the past, where she belonged. My daughter was all I needed. Stu would make an adequate father. We'd grown used to each other over the years, it was easy, so I decided to keep him, allow him to benefit from a family he'd made no effort to contribute to. He threw my charity right back in my face.

Over a glass of iced water in a cafe, I remember our last visit to Nice. I hate museums, art galleries, ancient relics. Stuart pretends to love the arts. We visited the Matisse museum. He was really hamming it up, standing for an age in front of each exhibit, going on and on about post-expressionism, as if he was a bona fide art critic. He even told a group of students that he was trying to see beyond the paint, see right into the artist's soul. The thing with Stu is, he cares about nothing, which makes him a master of pretending to care about everything.

I left. He didn't even notice. I went to her house. Alcoholics always blame other people for their own miserable lives. An absent father, disinterested mother, wicked uncle. It could have been anyone, but she chose me. When I couldn't get anything out of Auriel, I tried the hospital. The stupid little man was obsessed with her, anyone could see that, was almost as desperate to find out where she was as me. He turned out to be just as useless as Auriel. They stayed in Aix last night. He took her to a fancy restaurant, bought her expensive gifts. They stayed in a boutique hotel. He's out to impress. If I hadn't taken him on board, he'd still be working on a building site and living in a crummy bedsit.

After my first visit to France, I was certain the police would come. My parents didn't ask for details about my trip to Cornwall with Ellie and her parents. I was getting bigger by the day. The time was fast approaching, when I would have no choice but to break the news, to shatter the veneer of normality they'd worked so hard to spin like a web around us. The police never came. Not that time anyway.

She didn't believe me at first, thought I was making it up. She claimed to hate her father, but anyone could see she worshipped him. I got to her through him, her Achilles heel, and in the end he got the end he deserved. Over all the rich handsome boys she must have met during her weekends in London with Charles, the bitch chose Stuart as a replacement for me.

When Hesther was born, Auriel stopped drinking. She loved to tell me that she'd saved her own mother, just by being born. Charles finally had the wife he thought he wanted. But it turned out he didn't want a real woman at all. He wanted the fantasy, the dancer on a stage, the Auriel he saw performing at Giselle at Sadler's Wells. She found out he'd been sleeping with a much younger actress, subsequently resumed her relationship with the bottle.

When we were little girls, she said she wanted to be a ballerina when she grew up, just like her mother. She showed me an old photo of some impossibly glamourous creature wearing a ballet dress and a tiara. I couldn't believe the skinny lady in a dirty coat at the school gates was the girl in the picture. But it was true. Auriel had once been one of the most acclaimed dancers in the world.

Hesther's mother was not in a fit state to engage in any extra curricula activities, just getting to the school gates was a Herculean challenge, so we asked mummy if she would take us to ballet classes. From the very first second, I hated it. The teacher was an authoritarian cow. Hesther loved her. She adored Hesther. At the end of our first class she said Hesther was the most promising student she'd ever had, referring to the rest of us as a tribe of baby elephants. Mummy tried to cheer me up, said neither her nor daddy were blessed with feet that would obey their owner's orders. For the next few weeks, I practised for hours in front of my bedroom mirror, until my feet bled and my head spun like a top. It didn't make an ounce of difference, the teacher said I danced like an over wound clockwork toy.

The time came for our first exam. I was sick in the school toilets before mummy came to collect us. Hesther had talked about nothing else for days. When Hesther had a passion, nothing else mattered. The exams took place in a private room, with only the student and teacher present. She went in first. My nerves were like needles by then. But still, somewhere deep inside there was a faint glimmer of hope, if only I tried hard enough. She came out with the biggest smile on her face, but before I could ask her what had happened, the teacher called me in.

It was bad enough dancing in a room full of girls, but all on my own in front of that hateful woman was too much to bear. I never danced a single step. She said I was wasting my time and mummy's money, try something else instead. I was only in the room for a few seconds, choking back the tears as I left. The teacher had told Hesther that with the right training she could become a prima ballerina.

Next day at school, she said ballet was too easy, it was boring, she'd decided to become a barrister like her father instead. We never went to another class, or mentioned ballet again.

My daughter moves gently as I sip my water. The heat is oppressive. This really is a wretched place. I drift away to my parent's garden, a cool lawn under my feet, the welcome shade of the apple trees, mummy out pruning the roses, cold lemonade in a jug.

In the car I tie a scarf over my head, put on sunglasses. Driving, I try to ignore the niggling doubt in my head. Have I imagined it all, are the carefully wound threads in my head unravelling like last time. My daughter kicks. I know this time I'm right. This time it's different.

Chapter 27

Ron

It's three 'o' clock. Another four hours until they manhandle me out of bed. I'm too hot, my nostrils full of cheap disinfectant. Our house always smelled like a meadow, even after the stroke. Mary efficiently dealt with bodily fluids at the point of exit. We are both weak now. Both alone. Demons have no fear of the lonely.

    It was the same dream. Screams so loud, they still ring in my ears. Sometimes I join in, but not tonight. Tonight I was helpless as a spring lamb. Girls in green robes, ice white corridors with no beginning and no end. Eyes gouged out of shaven heads. Some ran, some skipped, tripped, got back up again. I wandered among them, searching, always searching. I thought I saw her, but it was only a trick of the light. They called out 'help me, please help me.' I should have tried to save them, but instead I pitied them, despised them, desired them. Then she came like she always does. Tonight Hesther had wings, her hair made out of liquid gold. She was naked and I wanted her. I wanted her so much that shame engulfed me, blazing flames of shame, until the pain woke me.

    I chance pulling the cord, in the vague hope they might bring pills. Ten minutes later the one they call Jenny comes. The one who told me staff here come and go like night and day. I don't blame them. What sort of person would want to care for the old, for the feeble, for the ones death rejected. The cavalry arrives. One I've never seen before. They embark upon the task of cleaning me, changing the bed, stowing me safely away again, until the morning. As they work, they chat. But not to me. Jenny's husband is a cheating bastard, the new girl Violet used to work in a children's nursery, thinks caring for the elderly will be less demanding. They reward my good behaviour with two pink pills.

When Hesther stopped coming to our house, I'd sometimes spot her from a distance in town, she was always accompanied by a gangly looking lad. I never approached her, it would have felt like a betrayal of my daughter. We thought Sarah would come round, get over the shock of her friend forging a teenage romance. She didn't.

In the days after her disclosure Hesther would often pop round with little gifts for Sarah, handwritten notes, bunches of wild flowers. Sarah wouldn't see her. As time went on she didn't want to see anyone, not even us, refused point blank to go to school, spent days alone in her room, sent trays of food back down untouched. Then one Wednesday morning, Mary tried her door and it wouldn't open. We found out later that with some miraculous feat of strength, she'd managed to drag her wardrobe across the carpet and barricade herself in her room. We should have acted then. Instead we waited two full days, before admitting defeat and calling for help.

Chapter 28

Stuart

She's not what I expected. I can't see anything of you or Marnie in her. She looks a hundred years old, even though she's only in her late fifties. Despite her condition, the house is immaculate. I perch on the edge of a cream leather sofa. She sips from a glass of amber liquid.

'Why did you bring her to my door … Haven't I been through enough. It's his child, isn't it. She said her daughter died … I knew she was lying … She was always lying.'

'You mean Hesther, did she -'

'No her friend … I refuse to say her name. I knew from the first time I saw her she was trouble. A peculiar little child. Hesther only became her friend because she felt sorry for her.'

'Look … I know this sounds odd … But Marnie, the girl outside … Well we only met on Sunday. Me and Hesther … We were together, for two years, before you came to France. Her name was in Marnie's file at the children's home where she grew up … Marnie thinks Hesther is her mother.'

She laughs, takes a long gulp of her drink. I could really use one myself right now.

'So they gave her away … That doesn't surprise me. Hesther is her half sister, my husband was her father. That's why they look alike. It was all her fault … Hesther's friend, she seduced him you see. He was weak like all men, that was his crime, and he paid dearly for it … That girl is nothing to do with me … You should not have brought her here.'

'Did Hesther ever mention me when you moved. Why was it so sudden … Oh, I see, was it because of -'

'She came all the way to France, just to tell us. Did you know she spent time in a lunatic asylum. That girl out there … You stay well clear of her, she'll turn out just like her mother, you mark my words. She came here … Wanted to know where

Hesther was ... As if I was going to tell her, after what happened the last time. She would have ended up in prison, if I'd called the police ... I didn't have the energy ... I'm dying ... Did you know that. I was never meant to be a mother. Hesther belonged to him, not to me. She didn't need me, so I drunk. Then I let her go. I knew she was spending time with a boy, back then ... I saw her once ... With you. Why are you here, I never asked, did I ?'

'Hesther do you know where -'

'I should have guessed, you think you're in love with her, don't you ... Everyone thinks they are in love with Hesther. Right from the day she was born, everyone fell in love with her ... But she's not real, you know that, don't you. There's something missing ... I could blame myself, but I'm not going to.'

The relief is immense. Marnie's not yours. You're her sister. I can't give up now.

'I want to see her ... Hesther. I don't want to hurt her ... I'm married, I don't want anything from her, I just want to tell her I'm sorry ... That I missed her, that I hope she's happy.'

She looks unsure, so I pull the picture of Sarah from my wallet. Without warning she hurls the remaining contents of her glass in my face, the liquor burns my eyes, blinds me for a few seconds.

'You'll regret this ... Both of you ... I should have known you were in it together.'

She comes at me, I hold her away, she falls, her head cracking on the stone floor. It gives me time to search, I find it in her bedside cabinet, a tatty address book. As I leave I feel for a pulse, she's alive, that's something at least. Now I can offer Marnie an explanation, a reason to meet you.

The van's empty. She's gone.

Chapter 29

Marnie

He's in the mood for mischief. I try to distract him, mess around, tell him his favourite jokes. The last time he got me locked in a police cell, they let me go. Matron said I was extremely lucky. I tried to be brave, like things like that happened to me all the time. But I was scared, really scared. One of the police men looked like Father Christmas, a big white beard and boots, a kind look in his eyes, like he should be showering children with gifts, rather than locking up criminals like me. He brought me a hot chocolate with marshmallows and a clean fluffy blanket. He was actually nicer to me than any of the staff in the home, said he had a daughter and would want someone to look out for her, if she ever found herself in my position, which I was pretty sure she never would, not with Father Christmas as a dad.

Anyway it turned out to be quite a nice day in the end, it was the only holiday I was going to get, so I tried to make the most of it. When his shift ended Father Christmas came into my cell with a chess set and a massive bag of sweets. So in the end Charlie lost out by letting me take the blame. This time it'll be different, if he gets me into trouble here, they'll probably chop off my head or something.

He wants to go to the wolf's, punish her for what she said. He wants to punish Stuey. So I try a trick, tell him there's a bar around the corner with a pool table, we can get vodkas and cokes and cigarettes. A woman gets out of the parked car, walks up to us. She looks like some kind of film star, with a scarf and sunglasses.

'Are you ok ... You just look a little lost.'

She's English. Charlie takes one look at her and runs for his life.

'I need to get home ... To England ... It's complicated ...

How I got here ... Why I got here I mean but it didn't work out, I -'

'You're in luck. I came to see my aunt ... A surprise visit, but her neighbour says she's away for a couple of weeks ... So I'm heading home, I could give you a lift.'

'The thing is ... I don't have a passport. I came with a man ... Hid in a van ... It sounds bad, but it really wasn't as bad as it -'

'Look, my car's just up there. Jump in and we can discuss it on the way. There are ways round these things ... It sounds like you need some looking after.'

I can't believe it, for once luck's on my side. It's over. I'm going home. Stuey's on his own now and he deserves all that he gets. She stops for fuel, brings me back a coffee and a ham sandwich. She's called Helen, says she can take me all the way to Chelmney.

'So what happened, the man and van thing?'

'Well it's complicated ... I didn't really want to come ... Well I sort of did ... He didn't actually force me. My mother lives here ... In France ... He used to know her, when they were kids.'

'You're safe now, it sounds as if he took advantage of you.'

She works in a school, is married to a man called Simon. They're having a baby, their first child. She's going to be a great mother, you can just tell. My eyes feel heavy, I want to talk to her, tell her about the home, about Stuey, but it's impossible, the last few days must have finally caught up with me. My body turns to stone, then darkness folds around me like velvet, so I give up the fight, submit to oblivion, to being safe.

Chapter 30

Sarah

She thinks Hesther is her mother. The likeness is quite uncanny. For a few seconds, I actually thought it was her. But my husband was not accompanied by his long lost love, just some young girl who looks like her. A man who loses sleep over a parking ticket, smuggled a child into France in the back of a van. For once I'm in awe of him.

We used to talk about boys. A likely topic of conversation for teenage girls, I suppose. There were no boys at school, so it was just pop stars, actors on the TV. We were never going to meet them in real life, so it didn't really bother me that much. For my part it was just playful banter, the thought of being anywhere near a boy made me want to vomit.

When we met, Stuart was still a virgin. He would happily have stayed that way, but I wanted it out of the way, to take something from him that she never had. We married a few months later. Hesther's not her mother, but there must be some link between them.

The pills work as quickly as I remember. She'll be out of it for hours. I keep a packet in my bag for emergencies, haven't had to use them since I married Stuart. In the so called clinic, they were our only chance of respite, given out like sweets, a reward for exhibiting pleasing patterns of behaviour. Some of the girls refused to learn. Went on and on with the same old performances, day in, day out. If you wanted to be freed, you had to learn how to demonstrate a sound and sustainable recovery. I soon started to master the rules. Rules which appeared to be different for each girl. I was advised to avoid close personal relationships with any of the other inmates.

You could tell Sheila had been pretty once, what was left of her hair was golden blond, her eyes clear sky blue. She hated eating. One of my rules was to demonstrate a healthy relationship with food. She began to follow me, to the toilets or the shower block, whispering things in my ear that I didn't want to hear. The so called nurses became suspicious, thought I was encouraging her. She was a pest and I had to do something about it, so I sacrificed two pills, spat them out instead of swallowing for three nights running.

They said she nearly died. When she recovered, they sent her to a high security institution. I felt guilty at the time. But now I know I did her a favour. None of us were going to get better in that place. Our only hope was pretence.

We make it back to Auriel's just in time. I watch him look for her, realise she's gone. There's clearly some connection between the girl and Auriel. Could she have got pregnant before they went to France. He said they never did it, but he said a lot of things. She certainly didn't look pregnant when I found them in Burgundy. I follow at a safe distance, we take the coastal road towards Cagnes-Sur-Mer. He knows where she is.

Her dress looks expensive, but it's been slashed with a knife down one side, leaving a gaping hole and there's a nasty red stain on the hem. Her arms are badly scarred. I remember Hesther's scars. She pretended not to care, said they were purely superficial, but I could see the pain in her eyes.

We were both only children. Mummy was old when she had me and Auriel not fit to have anymore. The bond between us became so deep, that in my eyes she was my sister. It used to seem silly having two birthday celebrations, when our birthdays were so close together, so we waited until hers, said it made us virtually twins.

We were nearly thirteen. Our last birthday together. Becoming a teenager was a big thing in those days. She thought she was in love with Mick Jagger. Was convinced they'd get married and live on a ranch with a hundred horses. It didn't really bother me, she was never going to meet him, was she. For the life of me, I couldn't see what she saw in him, he looked just like all the other scruffy lads who hung around the streets of Chelmney.

Mummy said we could have a small party at our house. I hated parties, wanted it to just be the four of us, but Hesther said a party was more appropriate, considering the circumstances. Auriel always forgot her daughter's birthday, Charles used to buy her some ridiculously expensive gift that she always pretended to hate. We didn't have any real friends as such, so just invited a few girls from our class. We planned our outfits meticulously, matching dresses which we spent ages choosing from the new boutique in town. On the day I spent an hour getting ready in my room, perfected my hair and makeup as we'd planned. Mummy made finger sandwiches, vol-au-vents with chicken in a creamy sauce, baked a cake, which I tried my best to ice prettily.

Hesther arrived an hour before the party was due to begin. I rushed to the door in excitement, expecting to see my twin looking back at me. Instead there stood a ragamuffin girl wearing a pair of threadbare jeans, a man's shirt at least three sizes too big for her, but worst of all, her hair was piled high on her head, like a badly built bird's nest, rather than gentle waves down her back, like we'd planned. She hadn't even bothered with any makeup, just drawn a flower in felt tip pen on her cheek. I wanted to slap her right there on the doorstep, instead as I let her in, she told me how sweet I looked, but now she was officially a teenager, she thought the dress was too babyish for her.

I ploughed my way through the party, forced myself to talk to some of the girls, dance to the hideous music. When everyone left, I ran upstairs, cut the stupid dress into shreds, found daddy's hammer and smashed all the Rolling Stones records into pieces. The next day she came down with a stomach bug, which meant she missed her birthday meal at The Ritz with her father in London. The raw chicken had done it's job. By Monday morning I'd already decided to forgive her.

At Agnes-Sur-Mer, he follows the sign to Grasse. We took a day trip there on our holiday in Nice. One guided tour of a perfume house was enough for anyone, but he put so much effort into trying to look interested, I suggested another. It was well worth two hours of tedium, to watch him try to maintain some facade of enthusiasm in front of an earnest tour guide. We took a late lunch in a pretty courtyard, consumed bowls of fat olives, fresh fish from the coast, homemade bread studded with fragrant rosemary, washed down with a bottle of local wine. It was the sort of meal that could trick a weaker person into believing they were in love, the sort of meal that could have ended tenderly in the cool shade of a hotel bedroom. He suggested the cathedral, said there was a painting by Rubens he was particularly interested in seeing.

She stirs in her sleep. She's dreaming, saying a name over and over again. It becomes clearer, she's calling for someone called Charlie. I should have given her three, she's starting to annoy me. We're getting close, I can feel it. I should never have given up looking for her, who would have thought it would take Stuart to show me that.

Chapter 31

Stuart

She has no money, no passport. Her only option is the police. There's a viper thrashing in my skull, I lose control of the van, swerve onto a grass verge. A car screeches to a halt behind me. What if it's them. What if I've come this far, just to end up in police cell and never see you again.

Me and Sarah never really talked about the past, our childhoods, the years before we met. Of course it's always been a mystery why she chose me, when she could have had any man she wanted. Now I think I know. It was because of you. The man in the hospital, Auriel, they recognised her face, she's been here before. She wanted me because I was her link to you.

When we met, you said you had a friend, a special friend, a friend you couldn't wait for me to meet. The weeks passed by, you stopped talking about her, I never got to meet her. Now I'm pretty sure, that friend was my wife. When Marnie said you were her mother, the weekends began to haunt me again. Ragged hours dragging by mercilessly as I lay on my bed, or walked the streets of Chelmney, my imagination running wild and free. Boys handsome, well groomed, boys with money, lineage, boys who could twirl you round the dance floor like something out of a Jane Austen novel. You rarely mentioned your time in London, but the snippets you couldn't hold back filled me with a deep dark dread. Marnie was right, this is wrong, I can't just turn up and crack your world into pieces.

If it's the police, surely they would have arrested me by now. What if it's worse than the police. What if someone's picked her up for the wrong reasons. What if she's dead and it's all my fault. For all the bravado, she's still a confused child inside. Being locked up may not be so bad, as long as I know she's safe. The girl in the village square with your father, I'm pretty sure that must have been Sarah. Auriel said she was pregnant, could Sarah really be Marnie's mother.

Chapter 32

Marnie

It feels wrong. Like I'm waking from a coma, like I've been asleep forever. My eyes feel like they're too heavy for my head. We must be in Calais by now. The car's parked in a street, Helen's not here. I try to unbuckle the seat belt, but my arms feel like they're made of granite. She must have gone to sort the passport thing out, but surely she would need me there with her. I'm dying for a pee and my mouth's like a rat's cage, so I force my eyes back open, almost fall out of the car.

The thought of Stuey all alone makes me want to cry. I never thought I would, but I miss him like mad. Walking's much harder than it should be. There's no sign of her. The road opens into a square. There's a man standing alone by a fountain, I can ask him where the passport office is. As I get closer he looks familiar, before I know it I'm running, he sees me and he's running too. This must be a dream, in a while Charlie will wake me and everything will be back to normal. He holds me in his arms like I'm a child, surely Charlie will wake me now.

'Marnie ... I was worried sick, but how did you know where _'

'Stuey, you're getting the ferry as well. I met this woman ... Helen, she's getting me a passport. You shouldn't have gone back to the wolf's, I mean grandmother's house, I warned you I'd had enough. She's taking me back to Chelmney. We are in Calais aren't we?'

My head feels like it's stuffed with cotton wool. He can help me find her, he owes me that, then we can all get the ferry together, and I'm pretty damn sure Charlie will be waiting for me at home.

'We're in Grasse Marnie ... The south of France, nowhere near Calais. She lied to you. I think I know who she is ... Helen.'

Stuey's gone into full out psycho mode. I could tell he was mentally unstable but he's lost it completely. Why's he talking about grass, has he taken something. Me and Helen can look after him, make sure he gets home safely, call his wife if need be.

'It's ok Stuey, I'm here now, you don't have to -'

'Didn't you notice you were driving in the wrong direction.'

'I was asleep ... After everything you put me through, I was tired, she felt sorry for me, wanted to help me.'

She's heading towards us across the square.

'Helen ... Have you got my passport ... This is Stuey, the man I told you about ... But he's confused, needs help, I know it's a lot to ask, but can you help me get him home, I know what he did was bad, but he's my friend, I can't just leave him here.'

'Sarah ... I thought it was you.'

He's white as a ghost, even though it's a million degrees. He's delusional, this Hesther thing has really got to him.

'It's ok Stu. I know why you're here. Don't bother lying. It's over. She's here, isn't she, you've arranged to meet her. Is this Auriel's daughter? She couldn't even look after one child, no wonder she gave her away.'

A Catherine wheel explodes inside my head. They know each other. They both tricked me. That wolf in sheep's clothing is nothing to do with me, none of them are. Were they all in it together, the estate agent, the bar woman, the weasel at the hospital, the wolf. Was this all just a big plot to kidnap me, Stuey never knew my mother at all. I have to escape, before the nightmare gets any worse.

Chapter 33

Ron

Mary glides through life like a swan. Or so one would believe from appearances. Those who know her would imagine she has full control over her life. They're wrong. All the planning in the world can't beat destiny.

Her feathers were ruffled today. But only I would have noticed. Sarah and Stuart are in Paris, celebrating their baby. When they travel Sarah always calls her mother on arrival at their destination. Mary forgot to ask her which hotel they were using, and so far Sarah has not been in contact. Mary and Sarah are too alike for intimacy. In the conventional way, at least. After what happened to Sarah, Mary constructed a wall around herself for protection, around us both, I suppose, but I could see the cracks beginning to appear, while she tried to plaster over them. Sarah is the only one with the power to bring that wall crumbling down around us.

She took me out into the garden. Talked to the back of my head. I tried to listen, but childish giggles blocked out her words. They skipped along beside us along beds of dying begonias, across the dehydrated lawn, to an arbour under an oak tree. We sat for a while in silence, so tiring of our company, they ran off to hide in a row of hydrangea bushes, a blackbird singing to them from a broken branch on the tree. When she pushed me back, they returned to the dark, damp crevice of my memory. That's where they live, their home.

When Sarah said they were moving to London, I expected Mary to fragment into pieces. Instead she thrived. We backed them financially. I thought doing so would help us as well. It did not. Sarah's monthly account of the refurbishment of her home simply acted as a further drip feed of guilt. Stuart's parents were deceased, failed to leave financial compensation for their early departure from his life.

When Sarah brought Stuart home, we were shocked. What on earth could our beautiful daughter see in this dull looking lad who worked on a building site. I expected Mary to stop the relationship in its tracks, but Sarah was unyielding in her determination to have him. She was well, had some sort of purpose in life, and that seemed enough. We never said as much, but Stuart took the burden from us and we gratefully passed it on to him.

There were certain advantages to the union. He was malleable, bland, polite, didn't question Sarah's past. He seemed happy enough to live in the moment, and in doing so made our daughter whole again. He made up for charm and pedigree with predictability. He would never achieve any honour or prestige, but could be trusted to tow the line, be a kind and faithful husband, protect our fragile daughter from the rough seas crashing at her door. They married. It worked. But now there's a baby in the equation and Mary's anxious, I can see it in her eyes.

They put up a small bookshelf on my wall at my wife's orders. It seems even prisoners are allowed books. She brought in a selection of my favourites; general law, historical biographies, war novels. But I know I'll never read another word. My world now is the ones who inhabit my head. I broke rank. Treachery is a crime that deserves no reward for good behaviour.

Chapter 34

Sarah

At first she seemed happy to see me. A familiar face from home, come all the way to France to make amends. We went up to her room, she told me they'd been forced into hiding, some gangleader her father was prosecuting, threats of murder or kidnap. He lied to them, it was me he was hiding them from. She didn't mention my belly. I wanted to tell them altogether, and luckily Charles was back from London, out for a walk, would be back soon.

I heard the door slam behind him, a high pitched scream from Auriel who was asleep when I arrived. It was time and I was ready for it. We went downstairs and I blurted it out before he had time to take off his coat. Hesther refused to believe me, said I was still ill. He grabbed me by the arm, puffing like an angry ox, dragged me away from the house, into the village, a strange gloomy little place, with as much life as a morgue. He called me a cunning little bitch, said they'd never believe me, told me to say I'd made it up, someone else was the father of my baby. I agreed. We went back to the house.

He called Hesther downstairs. There was a deep scratch down his cheek, where I'd caught him earlier with my nail. He expected me to retract my statement. I said I needed a glass of water, went through to the kitchen and he followed. A towel and a gas flame was all it took. I pushed him hard, pulled out the table to block his way. He should have followed me out, but instead he tried to put it out. Hesther refused to leave without her father, thought she could save him. She couldn't.

I'd paid the taxi driver to come back for me the next day, so slept in a barn with the comfort of knowing she believed me. Before I left her crying out in agony from her burns, I told her he had a mole shaped like a spider on the inside of his right thigh, and for a final flourish that he sometimes called out her name in his passion for me.

I hated weekends. For two full days he took her away from me, paraded her around London, like a prize heifer. Occasionally they stayed in Chelmney and he allowed me to visit for an hour or two on a Sunday afternoon. I was never made to feel like one of the family, like she was at our house. I didn't belong in his world and he made that blatantly clear. My first plan when I left the clinic, was to tell Charles about her and Stuart. But I quickly realised that would be no punishment at all. She didn't care any more about Stuart than she did about me. Charles was her weakness. He was the one I needed to use in order to plunge the knife of betrayal into her heart, the same knife she happily plunged into mine.

So typical of her to live in Grasse. A town that literally smells of roses. He's drifting around like a tourist. Has he agreed to meet her somewhere. The pills will start to wear off soon. I don't want the girl escaping. It's just as pretty as I remember, honey and walnut buildings, narrow streets tightly crammed with houses. He lingers outside shops selling patisserie, lavender and coffee, explores cool recesses of ancient churches. The day begins to close, harsh sunlight softening into evening glow. He heads towards Place aux Aires, where we drank coffee after our tour of the cathedral, both exhausted, but neither one of us ready to admit defeat.

What if she's here right now, sipping a cold glass of wine. He stops to read menus, waves away emphatic waiters. I try a breathing exercise, this stress is not good for my daughter. I was fifteen, my hair had grown back below my shoulders. To my shame and displeasure, my body was blossoming out of control. Men who used to look straight through me, began to let their eyes linger longer than was polite. Boys were the enemy, so I hid away under loose childish clothes. Then one day it came to me. I had power, if only I was brave enough to use it.

Just before my fifteenth birthday, mummy took me for a day out in London. We spent the morning at the British Museum. I don't think she enjoyed it any more than I did, but it seemed a normal thing to do. Normality had been missing from our lives for a very long time. We ate lunch at the Savoy, daddy's treat since he was too busy at work to accompany us. After lunch we went to Carnaby Street. Showing pride in my appearance was one of the signs of a good recovery, well worth an outing of mummy's credit card.

One day the following week, daddy was at the office and mummy had one of her charity functions. I dressed carefully. The skirt was as short as mummy would allow, the shop girl explaining that since I had good legs, it would be a shame not to display them. I borrowed a pair of mummy's American tan tights, laced up my new knee high white patent leather boots, completed the look with a belted camel coloured coat.

I knew where his office was. Hesther used to go on about it all the time. How he let her wander through the hallowed halls of law. How she used to laugh at the men in silly wigs. How he liked to leave her on her own for an hour in Harrods with his credit card, then pick her up in a chauffeur driven car and take her to lunch at Claridge's, complete with a bottle of Champagne. I wanted to say that I was free to pop into daddy's office whenever I wanted, and if it was lunch time he'd willingly take me to the cafe across the road for sausage and chips. But of course, I never did.

It was too early for lunch, so I sat in a coffee shop across the road from his office, a grand, imposing building, nothing like daddy's little place in Chelmney. Twelve 'o' clock came and went, a stream of people coming and going through the door. Charles was not someone who could be easily missed, he was at least a foot taller than daddy, exuded power, wealth and privilege, took on an almost God like persona.

One 'o' clock came and went. The cafe was full of men in suits, I felt totally out of my depth, was about to abort the idea and go home. He was deep in conversation with a much shorter man, I ran out of the cafe, across the road, just in time to stop him from disappearing into the crowds.

He seemed annoyed to see me, tried to swat me away like a fly. I was desperate, this was my one and only chance. The words came out before I had chance to think, I said I had something important to tell him about Hesther, something he really needed to know.

Ten minutes later we were seated in a small Italian restaurant. I considered telling him about Stuart, after all. But she'd have loved the drama, taken his anger as a sign of just how much he loved her. My other plan seemed too improbable for words, now I was actually there and doing it. He poured me a glass of wine. I sipped it slowly, still on a reduced level of medication. We ordered, he seemed to mellow a little, asked me what it was I had to tell him. I tried to act like the women on TV, smile a lot, toss my hair, look interested in everything he said.

I told him that I missed her. That I was sorry. But after two glasses of wine, his interest turned to me. On the train home, I tried to imagine daddy taking Hesther out for lunch, buying her wine, topping up her glass, telling her she'd grown into a beautiful young lady, asking if they could do it again next week. I couldn't. That's when with dread in my heart I knew it had worked, and I had no option but to see it through.

I watch him like I used to watch them all those years ago. She runs into his arms, just like she used to, she looks so young, like time stood still for her. But it's not her at all, it's the blasted girl. Could there really be something going on between my husband and a teenage girl. They see me. I tell him it's over, there are no more lies to tell. She runs like a hare, melts away into the dusk. He looks awful, a pitiful version of the man I slept next to on Saturday night. I reach out, touch unfamiliar stubble on his cheek. Then, for the first time ever, I watch him cry.

Chapter 35

Marnie

Charlie pokes me in the shoulder. It's freezing. I tried to cover us with some newspaper and a broken up cardboard box. I should've known he wouldn't leave me. It chokes me up to think that I thought I didn't need him. Without him, I'm nothing, helpless as a newborn kitten. My head aches, my throat's scratchy as sandpaper. If I hadn't left him at home on Sunday, none of this would've happened. I'm just as dumb as all the other girls after all. I was lucky to get away, could've been locked in the back of a truck by now. I'm not smart enough for Oxford, that's what all this has taught me.

When I stopped running, he was there, right next to me. He didn't even laugh like he usually does, just rubbed my back until I caught my breath and was able to speak again. I was one of the top runners at school. The PE teacher was always trying to get me to join the running club, enter stupid competitions. I told him running is for horses, not for girls who have the brain capacity for a top university education. Girls who prefer to spend their time learning, not trotting round a track like a well trained pony. But in the end it was running that saved me, not education, so perhaps he was right all along.

One of the girls in the home ran away. She was gone for ages, no one made much of an effort to find her. Then one day she turned up again, all skin and bone, looked like she'd been sleeping in a skip. She said she'd had an awesome time, met a gang who taught her how to shoplift, make a fortune from begging on the streets. Tracy Webster asked her why she bothered coming back, if she was having such a bloody good time. She just shrugged her shoulders, and that was that. A few weeks later a rumour went round that she'd actually slept with a man for money. However bad it was in the home, I would never have run away, not unless I had pots of money. I was right. This is the least fun thing we've ever done.

I consider our options. It's getting light, so we have to move on. I've no money. Charlie can't stand the police, which is understandable. They might be looking for me, so we can't risk going back to town. We need a place of safety. A church is a place of safety, everyone knows that. People hid in churches in the war, didn't they. Priests don't ask questions, do they, not unless they're sin related. There's a spire in the distance, we'll head for that.

The pain in my head is getting worse. We pass a bakers. My stomach feels like it's been hollowed out with a carving knife. Before I can stop him, he goes in, grabs a loaf, and we're running again, then we fall down in a tangled heap on the steps of the church, stuff the warm bread into our mouths like we've not eaten for a month. When we're full, we laugh until our bellys ache and I feel sick. Two little boys watch us from behind a half open shutter. Charlie bristles with anger, he hates being watched.

The door is locked. How are people supposed to seek refuge, when they lock the bloody doors. Someone really should have a word. It's getting hot again, there's a fever rising through my body. Charlie snuggles into me and we lay our heads against the smooth warm wood of the door. Before I know it, I'm dreaming about my mother. She's so beautiful, it hurts to look at her. She's standing next to a priest. He looks like a film star, young and handsome, not like the wrinkly old man who used to come and bless us in the home. They lean over me, she strokes my hair away from my face, her hand is soft as rose petals, she smells like a wedding bouquet. My eyes close, but I can still hear them.

'She's got a fever, I'll take her home with me.'

'I'm sorry, Madame Hesther, but I saw her and … Well you can see why I thought of you, she is -'

'You did the right thing Father Decroix, I'll take it from here … If you can just help me get her into the car.'

I force my eyes open so I can look at her again. She looks like me, but better, more like an angel than a human, she even has scars on her arms like mine. She covers me with a silk scarf, it smells like the parma violets I used to buy from the sweet shop in Brimfield. I don't want to wake myself, so I close my eyes, submit to sleep. I want her to stay with me forever.

Chapter 36

Stuart

Couples generally have a story. How they met. A carefully crafted, frequently revised version of their first encounter. Humorous perhaps, or heart wrenching. So ridiculously romantic, they could easily have stolen the plot from a Mills and Boon novel. I can with all honesty say I have no idea where and when I first met my wife. She just sort of drifted into my life, like a solitary leaf you don't notice at first, until it turns into a pile on the lawn, or blocks the drains, and you're forced to take action. The last thing I was looking for was any form of romantic liaison, although you'd gone, in my mind we were still a couple.

She suggested a drink. Her face was familiar, I knew I'd seen her before, but couldn't pinpoint where or when, how many times. She was stunning to look at, so I felt safe, thought she just felt sorry for me, was offering an hour of companionship with nothing more expected. It seemed rude not to, so I accepted her invitation. She quickly turned me into her pet project. I was too weak, too empty to put up a solid line of defence. When we were out, I'd watch men stare, struggle to fix their eyes back on their own date. Somehow I'd won a prize, coveted by many, but of no value to me. I felt numb with her. Numb was good.

She didn't seem to care I had nothing to offer, refused to buy into the courtship dance, never gave her flowers, never showered her with shallow compliments. She was in control, for the first time in my life I didn't have to think for myself, and it felt good. She took me, so somewhere deep down in my subconscious I wasn't betraying our love. I was purely following orders.

For the first couple of months physical contact consisted of a chaste kiss on the cheek before we parted. I never walked her home. Then it changed. One evening she took me to Zefferelli's for dinner. I'd passed by the restaurant a million times, never once thinking I'd actually go in and dine there. The waiter was shameless in his desire, clearly saw me as no competition whatsoever. If he'd looked at you like that, I'd have punched the lust right out of out of his dark flirtatious eyes. He hovered at our table, topping up half full glasses, wiping away an imaginary crumb. I remember thinking this was it, anyone could see his charms far outweighed anything I could muster. She hardly seemed to notice him, appeared distracted. We finished the bottle of Chianti, left and I was convinced she was going to tell me that was it, we were over.

She said she wanted to come home with me. Home was a scruffy bedsit in the wrong part of town. My humble abode was no place for a girl like Sarah. I said it was late, but she was insistant. I had nothing to lose, so I gave in. What Sarah wants she nearly always gets.

We sat on the bed. There was nowhere else to sit. She calmly took in the bare floorboards, cracked walls, encrusted cooker and sink, pile of dirty clothes in the corner. I shared a bathroom down the hallway with three other men, was quite sure if she asked to use it, that would be the end. I offered her a cup of tea, she declined, told me to take off my coat as she removed hers. She spread them over the stained eiderdown, told me to take off my clothes. At first, I thought she was joking, but she started to remove her own, folding each garment carefully, placing them on top of the battered chest of drawers. I had no option but to comply.

I thought it would be impossible for me to give her what she so obviously wanted, but my youthful body took over and five minutes later my carefully preserved virginity was close to expiry.

The only thing left to do is to check into a hotel. We lie together in a narrow bed. She strokes my hair, then I make love to my wife for the last time. Your name floats above us in a sweet melody, but it's impossible to tell if it's coming from my lips or hers.

Chapter 37

Ron

The wedding came far sooner than we expected. We feared the worst, but her stomach remained steadfastly flat. The sight of her in her wedding dress almost brought me to my knees, something I never thought I'd see. The congregation in St Mark's church, made up mostly of Mary's charity acquaintances would have assumed our daughter was perfect in every way, intact, precious, undamaged. A daughter I could pass on to Stuart with pride. Not one of them could have guessed pride had long since forsaken me.

The wedding suit turned Stuart from a boy to a man. He was marrying the three of us in a way, appeared to accept that without question. He allowed us to smooth away his rough edges, turn him into a respectable white collar worker, someone we were not ashamed to introduce as our son in law.

It was a privately run sanatorium, took a whole three months before they let us visit. We approached from a sweeping driveway, impressed by the neoclassical manor house fronted by a small lake and formal gardens. If you didn't know what hell lay behind those elegant walls, you could easily have mistaken it for a luxury hotel. We were admitted through a small back door. It was the noise that hit me first. For some reason I was expecting a place of calm, church like even, a place of peace and healing. Mary said Sarah had a delicate demeanor, that's why it happened. There was nothing delicate about the cacophony of suffering that greeted us that day. Those certified clinically unstable of mind could be vociferous in their demands. It was like some sort of satanic opera was playing out around us. It shames me to admit it now, but rather than looking forward to seeing my daughter after our prolonged separation, I wanted to snatch the keys from the nurse's belt and run for my life.

She led us down a labyrinth of corridors. Mary appeared as

calm and composed as ever, used the time to ask pertinent questions, nodding her freshly permed head at the replies. We came to a halt outside one of the doors. As she unlocked it, a faint sound escaped from the half lit room, like the dying howl from a badly injured wolf. Our beautiful daughter was not in that room. In her place, a blank eyed skeleton, dressed in a shapeless gown, with a badly shaven head. The nurse explained they were keeping her under a light sedation, the bruises on her ashen cheeks resulted from banging her head against the wall. Mary showed no sign of shock, no emotion, seated herself on the plastic chair then proceeded to tell the stranger on the bed a potted version of out recent lives. Her fundraising activities, my exertions in the garden, the new wallpaper and carpet in Sarah's room at home. I hovered by the door, unable to think of a single word to say. The pitiful creature rocked gently on the bed, knees up to her chin, eyes as vacant as the moon. She was silent as she listened, and from that I at least gained a crumb of comfort.

The following months passed slowly and painfully. We adapted our home life to the two of us. Mary told her friends that Sarah was boarding for a term or two at an excellent finishing school, never quite giving away any details. Some topics of conversation were strictly out of bounds on our visits, Hesther of course being the main one. The doctors took an experimental approach to Sarah's treatment. If one thing didn't work, they simply resorted to another. We were powerless. There was nothing we could do to expedite our daughter's recovery.

The miracle happened one winter's day. The snow fell thick and fast, we were almost forced to abandon our journey. When we entered her room, she was back. It was Sarah, not a stranger, sitting on the bed reading a teenage magazine. She began to talk, after that, tell us about her drawing classes, playing tennis and winning. The weeks passed by and finally she said the words. She was ready. She wanted to come home.

That's when the pain cut deeper. We could accept her being there when she was so obviously in need of help, but now she seemed better, surely she belonged at home with her family. The doctors said otherwise, explained patiently that although on the surface it looked like she was cured, there were deeper wounds, issues she still had to deal with, in order to ensure there was no risk of relapse. She pleaded with her mother, cried, said we were punishing her, that we didn't want her at home with us. She said we didn't love her, that we were not fit to be parents. It very nearly broke us. Each word was a barbed arrow through my heart. I know now that I should have been stronger, took her by the hand and led her out of that place with authority. But Mary insisted, said the doctors knew best. So we waited, until some months later, after a meeting with the manager over our concerns about how to continue funding her care, one of the senior doctors told us there was nothing further they could do. She was free to come home.

When Sarah came home, I could see that Mary was on edge. No one else would have noticed, but hairline cracks began to appear. Little things. A glass unwashed in the sink, a smear on the coffee table not immediately polished away. We watched our daughter like she was a rare butterfly, liable to break a wing at any moment. We monitored her every word, every mouthful of food that entered her mouth. The doctor advised us not to send her back to school, so we hired a tutor, an odd little woman with a liking for loose leaf tea, served in a china cup. Sarah showed little interest in her studies, began going out for long walks. It pains me to say that we welcomed her absence, it gave us time to breathe, to drop our guard, to feel like ourselves again.

They put a tie around my neck, comb my hair, just in time for her arrival. The dichotomy of old age is time. It's rapidly expiring, but at the same time, there's too much of it. Sometimes I feel like we're drowning in time. Her two hour visits are almost enough to suffocate us. The time is unnatural, enforced, not like before when we both had our own pursuits to follow. She talks to fill the silence, but never says the right words, the only words I want to hear. Our confession. The words which could finally unlock the shackles and free us from each other.

If I could speak, would I tell her not to come tomorrow. I would not. We both need the anchor of time, otherwise we would tumble into the steaming abyss where time ceases to exist. She kisses me softly, then leaves.

Chapter 38

Marnie

Heaven is awesome. If I'd known heaven was this good, I'd have come here ages ago, not even bothered with the life bit first. The amazing thing is, Charlie's here too. Who'd ever have thought they'd let Charlie into heaven. Not Sister Morag for one, she used to call us Satan's fodder, said we were wicked through and through, like a stick of rock.

It was Sister Morag who told me about Charlie. She said I had a brother, and a twin brother at that. At first I thought she was making it up. She said it was my fault my mother gave me away for being a naughty, disagreeable child. Then when I was five years old, Charlie came to live with me. She was right all along.

There are a lot of flowers in heaven. More flowers than I've ever seen. The sheets smell clean and fresh in heaven. Heaven has the most comfortable bed in the world.

'You're awake ... I've been so worried.' My mother lives in heaven. My beautiful angel mother. 'My very own sister. I knew she lied, you didn't die ... You are my sister, aren't you. You came here for me, didn't you.' I must have died outside that church. So it is true, you can find refuge from the world in a church, well outside one at least. Me and Charlie are safe now, forever. 'I've made some fresh lemonade, try to sit up and drink some ... It will make you feel better. I promise.'

This is like no lemonade I've ever tasted. There are ice cubes floating in the glass with real flower petals frozen inside them. My heavenly mother is some class act. She must have been some sort of celestial being. Celestial beings can't keep earthly babies, can they, they just get them back when they die. The flowers are on every surface, in all sorts of containers; vases, jugs, bottles, tin cans, jam jars. There must be baked beans and jam on toast in heaven. She floats around, humming a strange tune, a tune only the angels know. The weird thing is, Charlie knows it too, they hum together in harmony. I've never heard him hum before, it's almost like he's been here before, without me. She lays a petal hand on my forehead, rearranges the covers on the bed. She's the perfect mother, I should have realised she was waiting for me somewhere.

'How did you die?'

'You're still delirious Darling. It's the fever. Try to rest. We can talk when you're feeling better.'

Surely in heaven there's no fever. Surely in heaven you don't need to rest. Charlie's purring like a cat now, heaven suits him, I've never seen him this happy before.

'How did I get here? Have you been waiting? Did you know I was coming?'

'My darling girl, you came here to find me. I wasn't expecting you, but I always felt your presence ... That you were out there somewhere. You can tell me your story when you're feeling stronger, we can get to know each other ... Just like sisters should do.'

'But you're my mother. We're both dead ... In heaven.'

She laughs and it sounds like raindrops on moss.

'Sweetheart, you collapsed on the church steps. You're not dead, and I'm your sister not your mother ... You're just confused ... That's all. I never even asked your name, you should -'

'It's Marnie.'

'Marnie, how perfectly charming.'

When she says it, it doesn't sound like my name anymore, it sounds like she made it up, like it's a brand new word, a word only she knows.

'I remember now ... Why I was at the church. I came here with a man ... Well with a woman called Helen actually. But they knew each other ... Stuey and Helen. Stuey's still in love with you. You are Hesther aren't you. I thought they'd kidnapped me ... Now I'm not so sure. You're right I am confused.'

'Stuey ... Stuart, you came with a man called Stuart, how do you -'

'It's a long story, but I met him at Chelmney station ... But

I've just remembered, he called Helen Sarah. His wife is called Sarah, we went to their house, I saw their -'

'Hang on a minute Marnie, let me find something to show you.'

She leaves me alone in the room. The sun streams through the window, all the furniture is white. Charlie doesn't belong here, but he acts like it's his home, trotted along after her, rather than staying here with me. I'm pretty sure this is not heaven, after all. But how can she be my sister, it doesn't make sense. She returns with a photo album and a peach cut up into slices on a china plate.

'Eat this, it will make you feel stronger.' She turns the pages slowly, until she finds what she's looking for. They're standing together in what looks like the park in Chelmney. They're dressed similarly, look about twelve years old. I have to look very carefully, but then I recognise her, it's Sarah, Stuey's wife, standing right there next to Hesther. Helen had sunglasses on and a scarf wrapped round her head, was she Sarah, but how could Sarah know where we were.

'It's Sarah ... Stuey's wife ... You knew her ... They're here, Stuey and Sarah, they'll be -'

'Marnie ... I think we should go away for a while ... Just the two of us. You can recuperate, and we can get to know each other properly, without any interruptions. My friend has a small villa by the sea, get some sleep, I'll arrange everything.'

None of it makes sense. I just want to go home, sister or no sister. They're all as bad as each other. It's a bloody good job I don't suffer from hay fever, I'd probably be dead by now, for real. What's the point of picking things, just to cram them into a vase and watch them die.

'Wake up Marnie ... I've run you a bath, then it's time to go.'

Go where. This is turning into a joke. I know she looks like me and everything, but she's still a stranger. Stuey was a stranger, Helen was a stranger, but I went with them, didn't I. I'm way more dumb than I thought, Charlie's was right, I was kidding myself about the university thing. The steamy rose scented water helps clear my head. Even her towels smell of flowers. If heaven is anything like this, me and Charlie need to seriously up our game if we're going to get there. She's laid out some of her clothes for me, silk underwear, a flowing sunflower printed kaftan. I throw my ruined dress from yesterday into the bin.

We drive out of town. If I didn't know better, I'd think Charlie really had turned into an angel. He's good as gold in the back of the car.

'I want to tell you a story, Marnie. Your story.' Her voice is like that honey and lemon drink they give you when you've got a cold. Soothing at first, but then too sweet and sickly as you get to the end. 'When I was a girl, I had a friend. Sarah. We were close. Then I met Stuart who I'm presuming is your Stuey. He reminded me of a stray dog, all skin and bone, pleading eyes ... That sort of thing. He obviously needed someone to take care of him, and that someone turned out to be me. I expected Sarah to help with the mission, but she wasn't up to the job. I didn't see it, but she was disturbed, seriously disturbed ... I'm sorry to say it Marnie but she ended up in a mental institution, so I was forced to look after Stuart all on my own, and it wasn't easy at times, let me tell you. He began to depend on me, it would have been just plain cruel to let him down ... Oh, you must forgive me, I left out the most important bit, didn't I ... I said it was your story, but I've made it mine, haven't I ... Our father, yours and mine, was a barrister by profession, did you know that, no you probably wouldn't, would you. Sarah is your mother, but you probably know that, don't you. I went to see her once, in the institution. They didn't want to let me in, the staff were terrible, but I insisted, told them I was her cousin, come all the way from America to see her, the accent was tricky, but I got there in the end. You must remember Marnie, most things are achievable, if only you try hard enough.'

I wait for her to finish the story. Seconds tick by, but she looks like she's gone into a world of her own. Then her and Charlie start to hum again, as if I'm not even here. She can't just throw all that at me, then stop half way through.

'What happened ... Did you see her ... Sarah ... How do you know she's my mother ... I look like you, not her, it doesn't make any -'

Charlie pokes me in the back, angry I've interrupted their symphony.

'It's all terribly tedious ... I'll tell you about it some other time.'

For the rest of the journey she drives in silence. Charlie sleeps like a baby in the back seat. We have to drive for miles down a private drive to reach the house. I thought it was going to be like one of those wooden huts on Chelmney seafront, but it's a bloody great mansion, like those movie star's houses in California, painted white, all on one level and next to a golden expanse of beach. The sea is the colour of a swimming pool, she says we're miles away from any other houses, which I'm not sure is a good thing or a bad thing.

She writes, has brought her typewriter along, says when she's writing, she mustn't be disturbed. The house is what they describe in magazines as minimalist in design. That means there's hardly anything in it and it's all painted white. I wouldn't under normal circumstances trust Charlie for a second, but he's on his best behaviour, trotting along behind her like a well trained puppy. We change into shorts and swimming costumes. She lays towels on two loungers and we sit and watch the water move leisurely in front of us. There are questions buzzing in my head like flies, so many it's impossible to untangle one from the other, so I close my eyes, let the sound of the sea send me into a dreamless sleep.

'Come on let's swim, the water's lovely here ... You can sleep some more later ... When I'm writing.'

The last time I went swimming was at school. They used to make us take swimming lessons, claiming it was for our own safety. Even make us try to save one of the other girls wearing pyjamas from drowning. Like from all the dangers in Brimfield, drowning was the thing that was going to kill us, especially in the night when we were wearing pyjamas. The nuns, fosterers, creepy men in town were never mentioned in the danger stakes. Instead they made us shiver in the changing rooms, learn how to dive, master at least three styles of swimming strokes, all the time living in fear of Mr Archer holding your head under the water until you choked. Mr Archer was the only threat of danger around water in Brimfield, so after a while I opted to sit in detention with Sister Morag, at least I could study there.

The sea is clear and warm. I've never been in the sea at

Chelmney, but heard it's freezing and half made up of sewage. Charlie's having the time of his life, splashing her gently, Charlie never usually does anything gently. She doesn't seem to notice, swims lengths, while I drift around aimlessly in the shallow water. Swimming is just as boring and pointless as I remember. My head starts to clear a little, the questions lining themselves up into some sort of order.

'I'm getting out now, I need to write, I'll see you later.'

Charlie trots along behind her, leaving me alone. After an hour in the sun, my skin feels like it's on fire. I can't remember seeing any books in the house and I can't very well nip along to the local library. If I don't die of anything else out here, I'm going to die of boredom.

I press my ear against the door, listen to the rythmic click of typewriter keys. It's ages since I've eaten, we didn't bring any food with us, what are we going to do, there are no local restaurants. The fridge is full, her friend must have stocked it for us. I want to make myself a snack, but it seems rude to help myself, even though we're supposed to be sisters.

'Darling, I'm sorry I left you for so long ... When I write time becomes a hindrance, passes far too quickly for my liking. Shall I make us an early supper ... Then we can talk properly.'

At last she's going to tell me the rest of the story, fill in the details. She chops up a lettuce and some ruby red tomatoes, puts two steaks under the grill. She has this thing, where she makes me feel awkward, as if she's not really from this world, so by being a mere mortal, I'm not worthy of her company.

'Do you want me to help ... With the supper?'

Charlie looks at me like I'm the dumbest girl on earth. She doesn't answer, tosses the salad with oil and vinegar, slices a golden loaf into inch thick chunks.

'We can eat on the terrace, it's too nice to be indoors. Why don't you open a bottle of wine, it is a celebration after all, isn't it Marnie dear. Our father had the strongest genes, that's why we look so alike, but I can see her in you ... Sarah.'

The food is delicious, the cold wine soothes my aching throat.

'Look Hesther, I wanted ... I mean, I need to ask you about -'

'It was a mess ... She tricked him, you see ... Our father, to get at me. She hated me by then, still does, I suppose. I tried to save him, from the fire ... Do you know about the fire ... No, I don't suppose you do. He was only human, a man, she threw herself at him.' She pauses, runs her hand down her scars. 'It should have been me who died, that's what she wanted. Anyway back to the hospital. It worked ... They let me see her ... I paid them quite a substantial sum of money not to tell her parents. It was the most dismal place you've ever seen ... All they could afford, I suppose. They should have sent her to a proper hospital, but they were ashamed, paid to bury her away in the countryside, just too middle-class for their own good. I expected her to come at me, like she did the last time I went to her house ... She just pushed herself into a corner, started whimpering like some animal caught in a trap. After all those months, she was still playing the victim, no nearer to getting better than when she went in ... It was a sorry sight to see, so I didn't stay ... But do you know what ... Marnie ... As the nurse let me out, she called out my name, the first time she'd spoken to me since I told her about Stuart ... And do you know what ... It made me want to cry. Now let's go to bed ... It's been a trying day.'

Chapter 39

Sarah

I made love to my husband for the last time. It was a strangely moving experience. Now he must go home, so I can get on with what I need to do. His usefulness has come to an end.

The house is just as I imagined. Picture postcard perfect, built from toffee coloured stone, the front garden a pretty tumble of half feral flowers. When we bought our nineteen-thirties semi, I tried to kid myself it had a degree of urban charm, I was wrong. When my daughter comes, we'll move to the countryside, maybe keep chickens and grow our own vegetables.

A thorough background check is vital, even when buying a secondhand car. Stuart would no more buy one without a full examination and service history than eat a plate of sushi. With me it was different. He asked no questions, expected no backstory, and that suited me fine.

When we woke, his first concern was for the girl. For some reason, he thinks she's mine. I offered to help him look for her. After three hours we were both exhausted. I suggested lunch. We ate olive tapenade on freshly baked bread, he told me to go home, to think of the baby, he could take care of things here. I almost laughed in his face.

I always knew I wasn't the only one, Charles had quite an appetite for the ladies. I was the youngest, he told me that many times, it was hard to say if it was out of guilt or pride. I already hated him, there was nothing he could say or do to make me hate him more. The girl is one of Charles' little bastards, I'm pretty sure of it. Typical Hesther to end up with a real life sister of her own.

I said we should go to Hesther's together. Tell her everything. The look of panic on his face was a sight to see. His hands were tied, so he agreed we should both make our separate ways to Calais, catch the ferry together, talk. I watched the last grain of hope drain from his body, almost felt sorry for him, after everything he'd put himself through to get here.

I went through his pockets while he slept last night, carved her address into my brain. I bang the brass knocker as hard as I can, shards of paint fly from the door, but no one answers. There's a low wall to the rear of the property, I climb over, careful not to harm my baby. The back garden is more organised than the front, masses of flowers, carefully weeded beds, a small vegetable patch next to a cherry tree, and a lawn which looks like it's come out of an English country estate. The shutters are closed, not unusual on a sunny day in southern France. My fist pounds into the door, then I try the doorknob, it turns easily and the heavy wooden door creaks painfully open. I call her name. Nothing comes back, so I cross the threshhold into the sweetest smelling room, and it feels like I've come home.

Chapter 40

Stuart

I'll never forgive myself. Anything could have happened to her. I've failed her in every way possible. Now I'll have to live with the guilt for the rest of my life. How can I ever come back to you, tell you I lost your sister, smuggled her across the channel, then left her to her fate with no money and no passport.

At the spot we're supposed to meet, I watch the ferries depart, one by one. Was there an accident on the motorway, Sarah dead or gravely injured. Far worse, her hands around your neck. Kaleidoscope images swirl round my head. Prison cells, hospital wards, a morgue, Mary's face, cool granite handcuffs, Marnie's beautiful face bruised in a hedgerow. I should have left the past alone, instead of raking it up and leaving the debris in all the wrong places. What to do now. I ask the question over and over. The only answer is, go home.

Brutal sunlight explodes into my dream, the space where my wife should be lying is empty. I try to move, but my head's pounding, my body fails to comply to orders. When I wake again, four hours have passed. With a superhuman surge of energy, I haul my limp body from the sweat soaked bed, stumble downstairs to the plaintive wail of the telephone.

'Stuart … Thank heavens … I've been worried sick. Why didn't Sarah call me … How was Paris … Let me speak to her, you really should have -'

'She's at work … We came home and they needed her in, she had to -'

'Oh, Stuart this is ridiculous, she should be resting, not racing around Paris, then doing a shift at work, you should have -'

'Look Mary, I'd love to chat, but I'm running a bath … She'll call you later … There's someone at the door, I have to go.'

I drop the reciever like it's made of burning coal. If Sarah missed the ferry, decided to fly instead, she'd be home by now. My only sanctuary is bed, in minutes I'm out cold again.

As night falls, I dial the operator, request the French emergency services. As she starts to recite the number, there's an unfamiliar sound, the doorbell. It's an extremely rare occurrence for anyone to come to our door unannounced.

I expect two of them at least, maybe a van load like you see on those real life cop shows. But instead of a crew of police offices poised with a battering ram at my door, there's the diminutive figure of my mother-in-law, a small suitcase in her hand. For the first time in my life, I find myself flinging my body into her arms.

'Whatever's wrong … I thought you sounded odd on the phone, so I took the first available train. Sarah … The baby … There's nothing wrong is -'

'We were in France … It's all my fault, I don't know where she is. Sarah's missing, Mary.'

She ushers me into the kitchen, makes tea in the china pot they bought us for our first wedding anniversary, the china pot we only ever used when they visited. Outward signs of emotion are to be avoided at all costs in the Parker-Forest family, but I can't hold the tears back any longer, force the steaming liquid down my aching throat, the pain helping to focus my thoughts. It's pretty obvious I'm incapable of dealing with the chaos I've created. If the police aren't going to take over, it might as well be my mother-in-law. Mary is someone you want by your side in a crisis. She never panics, is always capable. If anyone can sort out this mess, it's her.

'We went to France … Well I went to France and she followed.' Her face remains impassive. She would have made an amazing poker player, but she's more of a bridge sort of person. 'I met this girl … That sounds worse than it was … At Chelmney station, Sunday morning. I was going home, giving you space to deal with the Ron thing without me. When I was a kid, I had a girlfriend, this girl looked exactly like her, so I -'

'Sarah said you were going to Paris. You mean you met this girl in the hotel and you and Sarah had a row. These things happen, Stuart.'

She's offering me a way out, but I don't want it. If she's

going to help me, she needs to hear the truth.

'No … There was no Paris. I went to France with the girl without telling Sarah. The girl, Marnie, thought my old girlfriend Hesther was her mother. I was helping her … Look for Hesther.'

Her left eye begins to twitch, there's a bead of sweat on her upper lip. Mary never sweats, not even on the warmest of summer days. 'We found out the family moved to France … That's why me and Hesther split up, her family just disappeared overnight. I should have phoned her … Sarah, but the time went on and it just didn't -'

'Is Sarah in France … Does Sarah know where Hesther is?'

'She lives in Grasse … Sarah contacted the credit card people … Followed me … She used to know Hesther, didn't she … I think that's why she married me.'

Her forehead gleams with perspiration, the colour drains from her face, leaving a clown like arc of rouge on each cheek.'

'I'll ask again, is Sarah with Hesther?'

'I don't know. We arranged to come home … Meet at Calais, but she never turned up. I think we need to contact the police, I'll take all of the blame, they can check the hospitals, the -'

'No … Not the police.'

'There's no other way. Look, I know you're going to hate me, but I never got over Hesther. I married Sarah because it was easy … I'm still in love with Hesther, Mary, that's why I took Marnie to find her.'

I wait for the slap, the sour recriminations. I've never seen her like this, her hands trembling in her lap, her face contorted with what looks like pain.

'Promise me Stuart … No police … Say you promise, please.'

Her breathing's laboured, there's something badly wrong, she clutches wildly at her chest. As we wait for the ambulance, I hold her hand as she drifts in and out of consciousness, tell her I'm sorry, that I'll do whatever it takes to find Sarah, to bring her home safely. Before they carry her away on the stretcher, she grabs my arm, uses her remaining strength to whisper in my ear.

'Find her yourself … Don't tell the police … Go back, save Hesther … Save them both, for God's sake Stuart … And

Stuart.' Her voice gets weaker, until I can barely make out the words. 'It's not your fault, none of it's your fault ... It's mine.'

Chapter 41

Ron

They told me my wife is in hospital. A heart attack. So things change. They leave tepid tea just out of my reach, fail to shave me, leave me in pyjamas, rather than taking the trouble to put me in a suit and tie. There will be no inspection today, so standards are permitted to slip. If I could speak, I would ask them about my daughter. But I don't have the right to. I am the worst father in the world.

I was in London for the day, some law conference my partner was supposed to attend, but couldn't for some reason that evades me. They were walking together, her face turned up to his, she was laughing, and it shames me to recall that was the thing I found most disquieting. It was the first time I'd seen her laugh since her release. Charles could make her laugh, when I couldn't. Now I see that I never even tried. She was dressed in an outfit I'd never seen before, a skirt too short for decency, her legs open to the elements. I wanted to wrap her in a blanket and take her home. Instead I played a game with myself. Pretended the girl parading herself around London with a man old enough to be her father, couldn't possibly be my daughter. In those days young girls often looked very similar, as was always the case with Sarah and Hesther. The girl clinging on to Charles's arm was his daughter, not mine.

For the weeks, months and years that followed, I questioned myself daily on the correct course of action to take in such a situation. Of course the answer was so self-evident, it was hardly worth asking the question. However for some unknown reason, perhaps a fear of rocking the apple cart, instead of removing her from him, punching him firmly on the chin, I simply crossed over the road and proceeded on my way to the conference hall.

When I arrived home that evening, supper was waiting on

the table. It was my favourite, beef braised in red wine and creamed potatoes. I half expected her to be absent, but there she was, lounging on the sofa, magazine in hand, dressed in her favourite jeans and a baggy jumper. So I tried again to convince myself it was Hesther after all. Sarah was functioning and that trumped everything.

When she told us she was pregnant, Mary wanted to call Dr. Burrows, one of the consultant psychiatrists at the clinic. We never spoke about the abnormal roundness of our daughter's stomach, but I convinced myself it was a positive sign, a healthy appetite was one of the indications of recovery. Mary said Sarah was imagining it, Dr. Burrows would know what to do. It was nothing more than a minor setback, something floating in Sarah's head, rather than her belly. She'd made a new friend, even been on a short holiday with Ellie and her parents. So I persuaded Mary to wait, terrified Dr. Burrows would drag my daughter back to that hell hole.

The weeks passed slowly. By that time Sarah stopped leaving the house, but she seemed cheerful enough, so we were under the illusion, that if we didn't speak about it, it would go away. Her stomach got bigger, until there was no denying the existence of another life. I was well aware that she was in need of medical attention. But we let it drift, until the prospect of taking her to a doctor became impossible. Our family GP's wife was a member of the Rotary Club, one of Mary's fundraising cronies, so a visit to Dr. Chambers was out of the question. We were in denial. The fifty foot elephant in the room, was the fact that before long there would be a real life baby, something we couldn't hide in the closet, a mark of disgrace on our family. Our daughter would be an unmarried teenage mother, someone who in other circumstances would qualify as a recipient of the proceeds from one of Mary's gala dinners.

Reluctantly, in preparation, I secured a place in a private clinic, miles out of town. A clinic which offered a solution in cases such as ours. Without discussing the matter with Sarah, we were both quite sure she wanted a quick and painless answer to her problem as much as we did. When there was no doubt the baby was coming, we made the hour long journey, Sarah covered in a blanket on the back seat of the car.

She refused to tell us who the father was. I knew. She'd used him to reconnect herself in some way with Hesther. I locked the knowledge away inside my head. It was far to late to share it with my wife. I was a coward, a deserter, and my punishment was to live with that fact for the rest of my life.

Between the screams of agony, she talked. The names she'd chosen, the make of pram, the love she felt for her yet unborn child. The child which was going to make her whole again, complete our family, make our lives worth living.

It was too late. The arrangements had been made. There was nothing in our home for a baby. No nursery, no pram, no tiny clothes, not even a single nappy. We had assumed complicity, without bothering to draw from any evidence. She'd made her own assumption, we would provide for the child's needs, while she recuperated in hospital with a baby in her arms.

The procedure was booked in advance. We both considered it kinder to have our grandchild removed from its mother's stomach with a scalpel, rather than making her push. At the clinic, Mary ordered the nurse to sedate Sarah. By that point she'd reached a state of euphoria which appeared to eclipse the pain. I could clearly see my daughter, the old Sarah, the Sarah with something to live for again.

They knocked the elation out of her with drugs. Left us sitting in a stark room with no offer of refreshment. We bowed our heads in shame as staff drifted in and out. Now I'm left to bask in the full force of pain my daughter deserved to feel in order to claim what was rightfully hers, to hold in her arms the very thing that could have saved her. For the first time, I'm on my own. My wife isn't here to join in with the charade we created on that day in order to carry on living.

We saw them. At first, I wasn't sure. But Mary said if we could see for ourselves that they were healthy, we would feel better about leaving them. Of course we had no idea there would be two. We had only made provisions for one. Mary spent many hours deliberating over sets of possible parents. She opted for a couple from Scotland, a doctor and his wife in their early thirties. A couple who had been trying to conceive for almost ten years. A couple of considerable means who wanted the peace of mind a private adoption would offer. A rock sure guarantee that the mother would not turn up on their doorstep at some point in the future. The price we put on our grandchild's velvet head was immense. Mary claimed it was proof of their good intentions, evidence they could provide the child with the life it deserved. I tried to pick her argument to threads, but in some other parallel universe it made perfect sense.

Sarah was big, we could see that, but we were so wrapped up in the shame, we failed to consider the possibility of twins. That's where our carefully thought out plan came crashing down around us. There were two robust, dark haired infants lying in the crib. I said a silent prayer to ask that the couple would take them both. They didn't. The nurse told us they wanted the boy. We must decide what to do with our granddaughter. They had a list of places, if we were struggling for ideas.

When Sarah came round from the anesthetic, there was a calmness about her, a sense of peace I'd not seen for a long time. She asked to see her baby, held out her arms, and I truly thought I was going to die there and then, the pain was so intense. Mary held her hand, explained gently, she'd given birth to a beautiful baby girl. Her eyes lit up like stars, then she gave me that same questioning look she used to give me as a little girl. That was my chance. My opportunity to tell her everything was fine, ask them to bring her daughter to her. But I was powerless as a kitten in the presence of the lioness sitting next to me, so instead through bitter tears, I watched my wife wipe the joy from my daughter's eyes with a razor sharp claw.

The baby was too weak to survive. The doctors did all they could. The baby flew straight to heaven, too precious for the indignities of life. At that point we heard the shrill cry of a baby coming from the next room. She held out desperate arms in the direction of the sound and it was the most pitiful thing I ever had the misfortune to witness. Mary had decided that to lose one baby was enough, two would have been too much for Sarah to bear. To this day I wonder if that cry came from one of my grandchildren, perhaps my grandson being dragged away from his rightful family.

We were told there was an excellent home, governed over by nuns, they were willing to take our baby girl, if need be. She would be cared for there, until they found a suitable family to adopt her. Mary said we had no choice but to accept the offer.

Two days later we drove Sarah home. I expected her to disintigrate under the burden of grief, resigned myself to the fact she would end up back in the sanitarium. Instead she seemed to cling on to some greater purpose. Something we were not privy to at that time, at least. She was calm, rational, spent long hours in her room, but appeared at meal times, cleared her plate, washed and dressed herself, even went for the odd walk. It was nothing like the last time, so we naively allowed ourselves to relax a little, resume some fragile sort of normality. A normality which would crumble into dust by an unexpected knock at the door some months later. An event which for the first time since we met would render my wife impotent.

My twins were like an itch that never went away. An itch it was impossible to scratch. My life was consumed by grandchildren I couldn't see, couldn't touch. I was envious of Sarah, for her ignorance of their existence. She could grieve, heal, was not living her life saddled with back breaking guilt. Mary and I made a silent pact never to speak of the matter again. I constantly wondered if she truly believed our babies were better off without us, or if we were better off without them.

About two years before the stroke I cracked, betrayed my wife. The frustration of not knowing how they were, where they were, built up to a crescendo inside my head until I thought it would burst. If only I knew they were well, cared for, perhaps the weight would lift a little. The clinic where they were born had changed hands by then. However, on my third visit, there was one nurse who looked familiar. It took a substantial sum of money to break her silence. My grandson was living in relative luxury in rural Scotland, but my little girl had not been adopted, was still living in a home for girls. My own flesh and blood was growing up in a children's home, when we had a spare bedroom and all the money in the world to care for her.

It lay like lead in my brain, which I'm pretty sure eventually caused the stroke. I offered her more money. She said she could give the home our details, my granddaughter would gain access to them when she turned sixteen. That wasn't an option. But I owed her family. I could give her a sister, Hesther would look after her. We learned from the knock at the door that Charles had passed away. We were not privy to Hesther's current whereabouts, due to the restraining order. So the only piece of information I could provide my granddaughter with was Hesther's old address, the rest was up to her.

After that, a creeping void began to open up between myself and my wife. I broke rank. We barely communicated, about anything important anyway, began to make excuses to be apart, pursue our own interests, spend less and less time together in the house. Then came the stroke. I needed her and willingly she took me on board. She had full control. The risk was over. I couldn't blow and tell Sarah everything, tear apart the web we'd so delicately woven around our family.

They will come tonight. The wild eyed babies, morph into child sized crows, tear puckered flesh from my brittle bones, peck out my jaundiced eyes so I will never see my little ones again.

'Let's get you ready Ron ... You're going out.' I knew it was coming, they're taking me away, somewhere far worse than this. I don't deserve such comforts as these. 'Your wife has asked to see you. Theresa is going to take you to the hospital.'

She pulls me into a suit, forces my intractable feet into a pair of nearly new leather shoes. I open my mouth to scream, nothing but a puff of air escapes.

Chapter 42

Marnie

My sister comes and goes. I don't mean physically. She can be sitting right next to me, but she's not here, not in her head, anyway. I can speak, but she doesn't hear me, wave my arms, but she doesn't see me. I suppose I should be jealous that Charlie likes her more than he likes me. But to be honest, it's a relief not to have him whispering in my ear all the time. She never raises her voice, never gets angry like I do, so it's understandable, I suppose. Once she starts to hum, it's over, I know that now, so I don't even try to reach her anymore.

I keep thinking about the flowers. The waste. They'll all be dead when we get back, rotting in the vases. She won't talk about the future. Will she send me back to Chelmney, or will I stay with her for a while in Grasse. For now, it's as if this is all that exists, this house, the sea, her, me and Charlie. I had a list of questions in my head to ask her over breakfast, but to spite me Charlie started humming and she joined in. So I ate my fruit and yoghurt in silence, pretended that was what I wanted to do anyway.

I swim for something to do. She goes to her typewriter. It's starting to freak me out, being here on our own. In all the days we've been here, I've not seen another person. I could literally drown, right here and now and no one would notice. Sometimes I think if I did, she'd have forgotten I ever existed by the end of the day. Later I lie on a lounger, life without books is hardly worth living. What sort of person has not one single book in their house. My tan's coming along nicely, but there's no one here to notice, so what's the point. Eventually she glides across the beach towards me. She's so beautiful, so elegant. Why can't I be more like her. Whatever I wear, it's dirty within minutes, however much I brush my hair it tangles again. Maybe, if I could be more like her, Charlie would come back to me.

'Darling ... My head's aching. I've been working on a rather tricky paragraph ... You wouldn't understand. You're lucky you're not a writer.'

She arranges herself on the lounger next to mine, pours iced tea from a flask into two glasses.

'I wanted to ask you about Sarah ... You said she was my mother ... Gave birth to me, I mean. Did she say why she -'

'Did you know my own mother is a sot ... Do you know what that means, Marnie. She drinks, not in a normal way, but in a determined way ... She's dying. She once said that -'

'I know, I just read this book ... One of the men was a drunk ... I never told you, but one day I'm going to Oxford ... University, I mean, to study. In the book the man, he wasted his place by drinking too much, then he -'

'Yes, I know the book well ... Literature is by far the best way to learn about life ... But you obviously know that, don't you. The thing was ... Is ... Marnie. Having a sot of a mother, afforded me a very special sort of childhood. It is frequently viewed as the responsibility of the mother to smother the life out of their offspring. To mould them into some sort of distorted model of their own image. Sculpt them into the wrong shape, stunt their lives, quash their freedom of expression. But you see, my mother wasn't like that ... What I'm trying to tell you, is that you're the same as me ... Intact ... We are two of the fortunate few. Your mother gave you the best gift in the world. She gave you away, just like my own mother gave me to the world ... Allowed me the freedom to form my own shape, undistorted by her own wishes. It gives us an advantage over other people, do you see that, Marnie. I can see Sarah in you, but the most important thing is, you can't. You're not designed by her weaknesses, her flaws, she never had the opportunity to -'

'But she abandoned me ... I grew up in a children's home ... Your father ... I mean our father, he wanted you, didn't he.'

'She said he raped her, Sarah, our father ... Did I tell you that. But it was her fault. She wanted to destroy me, but all it did in the end was destroy her ... But it didn't destroy you, and that's all that matters now, isn't it.'

'I met your mother ... Me and Stuey went there, she said -'

'Did I tell you Sarah wants to kill me ... Now she can use

you, to get at me, that's why we're here. Now she knows where I am, we're both in danger. She thinks she hates me, convinced herself of that years ago.'

'But because it was your name in my file ... I thought it was you, that you were my mother. That's why I went with Stuey ... At first ... I thought he might be my father, I mean -'

She laughs. Charlie comes running out of the house, settles himself down next to her.

'What a thought ... No, me and Stuart were close for a while, but nothing like that. But I want to tell you about Sarah ... Your family, they were -'

Just to spite me, even though he wants to know just as much as I do, he starts to hum. I hate him. I wish he was dead.

'Tell me about them ... About you and -'

She sighs deeply.

'There's really nothing to tell.'

She joins him in his strange little tune. I've lost her and it's all his fault. Ten minutes later he trots behind her, back to the house. An urge washes over me, so strong it feels like I'm drowning, a burning need to go home, back to Chelmney, away from the lot of them. I never realised how lucky I was not having a family, I wouldn't even care if Charlie stayed here with her, they're welcome to each other.

For the next few days we fall into some sort of routine, me doing pretty much nothing, her locking herself away all day and writing. Then one afternoon I watch her from the kitchen window as she gets in the car and drives away, Charlie in the passenger seat next to her. I'm all alone, with no idea if she's ever coming back. Her stuff's still in her room. More importantly her typewriter and piles of paper are still here, I'm pretty sure she wouldn't leave those behind, if she had no intention of coming back. As much as I try, I can't make any real sense of the words. It seems to be a story about a dancer, set in a village in Russia, but the sentences are too long, sort of run into one another, as if she can't be bothered finishing one, before starting another.

After a bowl of soup, I go upstairs. I've not been in her room since we arrived, it didn't seem polite somehow. The wardrobe's full of the floaty type of dresses she likes to wear. Her bed's neatly made, unlike my own tangled mess across the hall. There's a single pebble from the beach on her bedside cabinet. The drawers are full of silk underwear, a bottle of jasmine perfume. I spray some on my neck, put on some of her pale pink lipstick, drag her comb through my knotted hair.

In the bottom drawer there's a pile of silk scarves that I've never seen her wear. The fabric is so soft, I'm dying to try one on, but know I'll never fold it properly again and she'll know I've been snooping. There's something hard underneath, curiosity gets the better of me, I pull it out, careful not to ruffle the delicate material. My angelic sister owns a real life gun. I can't bloody believe it. It's much heavier than I imagined a gun would be, I really wouldn't fancy carrying all that weight around in my handbag, like they do in America. It feels good in my hand though, solid, reassuring. I point it at the wall, run my finger carefully over the trigger. I can see the appeal now, just knowing it's there makes me feel better, safer, not that there's anyone around here to be safe from.

Charlie would be shitting himself with excitement, serves him right he went with her. What if I took it down to the beach, there's no one around to hear a single bullet shot. This is probably my only chance to shoot a gun, I should definitely take it while I can. The car screeches to a halt on the driveway. I put it back, smooth the fabric, close her door behind me.

We sit down for supper. She produces two steaming bowls of pasta and a green salad, opens a bottle of wine.

'Did you have a good day, Darling ... I've been thinking, it's time to go home tomorrow ... Don't you agree. I've been meaning to ask you ... Your arms, the scars, what -'

Charlie jumps about in rage. He likes to use his penknife, but doesn't like owning up to the consequences.

'It's nothing ... I mean they're nothing, just some old -'

'When I was in hospital ... After your mother tried to kill me ... It was weeks before they let me see my scars. By then it was purely a bore to have to look at them. I mean scars are only skin, aren't they, just in another form. Mine were a result of trying to save our father ... Who were you trying to save, Marnie?'

She's waiting for an answer. She never waits for an answer.

Charlie comes over, digs me hard in the ribs. She's still waiting, a look of grave concern on her face.

'It was my fault ... I mean, I wasn't trying to save anyone. I deserved it ... I mean I -'

'Who did it to you, Marnie, you can trust me, we're sisters aren't we.'

'It was my ... I mean our -'

It happens in a flash, but I watch it in slow motion. He picks up the glass salad bowl, smashes it with all his might on the tiled floor, she raises her arms to shield her face, shards of pale green glass dance like raindrops in the sunlight. One of them makes its home in her right arm as the rest form an abstract pattern on the floor. Crimson beads of blood drip from her wound, completing the composition on the floor. He runs from the room, laughing like a ghoul, leaving us alone together. I reach out my hand to help her, she pushes it away, goes over to the sink, extracts the glass, washes the wound under the tap, then starts to hum. It's much louder than normal, a tuneless melody. Music that reminds me of death.

Chapter 43

Sarah

On the second day, there's a knock at the door. It's a petite lady in an apron. She asks for Hesther, I explain she's away on vacance, left me, an old friend to housesit for her. She looks unsure, but goes away anyway, leaving me to continue with my research.

Hesther never does anything by halves. The house is crammed full of flowers. I've already got through a full box of tissues, should have thrown the wretched things out the minute I got here. She always loved writing, but now it seems she does it for a living. There's a whole shelf of books with her name on the cover. At first her writing used to irritate me, when she had a pen in her hand, it was as if I wasn't there. Her scribbles took her away from me, and that was hard to cope with. But it was something I had to learn to live with, writing was deep within her, writing was something we couldn't share.

Our English Teacher, Mrs Shaw, claimed Hesther to be the most talented student she'd ever had the good fortune to teach. I hated English lessons, especially when we had to write our own stories. However much I tried to create charming little tales or poems with no meaning, just like the ones Hesther made up and still does by the content of her books, the comments always came back the same; dull, unimaginative, hackneyed, try to let your mind fly free. Other subjects like maths or geography were different, we could study together, she could help me with the difficult bits, but in English, I was on my own. She's dedicated each of her books in fountain pen to herself on the date of its publication.

If she'd been a painter, she'd have most definitely fallen under the umbrella of abstract school of art. That was the thing that annoyed me most, even when she let me read her work, I couldn't understand a word of it. It was like she wrote to spite me. To show me there was a part of her I'd never know, no matter how hard I tried. Next to her desk there's a bonfire sized pile of screwed up paper. Pages she's abandoned. She uses a typewriter, but it's not in the house, so she must have taken it with her. I'll wait for as long as it takes. After all I've nothing to rush back for, have I.

Stuart's home. I called, blocked the number, hung up when he answered. He won't come back to her until he knows where I am. I'm trusting he's made up something to appease mummy, for the time being, at least. She's kept the photos of us together, two little girls, running in the park, eating a picnic under one of daddy's apple trees, standing like shop dummies in identical school uniform. There's something in my eyes I've never seen before, a look of trepidation, something lurking in the shadows of my soul, waiting patiently for me to trip and fall.

She keeps an ebony box in her dressing table drawer, there's a tiny brass key to open the lock. It's the twin of Stuart's shoe box, her remnants of my husband. Tattered cinema stubs, torn bus tickets, sweet wrappers scribbled on in felt tip pen, a solitary out of focus polaroid. I almost laughed when I found it, at the pathos of it all. Two fully grown adults, clinging like limpets to the debris of their childhoods, after all these years. As I returned the items, the bottom of the box didn't look quite right, a shade lighter than the dark ebony of the box. When I gave it a good shake, the bottom fell out, revealing a deep red velvet pouch. There was a ring inside. Not the sort of ring you could buy in Woolworths in those days for a few pennies, the sort of ring a young lad would have saved up for, in the hope of surprising his sweetheart. No this was a special ring. An expensive antique ring. It fits me perfectly, I twist it round my finger, watch the sparkles catch in the sunlight. It's the most exquisite piece of jewellery I've ever seen; twenty-two carat honey coloured gold, a single flawless diamond resting daintily between two perfectly cut emeralds. It's mine now, just as it should have been all along. The words carefully written on the tiny scroll of paper are blistered onto my brain. 'To my own dearest Hesther. My Grandmother gave me this ring for safekeeping, and you are the safest place I know. Yours for eternity, S xxx'

On the fifth day there's a heavy knock at the door. It's a man, one of the most strikingly handsome men I've ever set eyes on. He doesn't seem surprised to see me, which immediately puts me on my guard.

'Bonjour, I am Henri, a good friend of Hesther.'

'She asked me to housesit for her … She had to go away … Last minute … I'm her best friend from England.'

He nods his head, as if she's already told him everything, offers up a perfectly manicured hand for me to shake. He doesn't look real, is dressed far too elegantly for this time in the morning. I run my hand down the voluminous dress I'm wearing, one of the many I found in her wardrobe. For some reason, I feel vulnerable in his presence. Without waiting for an invitation, he pushes straight past me into the kitchen.

'Madame, permit me to make us some tea.' He moves around like he lives here, opening cupboard doors, spooning tea into a china pot, pouring milk from the fridge into a small jug. 'I'm enchanted to meet you … Dear Hesther, she said she was expecting someone. I think she will be back soon … Then we must all do something together, you will want to stay for a while, spend some time with your old friend, mais oui.'

'How lovely to meet you … Yes, it is very lovely here … It would be nice to explore the area … When she gets home.' I try to sound relaxed, conversational, but the baby kicks out in protest at the invasion and a tidal wave of nausea nearly chokes me. 'You must excuse me … I'm having a baby, you see, so really need to rest.'

He stands to leave, my breathing slows to the relief of my daughter.

'Please, before I go, I must … How you say in English … Use the little boy's room.' Before I can stop him, he's skipping up the stairs two at a time. Her bedroom's a mess, the door's wide open, the contents of her drawers scattered on the floor. It's too late, there's nothing I can do now but wait.

He trots down the stairs, a dazzling smile on his chiselled face.

'Au revoir Sarah, until the next time.'

The door slams behind me as I run back to the kitchen to vomit violently into the sink. This was my warning. She knows

I'm here. I lay a comforting hand over my stomach, slowly climb the stairs and retreat to her bedroom to finish what I've started.

Chapter 44

Stuart

The sirens and blue lights signal the severity of the situation. She was meant to save me, to take over. Instead it's all a hundred times worse. The phone rings, I let it do its worst, then mercifully it gives up the fight.

When I wake again, I feel like I'm dying. It's hard to remember the details of what's happened, the timeline of events. All I know for sure is that it's bad and I'm not capable of making it any better.

The fever inhabits my body, the only thing I can think about is the fight for survival. For day after wretched day, my life is bed, toilet, sink. The phone is my torturer. I try counting the rings, to cling onto something other than the jackhammer pounding in my head.

Then finally, who knows how many days later, I wake and the malady has released me from its clutches. I can stand rather than crawl, my head feels like it's been released from a vice. After a bowl of soup and pints of hot sweet tea, some form of action seems inevitable.

My trousers hang forlornly round my diminished waist, the belt buckle reaching a virgin hole. Through the bathroom mirror a stranger stares back; gaunt of face, jaundiced skin with raspberry ripple eyes. Mary told me to save them. It turns out I couldn't even save myself. I resist the urge to crawl right back under the rancid covers. The phone rings, this time I submit to its demands.

'Stuart ... Thank God.' Her voice sounds weak, but she's alive, one disaster less to deal with. 'I've been worried sick. The silly little doctor refuses to let me out of this dreadful place, even though I'm perfectly fine ... Thinks he knows everything ... Power gone to his head, I suppose. Have you brought her home ... Is everything alright ... Can I speak to her?'

'I've been ill, Mary ... In bed mostly, I haven't been -'

'You must go now ... Back to Hesther's, we may still have time ... I'm going to get out of here today if it kills me ... Look just do as I ask ... You're the only one who can solve this, I -'

'But you never told me ... Anything about Sarah's past, I could have -'

'You never bloody asked did you ... We thought her illness was over, she seemed happy with you ... That's why we let you marry ... We thought she'd left all that with Hesther behind.' Her voice lowers to a whisper. 'Look Stuart, the police have been involved before ... She has a criminal record ... Sarah. She shouldn't be anywhere near Hesther. So enough talking ... Go ... Ring me when you get there.'

There's a click and she's gone. I'm on my own again. Ten minutes later I leave the house with only my wallet and passport for company.

Chapter 45

Marnie

Love is not a concept I've ever bothered too much with. You can't learn it at school. It won't get you into Oxford university. It won't buy you a big house. It won't allow you to travel first class around the world. So all in all, it's not something I've ever been concerned with. Of course there's Charlie. But that's different, not something you have to think about. She's humming as she drives so I can't speak to her. When we get back to her house, she says I can have my own room, decorate it as I like, even pick out furniture. She never mentioned sending me back to Chelmney. She promised to enroll me at the local college. So I suppose we love each other, even though neither one of us has said it. Sisters love each other, don't they, even if they don't like each other very much. That's how family works, or so I've read in novels.

With the fosterers, the teachers, the nuns, the so called carers it was easy. Love never came into the equation. If someone adopted you, they were supposed to love you eventually. Like you were their own. Like they'd given birth to you. But I never believed that, Charlie said it was a load of old crap and I believed that, I mean you can't just love someone because social services tells you to, can you.

It's different with your own mother, or so we learnt in science. There are hormones, genes, real things that bind you together. You actually live inside her for months and months, so really you're part of the same person. Now I have a sister, I try not to think about my mother very often. I know my sister loves me, because she never even punished me for the salad bowl thing. And even though Charlie doesn't show it any more, I know he loves me just as much as he loves her.

There's a car parked on the driveway of her house. I recognise it straight away, it's Helen's, I mean Sarah's, or whoever she really is. We park on the road. There's no sign of Stuey's van.

'She's here ... Sarah ... We should go back to the beach ... You said she wants to hurt you.'

'Marnie, my darling, everything's fine ... You can trust me, you know that don't you. You should meet her properly anyway ... Everyone should meet their mother at least once in their lifetime ... No matter who they are.'

This can't be right, not after everything she said about Sarah. My heart pounds as we unpack the car. I wish Stuey was here, I'd feel better then. The door swings open, and she's there on the doorstep, the women in the wedding photo dressed in what looks like one of my sister's dresses, acting as if it's her house and we're the visitors.

Charlie takes one look at her and runs for his life, it takes all of my self control not to run after him.

'You lied to me ... About taking me home to Chelmney ... About who you were ... You should never have -'

'Sarah, darling how kind of you to come all this way, just to see me. Or was it to see your daughter. Marnie belongs to me now, don't you darling. You can see we belong together, can't you ... She does have some of you in her ... But it's clear that our father had the stronger genes. If I was a few years younger, we could pass as twins, couldn't we Marnie.'

Sarah takes a step towards Hesther, and for a second, I'm sure she's going to slap her.

'My daughter is yet to be born ... I expect this girl is one of his little bastards ... Did she tell you he was a rapist ... Your father ... Had a penchant for little girls like his daughter ... He made me pregnant, but luckily his child went straight to heaven ... Now she's ready to come back as mine and mine only ... There are probably loads of you ... You all deserve each other.'

I should have gone with Charlie. She's crazy, they're all a bunch of nutcase liars, the whole bloody lot of them. But Hesther was right. I am glad I met Sarah. Who in a million years would want to be raised by a mother like this. Even the home was a better option than that.

'You've made yourself at home, I'm glad to see. It's a stunning ring isn't it. Your husband gave it to me ... So long ago now … When I met him, I somehow thought it would be the three of us … But that wasn't to be, was it … Such a shame, and to think you ended up together anyway … Keep it ... The ring, it's no use to me … You deserve it for putting up with him all these years. I think he truly believed he was in love with me, did you know that … But we were just kids … In the end you were the one to get saddled with him … My father did me a favour by bringing us to France.' Sarah looks like she wants to kill my sister, we should've stayed at the beach. 'But that was thanks to you … Wasn't it, so perhaps you and Stuart were meant to be together all along.'

Hesther's bag is on the table, the gun must be inside, I edge a bit nearer.

'You always did have an overly active imagination, I should have -'

'You know I should call the police, don't you … After last time … If I did, you'll have your baby in prison … You know that don't you … But I feel sorry for you, Sarah, I want to help you, I really do … You see none of this is your fault … Not really. The fault lays with your parents … They stifled you, and I know that because they tried to do the same thing to me. But I was strong, and unfortunately you were weak … Your mother was the worst culprit, but you know that, don't you … I'll tell you a little secret, I always had a soft spot for your father … And do you know what, I believe he had a soft spot for me.'

'You bitch … You know they both loved you … You never complained when you got a hot meal, a warm house with a real family instead of an alcoholic mother and an absent rapist father.'

This is getting way too serious, something bad's going to happen, if I don't do something soon. Where's Charlie when I need him. A sharp knock at the door shocks them into silence. I answer praying it's Stuey, or even the police. Instead the most handsome man in the world holds out a hand to me. He's so beautiful I can hardly bear to look at him, feel my skin burning up with shame.

'Bonjour … Marnie, I presume, just as charming as your sister.' He pushes past me, goes into the kitchen. 'Sarah … We meet again … Hesther Ma Cherie.'

He kisses her, not on both cheeks like the French do, but buries his tongue deep inside her mouth. Sarah turns away in disgust. The kiss is bad enough, but the fact that she never told me about him is worse. Sisters are supposed to tell each other everything, especially about hot boyfriends, aren't they. After what seems like an age, they pull away from each other, and I can finally breathe again.

'Henri, you've met Marnie ... My sister ... Now be a perfect dear and take her out somewhere ... Coffee ... Ice cream ... Whatever she wants.'

'But I can't leave you ... With her ... You said she -'

'Nonsense Marnie, you're in perfectly safe hands with Henri ... He's one of my oldest friends ... I need some time alone with Sarah.'

He takes my arm and it's clear I have no choice in the matter. All eyes follow us as we walk. His hair is so thick, dark and shiny, it almost looks like a wig. His suit is made from cream coloured linen, it's spotless and perfectly pressed, which makes me think of Stuey when I last saw him, so bedraggled, his thinning hair thick with grease. I'd willingly give a million pounds to have him here with me now, instead of this playboy mannequin. Henri looks like he should be in Hollywood sipping cocktails with some glamorous actress, rather than taking me for an ice cream like I'm a six year old kid.

He keeps looking at me, it doesn't feel good, dangerous, wrong somehow. A well dressed elderly couple stop in their tracks and stare, the man actually has the cheek to point his finger in our direction. If you did that in Chelmney, you'd get your head kicked in. No one seems to think staring's rude here, so I start staring right back. Charlie would be proud of me.

'We will sit here, get to know each other a little better.' He pulls out the chair for me, like I'm too weak and feeble to do it myself, puts a hand on my back to guide me into the seat. I want to punch him, can't bear him touching me. What she sees in him, I really can't imagine. 'You are just as beautiful as your sister ... But so young ... So perfect.' I really should have at least brushed my hair, but the threat of them killing each other was quite a distraction. What about the gun, will Sarah have a weapon too. I shouldn't have left them, but when Hesther says to do something, you do it, even if it's the last thing in the world you really want to do. 'Your sister lights up our dull little town … How we managed … Before, without her, I will never know.'

'Look … Henri … When we were away, Hesther told me some bad things … About Sarah. I think we should go back, we should -'

'Everybody here loves her … They say the English writer, with the kind heart. She helps out at the refuge … Helps people who are not as fortunate as ourselves. They adore her … So talented, yet so kind.'

The waiter brings out a coffee for Henri and a bowl of strawberry ice cream for me.

'We'll go back, after this, I really don't want to -'

'Ma Cherie … There is no rush in these things … They are old friends, they need time to, how you say … Reminisce.' He leans over, brushes a strand of hair from my face with his finger. His hands are too soft, like baby's hands, it makes me shiver and not in a good way. 'But I think that you have an interesting story to tell … Like your sister. I can see it in your face. Did I tell you that I write too … For my own pleasure, of course. I would like to write you … Your own unique story.'

A young man comes to our table.

'Henri, how nice to see you after all this time. What a charming companion you have today. But the clock is ticking now, is it not.'

He walks away, without waiting for an answer.

You are right, Ma Cherie, we should go back. The time is right to do so, is it not.'

At the door to her house he kisses me hard on both cheeks, his hand moving slowly down my back. Luckily for him there's no sign of Charlie. Then he leaves, when I was banking on him to come in with me, so I wouldn't have to be on my own with them again. The door's unlocked, but the house is empty. All the flowers are dead or dying. The typewriter's back on her desk, but there's no sign of the gun in her bedside cabinet. Without warning, Charlie swans in, like he never even left, tickles me because he knows that always makes me forgive him.

We find crisps in one of the kitchen cupboards, wine from the fridge, cuddle up together on the sofa, just like the old times and watch some dumb program about a farm. It's pretty lame, but it takes my mind off what might be happening with Sarah and Hesther. After nearly two bottles of wine, we both start to drift off to sleep, get woken by a knock at the door. Charlie tells me to ignore it. It's still unlocked so it won't be Hesther, if it's Henri it would be fatal to let him in with Charlie here armed and loaded. The knocking gets louder, then we hear the door open. Charlie waves his penknife around wildly, I grab a heavy vase from the table.

He looks a million times worse than when I last saw him. He's lost so much weight, his clothes are hanging from him, like he bought three sizes too big from a charity shop. His eyes are red raw craters sunk into his hollowed out face. It looks like he's not shaved for weeks. Without thinking, I push Charlie out of the way, knocking the penknife from his hand and jump into a pair of trembling arms.

'Stuey, you came ... They're gone, Sarah and Hesther ... They were here ... Arguing ... Henri took me out, and when I got back they were gone ... Hesther, she ... Stuey, Hesther has a gun, we have to find them.'

He peels my arms from his shoulders, sinks into the sofa, and it's clear from the state of him, he's going to be no help whatsoever, so I lay my head on his shoulder and we both give in to sleep, leaving them to their fate.

Chapter 46

Ron

Her face is scrubbed clean. She's dressed in a hospital gown. For the first time since I've known her, my wife has an air of vulnerability about her. She handled the birth of our daughter like an ox. The midwife said Mary was by far her least challenging patient. Mary said it would be silly to make a fuss over one of the most natural things in the world. She's connected by wires to various machines. I've never noticed before, but her hair is thinning, patches of white scalp clearly visible under the dying curls. Theresa parks me up beside her bed, the nurse acts like I'm not here, speaks directly to my carer.

'Mary's doing well ... Much better than expected, in fact she -'

'I'm quite capable of updating my husband on my health status, thank you very much. I may have a malfunctioning heart, but there's nothing wrong with my brain ... Would you both allow us some privacy, we have important family business to discuss.'

The nurse scuttles away gratefully, but Theresa's not so keen to leave, probably sensing some juicy gossip she can use as hard currency in the home.

'We don't like to leave our residents unattended, we have a -'

'Look my dear. My husband is in capable hands with me. I cared for him singlehandedly for years ... Why don't you get a coffee, they tell me there's a decent canteen downstairs ... Have a break, I'm sure not all your residents are as unchallenging as Ron.'

'Ok, but I have to have him back for supper, so I'll give you half an hour.'

Supper is the meal they serve promptly at four-thirty. It would be earlier if they could get away with it. The mantra is, the sooner we're fed, the sooner we're in bed. The night staff take over then, which means two people to care for thirty residents, instead of ten during the day. A more accurate description of the meal would be nursery tea. Mostly a piece of white bread cut into quarters, topped with ham so thin, even the bluntest of dentures could get in, followed by two pear slices out of a tin, served with condensed milk in a plastic bowl. On one occasion they even had the audacity to place a dollop of red jelly partnered by a block of jaundiced ice cream in front of me. I would have tipped the whole lot out of the window, if only I had the ability to open the damn thing.

'Darling, I'm so sorry.' She takes my limp hand in hers. 'It was the shock … You must listen carefully, but stay calm … I was worried, something wasn't right, so I went to London … There was no trip to Paris, I don't have time to go into all the details, but suffice to say … It's Sarah … She knows where Hesther is … In France, Grasse. But Sarah's different now, we both know that … Stuart … The baby … She wouldn't do anything stupid … Would she darling, not this time … But the thing I need to tell you, is this … The boy, Hesther's boy, the measles boy … It was Stuart … That's why Sarah wanted him, I can see that now, it was such a mystery at the time … When Stuart was leaving us, that Sunday morning, he met a girl at the station, she looked like Hesther … What if she is Hesther's and Stuart's … It will tip Sarah over the edge … I had to share it with you, my darling, you're the only one I can talk to, we must do what we -'

The nurse returns, pushes me out of the way so she can reach one of the machines then scribbles some numbers on my wife's chart. Theresa appears, staring with intent at her watch.

The last time Sarah found Hesther, she intended to kill her. Maybe Mary's right, with a baby inside her, she won't do anything stupid, maybe she wants to apologise, make amends for the past. When the police arrived at Hesther and Auriel's house in Nice, my daughter was found to be in possession of a knife, not the sort of knife you use to spread butter, the sort you would use in order to inflict serious bodily harm. We'd buried our heads so deep in the sand, we missed the signs again. Sarah blamed Hesther for her baby daughter dying, her greater purpose, the thing that was keeping her calm, was a plan to make Hesther pay.

Today supper consists of chalky tomato soup fresh from the packet, followed by a lump of mottled mashed banana topped with a drizzle of neon custard. For once, I allow myself the privilege of leaving it untouched. The pieces begin to fit together, slowly, like a jigsaw I've had sitting in a cupboard for years, and only just got round to opening.

My granddaughter was here, in Chelmney. She must have come to look for Hesther. Stuart is the lad who used to hang round with Hesther. Sarah's sudden desire for a boy with no charm or assets was nothing to do with Stuart. It was Hesther. It's always been Hesther, we just didn't match up the pieces. We were so relieved our daughter finally had the trappings of a young adult; a husband, a house of her own, good grooming, nice clothes, holidays and meals out in restaurants, we failed to delve any deeper, to see it was all a veneer. Underneath rage was still streaming like poison through her veins. Underneath all she was living for was Hesther.

One of the greatest regrets of my life, is the fact that Sarah unwittingly lives in a house purchased from the blood money of my grandson. Mary argued we were using it wisely, providing a stable environment for our daughter, helping to mitigate against any future relapse. I could hardly bear to set foot in the place, but Mary seemed happy enough to help with interior design options, the purchase of furniture and carpets.

When the police came to our door, they told us that Hesther was reluctant to press charges. Auriel on the other hand was adamant. In the end, Hesther's testimony meant they were lenient with Sarah, but by then it was too late for us.

As they opened the first drawer, Mary snapped like a well worn rubber band. A female officer was called in to restrain her. It almost broke me, to see my wife in handcuffs on the sofa, as two officers of the law meticulously worked their way through decades worth of debris, leaving it scattered like flotsam on the carpet. When they reached Sarah's wardrobe, six hours of solid graft threw up its rewards. The evidence safely stowed in a plastic bag, they proceeded to search my wife's lingerie drawer, pulling at items even I would never have dared to touch. Two hours later they left.

We were in shock. Both about the visit, and Sarah's whereabouts. Exhaustion and despair meant we failed to ask the right questions, at the time, anyway. It was much later when we were to discover just how dark our daughter's mind had become.

After supper, they come back to undress me. We retire at the same time as five year olds, although we have no exertions to recover from, and nothing to get up bright and early for the next day. But this evening I don't mind. Everything I need is in my head. I picture her face, but it's Hesther's face I see. My granddaughter deserves a mother. My daughter deserves her twins. Before I fall asleep, I make a pact with the heavens. If they grant me one final audience with Sarah, somehow I'll find a way to tell her her babies are alive. For the first time since I've been here, they don't come in the night. For the first time since I can remember, I'm granted the beatific slumber of the righteous.

Chapter 47

Auriel

We were both performers. That's why he chose me. We both performed the same role, presented a body of evidence to a room, in order to persuade the audience of the truth. My daughter does the same, to wide critical acclaim. Her books do not sell in the millions, but numbers don't matter in the arts. If I could have danced for just one person who took a grain of truth from my performance, it would have been a far greater achievement than to dance for one million unbelievers. Hesther writes for the initiated, for those who can see through to the honesty of her words.

Sometime when I wake in a morning, for a few seconds, I'm still worlds away from death. But by lunchtime I submit to my beloved, the fresh wind of mortality, allow the day to float away on the spirit of love. If I close my eyes, I'm with her once more, dancing on an empty stage, our limbs entwined in exquisite movement, until exhausted we fall, certain in the knowledge we'll rise up together again.

Back in those days London was a battle scarred skeleton of a city. To us it was our promised land. Helena was the most gifted dancer I'd ever met. Her grandmother trained her in secret, in a cellar, with a makeshift bar. Her father was captured, taken to Treblinka to work, her mother raped, shot between the eyes for daring to spit at a German soldier. They almost starved to death behind the ghetto walls, but even then, her grandmother made her dance, although some days they were both too weak to climb up the cellar steps at the end of the day. Her grandmother taught her that dance would make her free. She was right. Dance saved Helena. Dance destroyed me.

She was rescued from the ghetto by an English benefactor collecting children to take back to London. She came to his attention dancing in the street. In return for being saved, the children were given gainful employment in one of his London factories.

Helena had no beginning, no middle and no end. She'd witnessed so much horror, it was impossible to pin her down, she flowed like a river through the lives she touched, operated on pure elation at simply being alive, swept me up in her insatiable quest for pleasure. For eighteen months we lived a lifetime in each day. Then one night he came to the show, chose me, and it was over.

When he took me, the very thing that made him want me was ripped away. He couldn't bear to think of other men watching me dance, so he took me off the stage, forbid me from dancing. I became a girl, just like any other girl. I hated him for picking me, when it could have picked anyone.

Helena escaped from the factory for a few hours one day, after seeing her dance, our director paid off the benefactor most generously. He wanted her for his own, but Helena was free, as impossible to catch as a flock of wild geese. She died in her late fifties of a drug overdose. By then I was too numb to feel any pain.

I will never see my daughter again. Not in this lifetime. I set her free, imagined she would ascend like a bird of paradise. Instead she limped away like a wounded cub. I thought she didn't need me and when I found out she did, it was too late.

She was here this morning, his other child. It was Sarah who took my daughter away from me, made me think she didn't need me. Sarah and those conniving parents of hers. They thought I couldn't see what they were doing, stealing my child right in front of my nose. They thought the drink masked everything, when in reality it masked nothing. They wanted her for their own needs, the three of them. They wanted her because they were empty vessels, passionless, dull, living humdrum little lives.

The trouble was, although they took her from me, they could never steal her from Charles. So Sarah took it upon herself to steal Charles from Hesther. She said her child died. But today I saw clear evidence that she was lying. She blamed Hesther for the made up death, tried to punish her with guilt, but it didn't work. My daughter was informed that she could not have children, after the fire, her internal injuries were too severe. She pretended otherwise, but I could see the pain etched on her face, when the doctor broke the news. The scars, she could live with, but I don't think she ever forgave Sarah for her barren womb.

She came to us again. In this very house, more disturbed than ever. There was always something missing in her, I think that's why Hesther picked her as a friend. The first time I saw her at the school gates, I watched her follow my daughter, like a stray puppy desperate for an owner. I could see there and then that there was something not quite right about her.

I used to blame Hesther for my insobriety. Imagined that if she'd been the sort of girl to rely on her mother, I would have assumed the role, put her before the drink. But to all outward appearances, Hesther had no need for anyone except herself. Sarah didn't need a friend, she needed an identity, and Hesther had enough for two.

After Sarah, there was a boy. She assumed I didn't know, but I used to see them together, on my trips to the off licence. He was a ragamuffin sort of lad, not someone you would expect Hesther to choose. But my daughter has always had a penchant for waifs and strays, because somewhere deep inside she has a desire to be needed. Charles was only interested in Hesther when it suited him, so her teenage dalliance remained a secret, from him at least.

He was here this morning, with the girl. A banal sort of man called Stuart. At first he pulled at my heart strings. Anyone could see he was still in love with Hesther, or imagined he was at least. Then I found out the truth. It was Sarah who wanted to find Hesther. He was just a pawn in their game. I never told Hesther about the carefully curated collection the police found in Sarah's bedroom, it was bad enough one of us waking with night terrors.

It's too late now to save my daughter. The time is here and there's nothing I can do to delay it. I hear her call my name, hold out my hand and she takes it, absolves me with a gentle kiss. We dance. Dance in a spiral, higher and higher into the sky. Her grandmother greets us with a smile, turns to her and says 'It saved us all, didn't it, just like I told you … In the end.'

Chapter 48

Stuart

She looks amazing. But she's lost weight and there's something missing, the light in her eyes has dimmed. Her skin is glowing from the sun, scars barely visible, but it's clear to see she's not the girl I met at the station. I try to hold her, but the journey took every ounce of strength I had. We wake on the sofa two hours later.

'Stuey ... You look terrible by the way ... We should be out there ... Searching for them. They were arguing. Sarah was living in Hesther's house ... When we came back from the beach ... Hesther thinks she's my mother ... Sarah, I mean, but Sarah says her baby died ... None of it makes any sense ... But I'm glad you're here ... And you won't want to hear this ... But she's got a boyfriend ... Hesther ... Henri. But she never told me about him, at the beach ... The thing with her, Hesther, is you never get to know anything about her ... Not anything you want to know anyway ... I collapsed, outside a church, and the priest phoned her to come and get me ... My sister, she -'

'I didn't know, Marnie ... Any of it ... About Sarah and Hesther, that they knew each other ... I know it sounds strange, but ...'

'He's a creep ... Henri.' She takes a good look at me, I know I'm a mess, but the look on her face confirms just how much I've let myself go. 'Well he's good looking, I suppose, really good looking ... Dresses well, has hair like Elvis, but better.' This really isn't making me feel any better. I feel as weak as a tadpole. 'They kissed ... Like properly kissed, it was disgusting. I could've -'

'You said they were arguing, what were they -'

'It was just boring stuff ... About the past ... Sarah was wearing a ring, Hesther said you gave it to her, but Sarah could have it ... There were other things, but I -'

'Come on we're doing no good here, let's go out and search for them.'

Your house is charming, just like I knew it would be, but ruined by vase after vase of dead flowers. She shows me your study, the words in your books are beautiful, but they don't make much sense.

'She's had her books published and everything … But I'm not being funny, Stuey, they're really crap … I'd never tell her, of course … What if we just left … You and me, went home to England, left them to it … I mean Sarah's quite obviously a psycho, and Henri … He's way out of your league, Stuey … I'm not being mean, but it's a fact.'

'I have to find them, Marnie. I made a promise to someone, I would.'

The streets are crammed with tourists who refuse to move at anything other than a slug's pace. They clog up the narrow arteries of town, form unwieldy groups around tour guides brandishing umbrellas in the air. Marnie drags behind me like a petulant child, her heart isn't in it, and I can't say I blame her, it was me who dragged her into this mess. On more than one occasion, I place a hand on a dark haired shoulder, only to stare into a stranger's face.

I knew Sarah had a dark side. Most people do, some are just better at hiding it than others. Ron is one of the few people I've come across who's good through and through. He was the last person who deserved to have a stroke, that's why it pains me so much to see him. On the rare occasion Sarah let her Halo slip, I could see just how much it upset her, how eager she was to stick it back in place.

She announced that we'd spend our first wedding anniversary at Hampton Court Palace, then dine out later at a new Greek restaurant in the West End. That morning I managed to reach the bathroom just in time to vomit into the toilet bowl. She said I was being melodramatic, wanted to ruin the day, but the pain just got worse and worse. When she left the house an hour later, the pain was so severe, I was forced to ring for an ambulance. She appeared at the hospital that evening, armed with a hamper of tropical fruits, two new pairs of silk pyjamas and a wide array of reading material. It was a burst appendix.

To this day I've never asked her about her time at the palace and she's never asked me how I got to the hospital. For the following two weeks she turned herself into a nineteen-fifties American housewife, tending to my every whim. She was so convincing, I almost allowed myself to believe she cared. But when I was well enough, she turned back into herself, and that was that. Our domestic idyll came to a timely end.

'I need to sit down, it's too bloody hot. Let's just go back to the house. They're not going to kill each other here, in front of all these people, are they.'

She's right, this is useless, the crowds are getting thicker by the minute. We can't keep walking forever, I feel light headed as it is. So we trudge back to your house in silence, drained, dehydrated, devoid of hope.

There's a dull banging coming from the kitchen. Marnie barges ahead of me, flings open the door, and there you are, standing at the counter chopping tomatoes, humming some strange tune I've never heard before. You turn to us, and there's not a flicker of surprise on your face. then you honour us with one of those smiles that used to make me melt inside.

'Marnie, darling … There you are … Henri said he dropped you off hours ago. He's a dear … Don't you agree, and so very useful, I really don't know what I'd do without him you know … And Stuart, you're here for your wife, I presume … Did you know she pretends to hate me … No I suppose you wouldn't … You always were rather naïve.'

And with that, you start humming again, chopping the tomatoes in an erratic manner, as if your head is a world away from this room. I wait for Marnie to speak, but instead she grabs the sleeve of my shirt, pulls me out of the room, shutting the door behind us.

'Did she used to do that … The humming thing … When you knew her. It drives me mad, I'm sure she does it on purpose … When she can't be bothered to talk anymore. Once she starts it's pointless trying to get anything out of her … We have to find the gun.'

She runs upstairs, I consider following her, but the pull from the kitchen is far too great.

'Hesther, I -'

'I'm preparing a late lunch. I suppose you're hungry ... I've had a trying day ... But these things happen ... Don't they, sometimes.'

There's something different about the room. It's the flowers, the dead ones have been replaced with beautiful fresh blooms.

'Hesther ... I'm sorry, it's been so long, I -'

'You married her ... I'm not surprised, in a funny way, you suit each other ... Can you remember, I told you once ... About her ... So many moons ago ... Henri wanted to marry me Stuart, did you know that ... But between you and me, he's not the sort of man a woman like me would consider as a husband. So I keep him close, but not too close, if you know what I mean ... Now we must talk about my sister.'

'Marnie is amazing, isn't she, considering everything she's been through ... But your father, you must have -'

'I want to thank you for bringing her here to me. It all sounds a terrible mess, I couldn't take in all the details ... But she's here now, and that's all there is to it, isn't it.'

This is nothing like I expected, it feels like wading through mud. I keep reminding myself I'm here to take my wife home, so far, I haven't even asked where she is.

'But Sarah ... Look, I really didn't know ... That you were friends, she just -'

'Sarah needs help Stuart. Not the sort of help you or I could offer ... Did you know her parents pretended to help her, sent her to some sort of poor man's lunatic asylum. It was probably all they could afford at the time. I'm sure you've tried as well, but you don't look like you've got money to burn. So, I've decided to take on the burden myself. You don't need to thank me ... That's not why I'm doing it. It's a small private clinic, some of the most eminent doctors in the world ... I could have simply phoned the police and had her arrested ... But I feel sorry for her, always have, I suppose.'

Marnie attempts to creep in unnoticed. She really doesn't seem herself.

'Clinic ... But where ... Her mother wants to -'

'My dear Stuart ... So many questions. She needs rest, recuperation, help to get her brain cleansed of all those ridiculous notions ... She needs protecting from her parents, can't you see that ... You do love her, don't you Stuart.' Marnie rubs at an imaginary mark on the table. 'But of course you do ... You married her, didn't you. I want to return something to you, you asked me to look after it and I did ... You can give it to your wife, when she's well enough.'

My grandmother's ring. The ring she asked me to keep, in order to prevent my parents drinking away the profits. We'd been together for over a year by then. A real milestone, considering I never expected to see you again after that first day we met. By then you were my life, my everything, all the romantic songs in the hit parade made sense. We were at the beach, your hair flowing like silk in the breeze. You haven't changed, I can still see that girl, standing at your kitchen counter, a chopping knife in hand. The scars just make you look more beautiful. I chased you across the sand, but you were always a faster runner than me. You fell down by a rock pool, I joined you, panting like a dog, it seemed the perfect moment, so I pulled the pouch from my pocket, the ring slipped out, fell into the water, without thinking you reached a tanned arm deep into the crevice, laughed as a crab scuttled away, I expected your hand to emerge clasping a stone or a string of seaweed, but there it was sparkling in the sun, and without a word you slipped it on your finger, in that moment I truly believed you were mine forever.

You hold it out to me, and there's nothing I can do but take it. It's over. I can see it in her eyes. She's right, I did marry Sarah. It's impossible to explain that despite that, deep inside I'm still the boy standing outside her door, waiting for a miracle to happen.

'Sarah ... When can I see her, her mother will want to know where -'

'The doctors said she will only get well if we give her time ... We mustn't be selfish in the matter ... We must put her first ... Something her parents never did. Now you must eat with us, then it's time for you to go home. Tell her mother that she'll thank me in the end ... I heard her father had a stroke ... Such a shame ... Such a gentle man, some would say weak, but not me, I prefer gentle.'

It makes sense now, about the baby, she made it up,

imagined it, she was mentally unstable, but none of us bothered to notice. We eat a goats cheese salad and fresh bread. She opens a bottle of local wine. I don't taste a thing, force the food into my mouth and chew. How could it end like this. Does she look at Henri like she used to look at me, come alive under his touch. Marnie's subdued, she looks so healthy on the surface, but there's something missing inside and it's all my fault. What I'd give to go back in time, walk past her at the station, leave a feisty teenage girl to forger her own way in life, instead of dragging her into this tangled mess, none of which is her making.

When we've finished eating, Hesther starts to clear the plates, humming softly to herself, like she's forgotten that me and Marnie exist. Marnie retires upstairs, I stand in the hallway, want to follow her, check she's alright, but I hear her raised voice, like she's arguing with someone, she must be on the phone, so there's nothing for it but to go back in the kitchen.

'Hesther, look I really need -' The volume of her humming increases. 'I appreciate what you've done … With Sarah, but I really need to know where she is, her mother deserves that much at least … I know you probably won't believe me, but I didn't know, about you and Sarah … About her illness, it explains a lot, but I'

'Time to leave Stuart … Give me your number, I'll be in touch … You look dreadful by the way … I hope you don't mind me being frank with you … You should look after yourself … Well you'll only have yourself to look after now, won't you … It wasn't real, me and you was it … The strange thing is, that's what prompted Sarah's demise … I don't think she could stand the thought of sharing me, not even with you … I fear her parents got to you as well … I can see it in your face … Perhaps it all started with me, I could never resist a challenge.'

Her face lights up and she looks at me like she really sees me for the first time since I arrived.

'It was real … To me anyway, I always -'

'But now I have a sister … More importantly she has me, I don't think Sarah will ever be able to perform the role of mother, do you.' Her voice lowers to a whisper. 'She's a strange little thing, you know ... Marnie ... But I suppose that's what comes of being raised in the care system ... Do you know, I sometimes hear her talking to herself ... Quite sweet really ... I can see Sarah in her, you must have done too. I intend to keep her for a while ... My sister ... She can go to college ... Then she has some notion of -'

'Can I go up, say goodbye to her.'

She looks uncertain, so I leave before she has a chance to say no. There are three fresh wounds on her left arm, I dab at the droplets of blood with a tissue as she sobs, trembling on the bed.

'Look ... You're not happy here, I can see that ... Do you want to come home with me ... I'll get you a passport, take you back to Chelmney ... This is my fault, after all.'

'I want to ... I really do ... I missed you Stuey ... But it's not that simple, I ... I mean we, well she -'

Hesther appears at the door in a cloud of fragrance, her hair freshly brushed.

'Stuart's leaving now, darling ... Say goodbye and thank him for helping to bring us together.'

Marnie goes to her, links her arm. The likeness is uncanny. But now I look closely, I can see Sarah in Marnie, the curve of her nose, the shape of her hands, the deep amber flecks in her eyes.

'See you Stuey ... Thanks for everything ... It turns out I needed a sister, not a mother ... Drive safely.'

She offers me a diluted smile. A smile that makes me want to grab her, bundle her into the car, put her back where I found her. Hesther frees her arm, places it firmly round Marnie's shoulder.

Before I can think of anything more to say, the front door bangs firmly behind me.

Chapter 49

Sarah

She's making it too easy. Hesther all over, taking the fun out of everything. Why has she sent the girl away. She knows I wouldn't do it in front of the girl. She's acting like I'm here to drink tea and catch up on the gossip. I should do it right now, wipe that smug grin from her face. She's hardly aged since I saw her, probably got some hideous painting full of grey hair and wrinkles locked away in her attic.

'Let's go for a walk … It's a lovely day, you can tell me all about the baby.'

We wander through town, I try to block her words from my ears, then walk down a labyrinth of winding country lanes, until there's no one in sight but the two of us. She's offering herself up on a plate, which should make me grateful, but instead it's disconcerting, as if she's complicit in the whole thing, wants it just as much as I do.

I forgot how much I hate the countryside. It makes me nervous, too much space, unknown territory lying behind trees and hedges. Me and my daughter will live near one of the parks instead. Kensington gardens maybe, feed the birds in the safety of civilisation. Our house is worth a small fortune now, I can sell up, get a mews perhaps. The thought of a life with me and my baby sends waves of ecstasy down my spine. Once Hesther's dealt with, there will be no distractions, no Stuart to drag me down. I could sing with elation, if we weren't getting deeper and deeper into some sort of forest, if I wasn't starting to seriously doubt I could find my way back on my own.

Lies flow from her lips like toxins. The thing with Hesther is, she doesn't understand the difference between truth and fiction. That's why she writes, I suppose. She flaunts her scars like old battle wounds, I try not to look at them, they only remind me of how much she got away with in the past.

'You know I never loved Stuart, don't you ... I loved you, but it became clear that was not reciprocated ... When you refused to see me. I wanted us all to be together, for you and me to share the burden of Stuart ... But he's not a burden to you, is he, no he's your husband.'

The first time I saw her, she looked straight through me. A new girl at our primary school was a rare thing, everyone wanted to be her friend. Before Hesther, I never saw the point of making friends, it seemed like too much trouble for no apparent reward. Hesther was a novelty, and when it got round that she lived in one of the biggest houses in Chelmney, the competition was even fiercer.

On her first day, she chose to sit next to a plump girl called Martha. After that Martha guarded her like a mother tiger with a cub, expected the rest of us to pounce the minute her back was turned. A quiet girl called Daisy used to sit with me at lunch, but a few days later she had an unfortunate accident with a pot of paint. Her mother picked her up, and to Martha's displeasure at lunch time Hesther took Daisy's place.

We reach a thicket, both exhausted we sink down on the soft moss. For a moment I almost imagine we're going to spread out a rug, open a bottle of wine, sit talking for hours like we used to in the long grass at the park, laughing at the world beyond the realm of the two of us. My daughter kicks hard, a stark reminder of what I'm here for.

The only sound is birdsong, the movement of leaves in the gentle breeze. I can make it look like she'd had enough, the trials of life finally caught up with her. But what if that's what she wants. Yet again she's using me, getting me to do the hard work for her. This isn't how it should be, this is a punishment for what she did to me, not a reward. Before I can open my bag, she grabs my hands, pulls me to my feet.

'Come on Sarry, I've something to show you, something special, something I've never showed anyone before.'

She used the name. The name she used to call me when she wanted something from me, the name I used to love hearing above everything else. She pulls me along, the trees becoming ever more close-knit, until only tiny specks of sunlight dance through the leaves. In the shade it's cool, I can feel the goosebumps on my exposed skin. There's so much I need to say, but my daughter reminds me I'm not here to talk. Words mean nothing, it's the cool, hard blade in my bag that will bind us together forever.

She starts to hum, and it almost sounds like the birds join her in a strange melody. In a split second she darts away, disappears behind a tree. Panic rises in my throat, a stray branch catching my arm making my baby wince with pain. I'm supposed to be protecting her, she needs me to be calm, in control. Hesther emerges from behind another tree, I break into a jog to reach her.

'This is the place … I wanted to show you.' Is she mad, there's nothing here but more bloody trees. I hate her right now, more than I've ever hated her. 'The baby … Henri said you're pregnant … It is Stuart's isn't it.'

'My baby is nothing to do with you, she -'

'Why did you give her up … Marnie … You could have -'

'You bitch … You know my baby died … That girl is nothing to do with me … But she's come back now, my daughter. And that's something you'll never have, isn't it.'

The zip on my bag fights back as I try to open it. Finally I feel the reassuring weight of metal. Something scratches in the undergrowth, it sounds like an animal, too big for a rabbit. They have wild boar round here, don't they, maybe it's just a deer.

He comes at me from nowhere, looks so out of place in the middle of a forest, dressed like he's going to the opera then on for dinner at the Savoy, that I almost laugh out loud. He's going to ruin everything, what's he doing out here, I pull the knife from my bag. He smiles down at me, wraps his arms around my waist, then before I can force the metal into him, I feel a sharp scratch on my shoulder. The knife falls from my hand, and the world begins to fade away. Before I go, I hear her voice, soft and sweet, just like it used to be.

'Be gentle … Don't hurt her … Remember my baby.'

Chapter 50

Marnie

It's all his fault. I could've got out of here, let Stuey take me home, but Charlie begged me to stay. I pleaded with him, tried all the usual tricks. But he said we belong here now, with our sister. Then he punished me for being a traitor. He still loves her, even after what happened at the beach, so I watched Stuey drive away without me.

We eat a very late supper. She doesn't mention Stuey or Sarah, just sips a glass of red wine, hardly touching the omelette she taught me how to make. Stuey looked like he was dying of cancer or something, he did all this for her, and she acted like she hardly knew him. Rogue feelings swell up in my chest, feelings you really shouldn't have for your brother or your sister.

'What will happen to my flat ... In Chelmney ... There's a social worker, she comes on a -'

'Darling, you're such a little worrier ... Details, details. Details only drag a person into the gutter with all the other poor souls down there.' She spoons more salad onto her plate, even though she's not touched what's already there. 'I'm going to write through the night, it's been one of those days.'

'Henri ... Is he your -'

'Quite a find ... But everyone has their limits, don't they.'

The things she says make no sense half the time, just like her stupid books. Charlie gives me a warning glare, he always knows when I'm thinking bad things. I want to ask her why she was so horrid to Stuey, but Charlie told me not to upset her. He's never worried about upsetting anyone before, not even me. He's changed since we've been here, and not for the better.

After supper she goes straight to her study, Charlie creeps in behind her. How did she manage to fill all the vases with fresh flowers, find a hospital for Sarah, in such a short amount of time. I rip the petals from a yellow rose one by one, then clear up the mess for something to do, then listen at her study door, hear the steady beat of typewriter keys, so risk a trip to her bedroom.

It's there under the silk scarves. What if Sarah's not in hospital, what if she killed her. Why didn't Stuey stand up to her, say she had no right to lock his wife away, not without asking him first. It doesn't feel like my home. The flat in Chelmney feels like my home. Home is supposed to be where your family is, but it isn't, not when you've got family like mine.

Back in my room, I try to imagine having a murderer for a sister. As hard as I try, I can't see her doing it. But there's someone who would have done it in a heartbeat, someone who'd give their right arm to shoot a real life gun, someone who loves her so much, he'd pretty much do anything for her.

As I fall asleep, images flash through my brain, the teddy bear rotting away in a dump somewhere, Stuey's bloodshot eyes, Henri's tongue down her throat. I bite down on my hand until it bleeds to stop my screams filling the silence of the house.

Chapter 51

Sarah

Sometimes when I wake, for a few seconds I can't remember where I am. It started in that place they called a hospital. I have to lie very still, concentrate on my surroundings, then it comes back to me. It even happens sometimes in my own house, with Stuart lying right next to me, and the familiar smell of fabric softener on our sheets.

So I don't panic. The usual suspects are hotel rooms, so that's where I must be, in a hotel, one I've never stayed in before. I feel for Stuart, he's not here, but that's not unusual, he often gets up early on holiday, goes for a stroll while I shower and dress. It's taking longer than usual, nothing's coming back to me. I try to stay focused, but keep drifting in and out of consciousness, returning each time to a blank canvas.

Eventually I find the strength to force my self into a sitting position. The walls are bare, badly painted, it doesn't look like the sort of luxury hotel I usually pick. Maybe I had too much to drink at the bar last night, took a pill under the influence. I can't remember the last time I had a hangover, but my head feels heavy, my limbs stiff and sore, so that's the only thing that makes sense.

It's basic, even for a budget hotel, no television, no mini bar, not even tea and coffee making facilities, just a plastic jug of water and a tumbler. Then it clicks, he must have booked it. It's always a mistake to let Stu book anything, he has no eye for detail, would probably book a stable, if the travel agent recommended it. He's probably feeling guilty, that's why he's gone out, hopefully to look for another hotel. Heaven knows what the rest of the place is like, if we have to stay, we're most definitely dining out.

The curtains are so heavy, it takes all my strength to pull them open, this is the worst hangover ever, I must have taken at least two of the pills. Maybe he said something to upset me and I wanted to blank it out. The view is staggering, soaring mountain peaks with icing sugar tops, sweeping slopes enrobed in flawless white fondant icing. He must have chosen the room for the view, but there's no balcony and the window refuses to open. Some cool mountain air would help to clear my head.

I peel a nightdress which I don't recognise from my body, ready to shower and dress, but the wardrobe's empty, my suitcase nowhere to be seen. I bet he booked a budget airline as well and they've mislaid our luggage, I'm going to kill him when he gets back. There's not even a telephone so I can phone down to reception.

The bathroom is even worse than the room. No power shower, no free standing tub which he knows damn well I always insist on, no designer toiletries, just a bar of foul smelling soap and a solitary toilet roll. View or no view we're checking out the minute he gets back. Naked I drag a chair over to the window, then at last hear the key in the lock.

'Stuart, how could you -'

'Sarah ... You're awake ... Welcome.'

She must be the cleaner, how rude to come in without knocking, use my first name like she knows me. I'll demand a full refund and put in a formal complaint. When we find a decent hotel we can spend a day on the slopes. Stu's a hopeless skier, considers it a pointless activity, getting dragged up a mountain, only to navigate your way down without breaking a limb, or worse. I'm surprised he booked a winter holiday by choice, Alpine scenery isn't his thing, he's more of a culture vulture, or pretends to be, at least.

'Look ... My husband must have gone out for a walk ... Our luggage isn't in our room ... The room is dreadful, not even the most basic of basic facilities ... It may have been the airline's fault ... About the luggage.' I realise I'm naked, this is the worst holiday experience of my life. 'Go down to reception ... Ask them to locate my luggage, then we'll be checking out ... And you should knock before entering guest rooms, surely that's one of the first things they taught you.'

'There's nothing to worry about Sarah.' Perhaps he booked some kind of hippy retreat by mistake, somewhere people are free to wander in and out of each other's rooms without bothering to announce their arrival. 'Rest some more, you are still confused ... I will be back later.'

She has an accent, French mixed with something I don't recognise, so I try speaking slowly in case she didn't understand me.

'Look ... I don't need to rest ... And to be honest, even if I did, it really isn't your place to tell me to ... My request is quite simple ... Find my luggage ... I will get dressed, my husband will return, then we are leaving ... This hotel is way below the standard I would expect in a ski resort ... Please pass that on to the manager.'

'You are here alone ... Not with your husband ... To get better ... A very generous lady has paid for you to stay here, she said -'

'You're obviously mixing me up with someone else ... Look just ask the manager to come up here, then we can sort this mess out out.'

I'm struggling to control my temper. Stuart should have been back ages ago. We're flying home, I've had enough, will never let him organise anything again. She leaves and locks the door behind her. I can only imagine the sort of clientele they attract here, this warrants a serious compensation claim when we get home.

A key rattling in the lock wakes me. At last, maybe he got lost, fell in the snow, he really does have a poor sense of direction. But it's not him, instead a woman dressed in a smart suit enters the room, the manager.

'Finally ... You speak English, I presume. I want to issue a formal complaint ... Your maid was extremely rude, refused to help me, and to top it all locked me in the room, I -'

'We gave you a higher than normal dose of medication ... You were upset ... To help you get some rest. This is a private clinic ... We will only medicate you in future if necessary ... We have the baby to think of ... You must try to remember that.'

The fog clears in a heartbeat. My baby, how could I have forgotten about my baby. There was no holiday. I was leaving him. It was her. I waited too long, allowed her into my head, just like last time.

'But you can't just ... I demand you bring me some clothes and let me out of here.'

'We have quite clear instructions to keep you here until you are well ... The doctors are convinced that they can help you ... Given time.'

The scream explodes like a missile, rings painfully in my ears. I lunge forward, claw at her face, feel soft flesh lodge under my nails. She's quick, stronger than she looks, pushes me down hard on the bed, jabs a needle into my arm.

'You have to start thinking about the baby Sarah ... This will not do.'

Then a familiar voice, I recognise as my own.

'Stuart ... Come Back ... Help me please ... I'm sorry ... I love you.'

Chapter 52

Ron

My daughter is residing in one of the finest medical establishments in Europe. Entirely at Hesther's expense. My wife resumed normal duty, after being released from hospital. My period of respite was brief. It was either that or prison, so Mary says we must be grateful to Hesther and accept her gift with grace. There is no baby. That was part of her condition. Again we failed to see it. She seemed so happy, they both did, Sarah looked a little peaky, but she works so hard, I never thought too much about it.

My granddaughter is called Marnie. What would we have called her, we of course never debated the issue. I wonder who was given the great privilege of naming her. It feels like an arrow through my heart that she was raised in a home for delinquent girls. I liked to imagine she was adopted as a baby, lived a rich life with a couple who wanted her, perhaps never even told her she wasn't their own.

Mary just laughed at Hesther's notion of Marnie being Sarah's daughter. Our grandchild would surely resemble Sarah, not Hesther. I thought long and hard about what my response would have been, before the stroke took the gift of words from me. Mary said it wasn't normal for a man to live away from his wife during the week, so she was most likely the result of one of his affairs.

'Time for your bath, Ron.'

Choice is something alien to me now. When to rise, when to take my meals, what to put on in the morning. I'm like a doll, they can do whatever they want with me, but my limbs are as obstinate as plastic. They handle me roughly. I don't think they mean to, but it's the only way to handle someone like me.

The water is lukewarm, I take my baths on the hot side, let the water cool as I catch up on the daily news. They fail to acknowledge my shivers, their attention firmly fixed on last night's soap opera. When the water is officially classed as cold, they take me out.

In bed, I use memories to torment myself. Memories of how we thought we were in control, when all the signs were in place to prove otherwise. I'd read articles about girls who just stopped eating, could never understand why someone would willingly do such a thing. Was so rock certain something like that would never happen to my own daughter, I dismissed the whole idea as simply page filling on a weak news day. We took the stance that talking would make it real, if each of us kept our feelings to ourselves, it would all blow over, like a sand storm in a desert. Mary said that Sarah was simply a highly strung child turning into a teenager, and I never thought to question her logic.

The day they rescued her from her room. Her long dark hair scattered in piles on the Axminster carpet. Her scalp covered in molehills of congealed blood. The stench, which made me run to the bathroom and gag. The look of contempt on the doctor's face, as he gently led her out of our house. They wanted to take her to Chelmney psychiatric unit, one of the hospitals Mary and her cronies fundraised for. We said no, we had sufficient funds to pay for private treatment, so we had her admitted into a Sanatorium for Girls, situated in the countryside, well outside of Mary's circle of Chelmney based charities.

It took three days to clean her room, my wife toiled like an ox, a tea towel wrapped round her face, a butcherer bin liner to protect her clothes. She scrubbed at the walls until her hands bled, but we could still make out the words 'blood sisters' set in a badly drawn love heart above the broken dressing table mirror. The lengths of hair ended up in the tip along with everything else. When all you could smell was disinfectant, I commenced the redecoration. We purchased new carpet, curtains, bed linen, modern pine furniture. When it was fresh as a show home, we stood together to admire our work, then shut the door behind us and didn't open it again until the day we brought her home.

I imagine my wife now. Battling on bravely with her charitable concerns, telling her friends that Sarah is abroad for a while, volunteering in war torn nations, nursing famine struck children back to health in some part of Africa. Putting her own life on hold, for those less fortunate than herself. We lost the thread of truth many years ago, now the tangled web we've weaved threatens to enmesh us in its viscous fibres.

    For a second, before I fall asleep, I wish Hesther was dead. That my daughter was whole again, at home with her husband, a real life baby thriving in her belly. Then the demons come, and I know it was all my fault. I broke my daughter into tiny pieces and will never have the time or skill to put her back together again.

Chapter 53

Stuart

My days are made of work and whiskey. To my great disappointment, they welcomed me back into the fold of the office. The house, which my wife maintained like a palace, is now reduced to an oversized bachelor pad. The once gleaming kitchen could now quite easily be classed as a micro health hazzard. I feel nothing, because there's nothing left to feel.

Sunday is the longest day of the week. Sundays weren't designed for single middle-aged men. Sundays were designed for lovers, long lazy mornings in bed, leisurely lunches in some cosy country pub, walking hand in hand through the park as the sun goes down. Sunday was made as a test. If you pass, it proves you've made something of your life, got the icing on the cake, not just the raw ingredients. I seriously consider going back to bed with a bottle of whiskey, drowning the day away with spirit. But the sun winks through the curtains in a salacious manner, tempting me to go outdoors, feel her heat on my body. To be sure, I toss a coin. It lands as I feared it would.

I've no idea why I'm on the train, when anywhere else would be far more preferable than where I'm going. My first impulse is to cross the passenger bridge and take the next train straight back to London. Even here, in the station, it feels too raw, like all my nerves end here, in Chelmney. The streets are deserted, businesses sealed from the world until later in the year. A dimly lit corner shop provides me with my daily quota of cigarettes.

He's half the man he was since I saw him last, flesh dissolved from his bones, any last trace of light faded from his sunken eyes. He slumps awkwardly in the chair, an untouched cup of tea, just outside his reach. The room is too warm for comfort, the air drenched with human suffering. This place is even worse than I remember. At first it seems like he doesn't recognise me, so I perch on the bed intending to leave in a couple of minutes, but then he tries to lift his hand and it flutters briefly in my direction, so I go to him, take it in my own. It feels as cold as a corpse, but he makes an effort to grip, a lopsided smile lighting up his face.

'Do you fancy a spin round the garden, a bit of fresh air seems in order ... Don't you agree.'

He makes no response, so I maneuver him into the wheelchair, he weighs no more than a five year old child. As we walk, I talk. Sport, politics, current affairs, anything that might pique his interest. When my words run dry, I park him next to a bench, sit a while, allow him to drink in the fresh air in peace.

Back in his room, he becomes agitated. His eyes are bright, his body twitching. I need to make my escape before Mary arrives, but I'm reluctant to leave him like this, so with about twenty minutes to spare, I order us both a hot cup of tea. His cheeks are rosy from the spring sunshine, I wonder how often they take them outside, I suppse it's too much trouble. When our cups are empty, it's time for me to leave.

'I'm going now, Ron.' I think we're both aware of the fact that this will be the last time we see each other. 'Mary will be here soon ... I'm sorry it's been so long ... About everything that's happened ... With Sarah ... I want you to know, I take my share of the blame in the matter.'

His hand flutters wildly in his lap, his lips move, but nothing comes out. I've been selfish, disturbed his peace, but there was something deep within me which compelled me to see him one last time. His eyes bore into mine, like he's begging me to help him. Does he hate it here so much, he wants me to help him get out. Fearing the worst, I'm about to call the emergency call cord when he shouts out.

'No.'

'Take your time Ron ... If you want to say something, I can wait.'

'B ... Ba ... Bees.'

He thinks Sarah's pregnant, no one's told him about what happened to her. He props up his left hand with his right and manages to point two fingers at me. The sheer effort of doing such a simple thing is painful to watch.

There's a picture on his bedside cabinet. The three of them, standing in front of a Christmas tree, wide smiles on their faces. I wonder who took it, I've rarely seen anyone else in their house. Sarah looks about fourteen years old, I hand it to him.

'A lovely picture … You all look so happy … Sarah is lucky to have parents like -'

'No.' The power of his voice takes me by surprise. 'Ba … Bees.'

'Don't exhaust yourself Ron … Mary will be here soon … I should go now.'

He tries to push himself up from the chair, takes a laboured breath, steely determination burning in his eyes.

'Sarah … Mahn … e.' He does the two finger thing again. I move in close to hear, his voice no more than a fractured whisper. 'Twins … A …. A … Alive … Marn.'

His eyes close, his breathing barely audible now, so I leave without saying goodbye.

Chapter 54

Marnie

My sister says we inherited our brains from our father. We never speak about our mothers. It's like a pact. My French is so good now, most people can't even tell I'm from England. College work is so easy, it's a joke, so I get top grades without even trying. I'm counting on Oxford to be a bit more of a challenge, because it's pretty boring when you hardly have to put in any effort.

I soon realised, people are people, no matter which country you live in, dumb and uninspiring, so I haven't bothered making any friends. I won't be here that long, so it hardly seems worth it.

I've made a plan. Charlie likes to spend his days with her. That suits me fine. He's made his choice, so when I move to Oxford, I'm leaving him here, with her. For the first time in my life, I'll be free. She brings out the best in him, while I've always brought out the worst, so it's worked out fine in the end. When I leave, I'm never coming back, they're welcome to each other.

Stuey used to phone. She got fed up with it, told him to stop, so now I really miss talking to him, he's the only one who ever really listened. Our father studied law at Cambridge. She never went to university, says her intellect was unfettered by the crushing formalities of a hierarchical education system. I want my intellect to be securely tethered to the fine traditions of one of the most esteemed universities in the world.

Sunday's are such a drag. There's nothing to do, everything shuts, I hate it here more than ever on a Sunday. It hardly ever rains, but when it does it throws it down, thunder and lightening, the whole lot, so you can't even leave the house or anything. I miss Chelmney so much, it hurts, which is really weird because I didn't even like it when I lived there. What I'd give to smell the rotting fish on the harbour, have a mug of tea and a bacon sandwich in the cafe opposite our flat.

She's in her study writing, Charlie curled up like a cat in the corner of the room. There's nothing for it but to go out for a bit and leave them both to it. The locals are on their way to church, it's too early for tourists. People here are so serious about everything, even getting a coffee is like a one act play. I suppose that's why she loves it and I hate it.

'Bonjour ... Marnie.' It's Claude, a boy from my physics class, goes out with a girl called Odette, pretty in a studenty sort of way, wears her hair in braids and little round glasses she doesn't really need. I'm taller than most of the girls here, feel like a bloody giraffe, another reason to move back to England. 'It's early ... What are you up to ... We could go for a coffee, but yes ... Discuss our next assignment.'

The thought of drinking coffee with Claude hardly fills me with joy, but there's nothing else to do, is there. When she writes she locks herself away for hours and Charlie's no fun anymore. I want a coke, but order coffee, all the kids at college drink coffee and smoke, like it's the law or something. He offers me a cigarette, I take it to be polite. Everyone's polite here, no one shouts, spits in the street, scraps like cats in an alleyway. If they saw what happens on the streets of Brimfield they'd have a fit.

He's actually way smarter than he lets on in class. It's fun in a way, talking physics just for the sake of it. Then he goes and ruins it all.

'There is a gathering ... Later ... Just a few people ... Drinks ... Good conservation ... You must come with me ... I would like that very much.'

Under normal circumstances I'd make any excuse under the sun, but it will piss Charlie right off if I go out drinking without him.

'Ok, but I can't stay long ... My sister ... She'll worry ... I live with her.'

'I used to live in Paris ... With my parents ... But my father died ... I hate it here, it's too quiet, but it suits my mother. I'm going to study at the Sorbonne, take a small apartment, become a doctor like my father and his father before him.' His hand brushes against mine on the table, I make an effort not to appear rude and snatch it away. 'What about your parents ... Where are they ... We all love her, you know, the English Rose, our very own author, right here in Grasse. We were all sad for her ... After what happened ... She would have been so very well suited to the role.'

'My father died as well ... He was a famous barrister ... In London ... My mother was a scientist ... Medical research ... She died having me ... I'm going to study at Oxford... I'm not sure what yet.'

What's he going on about. What happened to her. I can't very well ask him, can I, I should know what happened to my own sister. But the truth is, we hardly know anything about each other, and even worse, she doesn't seem bothered in the slightest.

The party's in a house on the other side of town. As we walk in, he tries to hold my hand, but I manage to put it in my pocket just in time. Where's the table full of bottles and cans, the loud music. What sort of crappy party is this, I only came to get out of my face. Charlie's not going to be pissed at me for having a chat over a bloody cup of coffee. The cigarette smoke's so thick, I don't see him at first. He's deep in conversation with a girl, she looks about my age, but I've never seen her before. His mouth is close to her ear, even though there's no music, not even a raised voice. He's by far the oldest person in the room.

After that first time, Henri hasn't been back to our house. She goes away. For hours sometimes, sometimes even for days. I always assume she's with him, but she never tells me and I never ask. Through the fog, I pick out a few faces from college. Claude gives me a cigarette, leans in close to light it. There's no sign of Odette, but he doesn't seem to care.

'Look ... I can't stay long ... She'll worry ... My sister.'

He drapes an arm around my neck, as if he owns me or something. If we were in Chelmney I'd punch his lights out, but here it doesn't seem appropriate, so instead I try and act like it happens to me all the time. What I'd give right now for a triple vodka and coke.

Claude is not what you'd call handsome. His face is too pointy, his chin too long and sprouting a patchy growth of hair.

He reminds me quite a lot of the ferret one of the foster families kept as a pet. Charlie was obsessed with the thing, poking it with a stick whenever he could, picking it up and spinning it through the air. Then one day it bit back with tiny razor sharp teeth, drew a fountain of blood from his hand. Charlie refused to let it win, it's not in his nature. Two days later I helped him bury it under a hedge in the garden. They put up posters on lampposts, searched the streets for weeks. It was our little secret, made us giggle under the bedclothes, until one night we laughed so much we wet ourselves. The next day they sent us back to the home.

Claude's attempt at conversation is nearly as bad as mine. Polite conversation is largely pointless, but he doesn't seem keen to resume our physics discussion, so I let him talk, nod my head now and again and concentrate on Henri and the girl instead. She's much smaller than me, dressed in what looks like a tramp's overcoat, a purple band holding back a mass of curly hair. She's nowhere near as pretty as my sister, but he's looking at her like she's Madonna or Princess Diana, or someone. I need to get out of here before he notices me.

'I'm sorry Claude, this is great, but I've got to go now, my sister will be wondering where I am.' I can see her now, typing away, in her own little world. I honestly sometimes think she wouldn't notice if I just packed up and left. 'You stay ... I'll be fine getting home on my own.'

'But, I would love to meet your sister ... There is nothing for me here now ... I will walk with you.'

I can honestly say some of the nights doing homework and watching dumb detective shows in the home were more exciting than this. He tightens his grip on my shoulder, steers me towards the door. If Charlie was here, he'd know what to do. Getting shut of people is one of his specialities.

'Marnie ... What a pleasant surprise ... You must send by best ... No my warmest wishes to Hesther.' Claude's arm grows limp and slips from my shoulder. Henri grips me with both hands and lands a soft kiss on both cheeks, then for effect wipes a stray hair from my face. The girl smiles politely, but I can tell she'd throttle me given half the chance.

'We're going now ... Sorry we're in a rush.'

I grab Claude, pull him out of the door, now I just have to find a way to dump him and I can put all this nonsense behind me.

'The man ... In there ... Emanuelle you should not ... I mean, be careful, he is not a good -'

'No that was Henri ... A friend of my sister's ... I hardly know him.' His arm slips back round my shoulder, he's obviously confused Henri with someone else, but I don't like him, what's a man of his age doing in a room full of teenagers anyway. 'Look at the time ... I've just remembered, I have to go somewhere ... Before I go home ... See you tomorrow ... At college.'

As I pull away, he knocks me off balance, lunges, pushing me hard against a wall, then somehow my mouth opens and he forces his tongue deep into my throat. I gag, can't breathe, press my body against him to push him away, but he's stronger than he looks, his tongue delves deeper, and without Charlie I'm helpless as a newborn kitten. He groans, presses his body into mine until there's no space left between us. With no choice in the matter, I surrender, and slowly the rest of the world melts away.

Chapter 55

Ron

Stuart came today. He was a shadow of himself. Another victim of our crime. He was my last chance, and I took it. A chance I did not deserve. I will never see my daughter again, I know that now. I will never see my twins.

I will never know if anything came from my endeavors, if there is any good left to come by. I always saw the end as something vague, hard to put your finger on. Like a painting by Picasso, esoteric, to be understood by each according to their own unique vision of the universe. I can almost taste it now. Death. And it has taught me otherwise. Death is as much as a shared experience as being born. There's absolutely nothing abstruse about dying, it's the most natural thing in the world. Life and death, links that chain us all together, no matter where we come from, what we do, how much money we accrue. Not one creature can rise above mortality, however hard they try.

When the stroke came, they assumed my mind withered with my body. But it wasn't true and the only person who could see that was my wife. She wakes me with a kiss. I force myself to look into the eyes of the woman I've betrayed. The woman I'm leaving to bear the fruits of my sin. Later they bring food. I leave it. Instead chant a silent mantra of devotion. Marnie, Marnie, Marnie … The world I never had.

Chapter 56

Stuart

I spend the day drifting, battling with half remembered memories. Streets which lead to feelings too raw to linger on. When the sun starts to set, I know I have to finish what I've started.

She looks as polished as ever, slightly thinner, her face a little on the gaunt side.

'Stuart ... Darling ... Do come in.' She scours the street for unwanted attention from the neighbours. 'I'm just about to prepare supper ... Would you care to join me.'

'I want a divorce ... You should have told me you know ... I know I never asked, but even so, you -'

'I'll put the kettle on.' She ushers me into the living room.

'I went to see Ron ... This morning.'

She returns with a tray, pours tea into china cups, offers me the sugar bowl, even though she knows I don't take sugar.

'Well this is a surprise ... You should have called ... Let me know ... I could have made up the spare room.'

'I'm not stopping ... I've got work tomorrow.'

'Look ... I know we were not entirely honest with you ... When you met, you and Sarah ... I'll be honest now ... Well we never entirely understood why you were together, but you've been a good husband ... In the circumstances ... The girl, why ... Sarah was over Hesther, I'm sure of it ... Then you went and stirred everything up again ... But Sarah loves you now, even if she chose you for the wrong reasons ... You can start again, when she's better, try for a baby.'

Her composure's slipping, divorce is difficult to brush under the carpet.

'I can't have children ... A vasectomy ... Years ago now. She hadn't got over the Hesther issue though ... Had she, not really ... Things could have turned out far worse, she could have -'

'You took her chance away ... To be a mother ... You had no right Stuart ... I presume you didn't tell her, she didn't -'

'He was trying to tell me something ... Ron ... This morning ... I think it was something about -'

'Don't be ridiculous Stuart ... He probably didn't even know who you were ... You really should have asked me first ... He gets confused ... Doesn't like to be taken out of his routine, he -'

'He knew who I was ... He knows more than people give him credit for, we should -'

'Please don't offer me advice with regard to my own husband ... Don't think I haven't noticed you've been avoiding him ... Since the stroke. I was the one left to care for him day and night, you never even -'

'He was trying to say her name ... Marnie ... I'm sure of it ... And he tried to say babies ... And he kept holding up two fingers. Can you -'

'I think it's time you went Stuart.'

The offer of supper appears to have been retracted, there's something she's hiding, and I've nothing to lose any more, it's time for the truth.

'Sarah ... She had twins, didn't she ... They didn't die, did they.'

She pours cold tea into her cup, forgetting to offer me a refill. Her face crumples, and for the first time since I met her, she looks like an old woman.

'She was unwell ... Some boy took advantage of her ... We never found out who ... It was a girl, she died ... Before we could bring her home.' She takes a perfectly pressed handkerchief from her pocket, dabs at dry eyes. 'Here you go again, dragging up the past ... Upsetting everyone ... Just go home, wait for Sarah, you can make your decision about the divorce when she's better ... She was sixteen ... Far too young to be a mother, and now because of you she -'

'I need to use the bathroom, before I go.'

Splashing cold water on my face, I try to picture Marnie as she was at the station. All I saw was Hesther, my childhood standing before me. The two things I wanted back so badly that I failed to see my own wife in her. When I started going out with Sarah, her physical resemblance to Hesther was both disconcerting and beguiling in equal measure. The colour and length of their hair, similar height and build, matching mannerisms. Sometimes when I closed my eyes and kissed her, it was Hesther standing there. Sarah's Marnie's mother, that's what Ron was trying to tell me, she must have had an affair with Hesther's father.

She's waiting by the door, composure carefully restored.

'Well thank you for coming ... You must -'

'The baby ... The girl ... She didn't die ... Did she ... She had twins, didn't she ... You gave them away ... How could you ... Does Sarah even -'

She walks back into the living room, I follow and she pours an inch of Sherry into two crystal glasses.

'Life isn't always easy Stuart ... We made yours go smoothly ... Helped you along the way ... But ours wasn't ... We were forced into to make difficult choices ... Think on our feet ... Yes she had twins ... But we honestly didn't know, times were different then ... There was no advice, support, for people like us anyway. We wanted to protect her, make it as pain free as possible, so we found a good home for the baby ... We were fearful of a relapse ... You should have seen her, in the clinic, it really was too much to bear ... We thought she could move on ... It was kinder to tell her that her daughter died. When she told us ... About being pregnant ... We thought she was making it up, acting out as the doctors at the clinic told us ... Some of the girls used to say the most outrageous things ...Even about their own parents ... Attention seeking, I suppose. The doctor said it was their way of fighting back, punishing those who loved them, who were trying to help them ... So as you can imagine, we were confused, conflicted. The doctor said it was all part of the recovery process, clearing the poison from the brain, like lancing a septic boil.' She takes a sip of her Sherry, is shaking, the colour drained from her face. What if she has another heart attack and it's all my fault, again. 'Yes she put on a little weight, but it suited her, she was too thin ... By the time ... By the time we realised, it was true, she really was pregnant, it was too late ... We -'

'But the doctor ... Surely the doctor told you she was having twins.'

'I just told you ... It was too late ... She didn't see a doctor ... Until the birth ... We never asked for any of it, you know ... It wasn't our fault, she came from a good family, we were good parents ... You know that Stuart, don't you ... Things like that were not supposed to happen ... Not to people like us.'

I can hardly believe what I'm hearing, Sarah was pregnant and her own parents never even bothered to take her to a doctor. I down my Sherry in one and without waiting to be asked refill the glass to the brim.

'But surely that's a case of neglect, you should have -'

'Oh, Stuart, always so bloody idealistic ... We were in a crisis situation so acted accordingly.' Her eyes burn with the contempt she must always have felt for me, but hidden so successfully over the years. 'We made more than adequate provision for the child ... How could we possibly have known she was having twins.'

'Provision ... You mean you -'

'They were a good family ... A family who could provide well for a child ... They proved that with a healthy contribution.'

'You mean, they -'

'They gave us a generous donation, and we took it as evidence they had the means to care for a child.'

'You sold your grandchild, for cold, hard -'

'Oh Stuart, don't be so bloody sanctimonious, we did what anyone else would have -'

'What sort of people are you, I can't believe -'

'When Sarah dragged you out of the gutter, you had nothing, you were nothing ... Where do you think all the money came from ... The wedding ... The house ... The furniture ... You didn't care did you, never bothered to ask. You were unable to provide for your wife, so we did it for you ... Now you've got the audacity to stand here and judge me ... For what, protecting my daughter ... Providing her with a home, a life, cushioning her from the problems of the world, keeping her well.' Her hands flutter round her face like moths. This is a side to her I've never seen before. 'You couldn't even afford a broom cupboard in London on your salary, forced your wife go out to work like a common labourer ... Without us you were nothing Stuart ... So you're just as guilty as me in all this ... And don't forget it.'

I've heard enough.

'I'm going now ... But the father, of the twins ... It was Charles, Hesther's father, wasn't it ... Hesther's Chelmney address was in her file ... Marnie's ... At the children's home ... Where you left her to rot ... Why didn't you report it to the police ... Having sex with a minor ... You were scared the story would get out, weren't you ... You failed to protect you daughter ... You sold your own grandchild, and all so that no one would find out what terrible parents you really were.'

The slap stings in a gratifying manner, blood pours from where her diamond engagement ring catches the corner of my eye. She slams the door behind me, even though one of the neighbours is watching from his garden.

On the crowded train I try to remember every detail of my wife, the woman I thought was strong and capable was actually fragile as a piece of damp tissue paper.

Back at the house, I stuff a bundle of clothes into my bag, a faded black and white photo, my parents on one of the few occasions they left the house together, her hair tamed into a neat bun on the top of her head, a new dress showing off a tiny waist. A woman I rarely caught a glimpse of, the man standing next to her, a virtual stranger. I empty the contents of the shoebox into the bin, add my personal documents to the bag. Then, sit in the kitchen I used to call my own and regard my whole life now contained in a single leather holdall. Much later I leave the house that was never mine to occupy, a house purchased with blood money, a house that by all rights should belong to Marnie.

At the station I play Russian roulette with the trains. It dumps me out at some nondescript northern town. A run down affair, most of the shop fronts boarded up years ago, a satisfying air of despair wafting through the litter strewn streets. I couldn't have ended up anywhere better if I'd tried.

The guest house fails to live up to its name. I commit to a month, feeling better that at least I've brightened someone's day, judging by the grin on the landlady's face. Six pints later in the local, it feels like this is where I belong, was always meant to be. I beat a young lad at pool three times in a row, he buys me another pint in admiration. A man covered in spider tattoos says he can get me a job on a building site. Closing time comes round too soon, I stumble home, grabbing a bag of chips on the way and the dark years dissolve into the night air as I shout a prayer up to the stars, a bearded man in a sleeping bag watching me warily.

After eight hours of the soundest sleep I've had for years, bedlam greets me. Stale cigarette smoke and worse seeping through the damp walls, a couple screeching at each other in some unfathomable language, punk music coming from upstairs at full volume. There's no en suite, a semi-naked man crawls out of the shared bathroom down the hall. After wiping a pool of vomit from the sink with toilet paper, I use the soiled toilet and leave.

For breakfast I ingest more saturated fat in one meal than Sarah's probably had in her life. Out in the street, the dank air feels like a balm. I start my celebration of gaining my freedom by generously compensating the bearded man for my drunken behaviour last night. After seriously depleting my wallet, he rewards me with a toothless grin. He deserves to enjoy today just as much as I do.

Chapter 57

Sarah

The hate comes and goes, like she does.

'Do you know Sarry, sometimes, I wish I could stay here with you. I chose it because of the view, of course … But there's Marnie … Even though she's seventeen, she needs looking after … You can't do it, can you … Sometimes, I wish I was you … No responsibilities … No deadlines to meet, not a single care in the world.'

In the beginning, I used to try and claw her deceitful eyes out, but she never comes alone, not anymore. So now I play with her instead.

'You're right … It feels safe here … Stuart never loved you … You know that, don't you … He loved me, couldn't wait to marry me, almost begged, he said -'

'Marnie's such a strange child, but I suppose that's only to be expected … Did I tell you she's got a boy … A funny looking thing … It was Emanuelle who told me … He knows everything.'

She thinks that girl is my daughter, which proves she's crazy, when we can both see my daughter growing right here, inside my stomach. She kicks, a reminder to me not to upset them, she doesn't like the needles.

'I think he forgot about you … When he met me, he -'

'Remember that day, your mother took us out for pancakes … I hated pancakes, so has ice cream instead, and you cried like a baby … Marnie's not like you … You did that for her, at least … She has brains, it surprised me at first … I don't know why, we share the same father, don't we … Did I tell you Emanuelle took quite a shine to her, but don't worry, I warned him off.'

There are no doctors, just the ones in green, she calls nurses. You must not trust them, not even an inch. They're on her side, every one of them. They say that when my baby's born, they'll let me out, but they're liars, just like her. They don't know my husband's on his way to rescue me.

Sometimes when the sun streams through the window, she comes, kicks off her shoes, brushes my hair like she used to, and I almost forget to hate her, almost believe she'll never leave me.

In the beginning, I tried to escape. But the window's too tough, too high, the door always locked, the needle always ready. My daughter's safe here, for now anyway, so I don't try anymore. She brings books, but I refuse to read them, games, but I won't play them. I eat the food, but only for my baby. She's big now, it's uncomfortable to lie down, but she needs sleep, so I sleep for her.

When we were nine, we both asked for the same board game for Christmas. She was away for days, with her father in London. I practised and practised with daddy, determined to master the complicated instructions and beat her. When she came home, I set up the board, filled a bowl with her favourite sweets, excited about our first game together. She tipped the pieces in the bin, said it was a silly childish game, pointed to her neck, where a beautiful gold and ruby pendant lay. She said that was her only present, purchased by her father from a jewellers on Bond Street. He said she was officially too old for toys, told her young ladies deserved real presents, not a heap of plastic toys. Mummy and daddy got me at least twenty gifts, toys I'd hinted at throughout the year, been eager to share with her. I wanted to rip the necklace from her throat, but instead took a felt tip pen, scribbled all over the board and put it in the bin on top of the tiny horse shaped pieces. She took the pen from my hand, pushed back my chest of drawers, scribbled one of her stupid poems on the wall, said I couldn't read it until she'd gone.

When she left, I tried to wipe the words from the wall, rescue the game, but it was too late everything was ruined. Daddy saw I was upset, took me to fly my new kite in the park. It got caught in a tree. Two of my favourite presents ruined, and it was all her fault.

'I was going to stay longer … This time … But I don't like leaving her … Marnie, on her own for too long … Don't forget the vitamins, will you.'

She brings flowers, puts them in a plastic pot. I hate them more than I hate her. When she goes, I'll rip each stem apart with my teeth. When my baby died, a secret part of me was glad. She was his, however much I tried not to think about it. Now it's perfect, she's mine and my husband's like she was meant to be, and no one, not even her, can take my daughter away from me.

Chapter 58

Marnie

When she goes away, Charlie goes with her. I've no idea where they go because she never tells me. The only thing I know, is that they always take the gun with them. I don't mind, not about her not being here, but it bugs me that she never tells me where she goes. She stays away for longer and longer, four days already, this time. The house is a tip, and I can't even blame it on Charlie. He knows I'm seeing Claude and doesn't care, won't even consider punishing me anymore.

Claude finished with Odette, soon after we met in town, then without asking me told everyone at college we were an item. She didn't seem to mind, even gave me a hug. It was too late by then for me to say anything, so now we're officially girlfriend and boyfriend. This girl at school stole Lynn's boyfriend and ended up in hospital with a broken nose. People here are too polite for their own good, and anyone else's for that matter.

The more time we spend together, the less I like him. He stinks of onions and some aftershave that smells like dirty leather. His favourite pastime is sticking his tongue down my throat and touching as much of my body as possible. The whole time he's doing it, he makes this sort of panting sound, like a thirsty labrador. Not only is it boring as hell, it's really disgusting, but the thing is he's so nice to me after, I can't bring myself to tell him to stop.

We sit on my bed eating crisps and drinking a bottle of her wine. Food and drink are the only things that delay the inevitable. Talking to him's not much better than the other stuff, for some reason his favourite topic of conversation is my sister.

'It was nice of you ... To feel sorry for her ... Because she would have been well suited to the -' He puts down his wine, pounces like a tiger, but today I push him away. It's his turn to do something for me. 'When she goes away ... Like now ... She doesn't tell me, where she's going ... I mean, would your mother just go away and not tell you?'

He runs his hand slowly up my thigh, it lands way too high for my liking.

'Ah, Ma Cherie, she is a witer, is she not ... You must not question a writer ... She goes away to make the research, perhaps ... So we must just be grateful of our time alone together ... How you say, make the hay in the sunshine.' His eyes glaze over and I know what's coming. His hand entangles itself in my hair, he drags my face close to his. 'My own mother ... She is not like Hesther ... That's why we did not question, her condition ... She is a free spirit, as all artists are.' He pulls a small packet from his pocket. 'But do not worry ... You will not end up like that ... You can trust me, I came prepared, we both want to, so why not now.'

His cheek astounds me. Bringing condoms into my house, thinking I'd ever take such a stupid risk. They split, don't they, if he thinks I'm missing out on Oxford, purely for his pleasure, he's got another thing coming.

'You're wrong ... My sister, she wasn't pregnant ... She would -'

'So tragic, one day so big, so radiant ... Next time no bump and no baby ... We all felt her loss ... Of course no one would have said so ... Not to her anyway.'

'No ... You're making it -' He attempts to silence me with his tongue, he's rough, but today I'm rougher. Our limbs untangled, it's time to talk. 'Are you seriously saying ... Hesther ... My sister ... She was pregnant, she lost a baby.'

'Of course, but you knew that, yes, she must have told you.'

'Of course she bloody told me ... I just wanted to make sure that was what you meant ... That you were all gossiping about -'

He comes again, stronger, harder, it's like trying to hold back a tidal wave. His tongue probes my mouth, his hands are everywhere at once. He pushes me down on the bed, the crisps prickle my skin, then before I can stop him, he pushes my dress high up around my waist, his hand reaching the point of no return. Just as I resign myself to what's coming, the front door swings open. Her voice drifts like nectar through the house.

'Marnie ... Darling, are you here ... I've got a chicken for supper.'

It's too late to get rid of him, there's no choice but to introduce them to each other. We straighten our clothes, I run my fingers through my hair. The house is in a right state and I've got a boy in my room, she's going to kill me, if Charlie doesn't do it first. As she appears at the doorway, he stands behind her, winks at me, and not in a good way.

'I see we have a guest, how charming ... You must stay for supper ... I insist.'

He looks nervous, turns red as a beetroot when she looks at him.

'The is Claude ... A friend from college ... We were just -'

'Oh, never mind all that now, darling ... I need to unpack, take a bath.'

'Help me tidy up ... Then you have to go ... She doesn't mean it, about the supper thing.'

We do our best, but it's not even close to her standards. Things are out of place because I can't remember where they belong, stains remove to budge from the kitchen table. I'm about to tell him to go, when she appears fresh from the bath, wearing a silk robe I've never seen before. He can't take his eyes off her, it's a good job I'm not the jealous type.

'Can you both help ... With the vegetables ... You can tell me all about yourself, Claude ... It's high time Marnie had a friend.'

I figure he owes me big time for all the hours I've wasted with his fumblings. Time I could've been reading, learning, educating myself, instead of trying to work out the quickest way to extract his tongue from my mouth. He can ask the questions I can't, to be polite, then she'll have to answer him, won't she. He's a guest, you have to be polite to a guest, don't you. If I ever met Claude's mother and she'd been away, I'd ask her about her trip, if she had a nice time, that sort of thing it would be rude not too, wouldn't it.

'Hesther ... Would you mind if I gave Claude a tour of the garden, then we can help you with supper ... He's really interested in plants.'

'Of course not, be sure to show him the hyssop, such a pretty colour at this time of year.'

He's seen the garden before, never showed an ounce of interest in anything but pushing me up against the wall and shoving his tongue down my throat. She watches through the window as I take his arm, point at foliage for good effect, and for once he's on his best behaviour.

'Don't be afraid to ask her things ... She'll be offended if you don't ... About her trip away, that sort of thing. Tell her you were sorry, about the baby, people don't usually say anything, she'll think you're a good -'

'I'll ask her about her books, she will like that, artists want to discuss their -'

'No ... You can read her books anytime. Make her think you care, about her, about me ... Then she'll let us spend time together ... In my room.'

I lead him out of her line of vision, push my body hard against his until he gasps with pleasure. She pours wine, Claude sips it, but appears to have lost his tongue, so I kick him hard under the table. Then to my surprise, Charlie comes to me instead of her for the first time in ages and whispers in my ear.

'Who's the ugly boy. Is that the best you could do. Get shut of him. It's just us three, family, you should know that.'

I try ignoring him, but Charlie hates being ignored.

'Well this is nice, do tell me all about yourself Claude ... I've seen you before ... I'm sure of it, such a friendly little town ... I've always felt most welcome here. Iwas born in a sweet little place by the sea ... In England, Marnie lived there herself, until I took her under my wing ... Do you have siblings ... Did Marnie tell you our father is no more, our mother's rather lacking in feelings of maternity.' She throws back her head and laughs, as if she's said the funniest thing in the world. 'I bet your mother is a perfect pet Claude, I can tell from looking at you.'

Our plates are almost empty, he needs to start talking and now. I kick him even harder.

'Did you ... I mean you just got back, so did you have an enjoyable -'

'Did Marnie tell you I was injured in a fire.' She shows him her scars, he looks mortified. 'Sometimes miracles happen ... They told me I couldn't have children ... but then -'

'Did you have a nice trip ... I mean you just got back, how

was your -'

'How sweet of you to enquire about my little sojourn. That reminds me, I'm tired, it's been a long day, I must leave you two to your own devices.'

The idiot's gone and ruined everything, she was going to tell us about the baby and he interrupted her to ask about her trip, he should have let her finish. He really is the dumbest boy ever, I hate him, this is the last time he's setting foot in my house. Before he follows her out of the room, Charlie sidles up to me and whispers.

'Do something about him, before I do. He's a fucking idiot, can't you see it ... And you really think you're smart enough for Oxford ... No way, you're a dumb whore, just like our mother ... Why can't you be more like our sister.' As they drift away they hum, a sad tune that prods something deep inside my memory. Then he starts to chant. 'Marnie is a whore... Marnie is a whore.'

I hate him, I hate her, but most of all I hate Claude. I rush out of the room and before he has chance to follow her upstairs, pull him into the cupboard in the hall.

'She's no angel ... You know that don't you. She was pregnant and everyone knows it except you ... She never even notices you ... You follow her around, sniffing at her heels, and half the time she doesn't even know you exist. She only loves herself, can't you see that. I loved you, even when you hurt that baby ... Forgave you, didn't I.' I've gone too far, but can't stop now. 'You know I'd have been adopted if it wasn't for you ... None of this would've happened ... I hate you, I love Claude now ... You always ruin everything for me ... He loves me, way more than you ever did.'

The wound is deep, it felt so good when he got his penknife out, cut into me, because underneath it all, it shows he still cares. Claude watches as I bathe it with the disinfectant she uses to clean her vases. Charlie's with her now, I should never have mentioned the baby thing, we made a pact never to talk about it again, and now I've broken my promise. After the baby I wasn't allowed to leave the home for months on end, had to beg for school books, fell way behind in all my classes. It took me forever to catch up, and all Charlie could do was call me a fat cow, when he knew damn well the chocolate helped me concentrate, which isn't easy when you've got someone whispering crap in your ear all day long.

It kept crying. I know babies cry, but this was different, more like a police siren going off for hours and hours at a time. Charlie tried everything to shut it up. They should never have fostered us, not with something like that going on. When it happened the parents refused to take any of the blame, even though they were supposed to be responsible adults and me and Charlie were only little kids. One of the nuns said it was fine in the end, the baby, no permanent damage, so it was a lot of fuss over nothing really, but we made the pact, just to be on the safe side.

'What happened, your arm. I heard you talking, who was -'

'Just go home Claude ... It's just a scratch, I caught my arm on a nail, that's all.'

'I did what you said ... Asked her, about the trip, you said we could -'

If it wasn't for Charlie, I'd throw him out and never speak to him again. But I need him. It's working, Charlie is jealous, he just proved it, Claude is my chance to take him back from her.

'I'll see you tomorrow ... I think she likes you ... You can come round again, soon.'

She comes downstairs, makes two mugs of chamomile tea. Claude was useless, so there's nothing for it but to try myself.

'How was your trip ... I missed you ...The baby ... I heard that you were ... I mean, you never said -'

She stretches out on the chair like a cat, takes a sip of tea.

'You can do better, than Claude ... But you already know that, don't you. You have charm, just like me, but you choose to bury it away, like a squirrel with a precious nut. I'll tell you a story. I was a little girl. I hated our father, but no one could deny he had charm. I watched him once, you know, in court, the jury were captivated, eating out of his hand. Anyway, I've forgotten what I was going to say ... Such powerful hands, my father ... Did I tell you that before.'

She shudders as if remembering something unpleasant, gets up and goes, leaving her tea behind. On my way to bed, I sneak a peek into her study. There's a crib, right there next to her desk.

A beautiful wooden crib that wasn't here earlier, complete with the softest looking blankets and a toy rabbit. But even stranger, Charlie's sat in the corner, all alone, rocking backwards and forwards like a clockwork toy, an injured expression on his ivory face. I want to go over, cradle him in my arms like a baby. Instead, I close the door softly behind me, climb the stairs to my room which is tainted by the smell of Claude. The place which should be my sanctuary feels more like a prison cell.

Chapter 59

Ron

She no longer comes every day, so they come every night. The surface water has been broken, and we will never know how to smooth it back into place.

They're still young, five ... six ... seven, it's difficult to tell. They live in summertime, somewhere they deserve to live. Miracles happen around them. I can run, jump over hedges, catch the balls they throw. I lift them high in the air, perch them on my broad shoulders as if they weigh no more than a strand of string. I push them high on a wooden swing, watch them soar like dragonflies, their cries of joy ringing out like church bells over meadows green, thick, fragrant with wild flowers.

They bat away the demon moths like flies, banish them forever with smoking cauldrons of love. We sing, songs of angels and doves, songs so sweet, the fairies shed crystal tears, draw near, throw confetti made of silken thread, which dances round our hallowed heads.

When she doesn't come, they reward me with pills. I sleep in the day, but they only come at night, don't care for the clatter of the day. When they go, each night they beg me to go with them. It tears my heart in two, but I choose to stay, filled with a creeping dread I'll never see them again. But they are faithful, my two, never let me down, hold out a hand to lead me from the dark into the light.

Tonight, sleep refuses to take me. I try to picture their faces, but it's futile, they only come under the cover of slumber. I listen to the rust creeping through my veins, the demons feed on it, gather together in foggy crevices, just before sleep takes over.

I hear them before I see them. A tinkle of laughter in the balmy air. But tonight, something's different, wrong. There are three instead of two, one far taller than the others. It's Sarah, but she looks transparent, ethereal, like a dream. My two are solid, real. I can touch them, hold them. I reach out a hand to my daughter, but it goes straight through her pale thin arm.

They dance, twirl round and round, until I'm so dizzy, I fall. Tonight my body fails me, and before I can pick myself up they begin to fade away. It's too soon, the pain is unbounded, like nothing I've ever felt before. The little ones free themselves from their mother, hold out their hands, beg me to follow them. The pain is so intense that I hold out my own hand and do as they ask, I've no longer got any choice in the matter.

We descend, the four of us, like stones through a cavernous well. When we reach the depths, they come to me, embrace me in their arms, and I know for sure this is where I want to be, this place of limitless love. My eyes adjust to the half light, I look into their faces and it's not them at all. Instead two pairs of demonic eyes stare back, their limbs turn into bindweed, twist and curl around me, until I'm lost in their clutches. Then clarity strikes a razor claw. It was never them, I just deceived myself into believing it was. They were playacting and I was complicit in their subterfuge. I put my trust in demons because it was easy, instead of striving, fighting for the light. It was my job to save them, that's all I had to do. Now it's too late, my fate is upon me.

Chapter 60

Marnie

For the next few days I hardly see her. Charlie's in a massive huff, refuses to look me in the eye, so I try to stay out of his way, bury myself deep in college work, the only thing that will rescue me from all this. Claude's even more of a pain in the butt than usual. He knows he can come round whenever he likes, and she probably won't even notice. There's only one thing he's after, but he's never going to get it, not from me at least. Charlie was wrong, I'm nothing like our mother, he should never have said what he did, but I suppose I shouldn't have either. There's only one way to make him notice me again, and I intend to use it.

'I hope you don't mind ... I've invited Claude for supper tonight.'

She floats round the kitchen like an angel, her hair catching the sunlight as she prepares eggs for breakfast. She doesn't appear to hear me, but then after a couple of minutes, turns and graces me with one of her dazzling smiles.

'Of course ... How lovely, I'll grill some steaks, we can have them with salad from the garden. But you must be patient with me darling, I'm at quite a crucial point in my story ... A tricky matter, you wouldn't understand.'

He's like an excited puppy all day at college, going on and on about her. Odette walks part of the way home with us, she's a trillion times more interesting than him, no wonder she was more than happy for me to take him off her hands.

'I can't wait to talk to her again ... Hesther ... She's such good company ... Can we go upstairs ... Before we eat, I've been thinking about you all day.'

Obviously he doesn't think I'm good company, only wants me for one thing. I hate him so much, I could die from it.

'I've got a headache ... Probably a migraine ... I need to rest, but you could talk to her, while she cooks ... She'd love that, she thinks you're good company too ... Fascinating, I'm sure that was the word she used.'

He looks so bloody smug, I could happily cave in his ugly ferret face, if I didn't need him so much. I make a show of taking two tablets, brew some tea, tell him I need to sit in silence for a while. She floats through the door, dressed in a silk kimono I've never seen before. He can't take his eyes off her, she has this thing, when she comes into a room, people can't stop looking at her, like she's a famous film star or something, like no one else exists. She pretends not to notice, but you can tell she loves it, evidence she's not like everyone else, me included, she's special, just like our father told her she was.

'Thank you for inviting me again ... I have very much been looking forward to seeing you, you are very kind to welcome me here like this.'

She throws back her head, laughs like a flirty teenager.

'Claude, my dear boy, it is an absolute delight. Now I must begin preparing supper ... You must entertain me, while I cook. Marnie, darling, could you gather some salad ingredients from the garden.'

I leave the door open, so I can hear them talk. She regales him with a boring story about some party she went to in London years ago, he laughs like it's the funniest thing in the world. He never laughs when I tell him stuff about Brimfield or Chelmney. I take my time, fill a basket with plump red tomatoes, crispy lettuce, a big bunch of punchy basil. To my surprise, Charlie comes out and joins me, prances round the garden like a pixie, tramples through a flower bed, so I drag him away and he picks a lilac rose, hands it to me, a stupid grin on his ridiculously handsome face. He knows purple's my favourite colour, he's forgiven me at last. Since the crib arrived, he refuses to go into her study when she writes, h sits sulking on her bed instead. I didn't realise just how much I've missed him.

Claude helps me chop and wash the salad, while she grills three thick juicy steaks and opens a bottle of red wine.

'I must tell you, about an artist friend of mine ... In Nice ... You would simply adore him, Claude ... He compels one to challenge their own conception of the relationship between land

and sea ... And you'll never guess how he does it, pure genius if ever I saw it.' She pauses, as if waiting for an answer, Claude turns bright red, stutters incoherently. 'Using the medium of brick dust and dried seaweed ... He imports the brick dust all the way from London, for authenticity, you see, in order to get the exact shade of colour.' Claude hates art of any description, he told me once when we were lying on my bed, after a particularly long and boring fumble. He's about to say something, which I'd have paid good money to hear, but she gets in before him. 'Did Marnie tell you, she intends to go to Oxford ... So tedious when we have so much to offer her here, you should tell her Claude, she refuses to listen to me ... Oxford is no place for someone like Marnie, a free thinker, like myself. She hasn't found herself yet ... Have you darling, that's the problem.' He nods enthusiastically, like she's giving him a rare insight into the universe, rather than spouting a load of rubbish about me. Does she really think I'd miss out on Oxford, just because Claude asked me to. Charlie tries to distract me, make me laugh. Now he likes me again, I can finally dump Claude and we can get back to how it used to be. 'Did you know she has a little friend ... Our Marnie here ... Someone in her head she likes to talk to ... It's nothing to be ashamed of, like one of my characters I suppose, I communicate through the page, that's the only difference. Well let's eat, so lovely to get to know you better, Claude ... I felt sure you of all people would appreciate my friend's preposterous talent, you're that sort of boy, I can see that ... Did I tell you I'm wring a sequence of poetry based on his work, I'll give you a signed copy when it's published.'

He looks like she's said she wants to marry him and have his babies. He really is the most pathetic boy ever. I never want to feel his creepy hands on me again.

'Thank you, Hesther, you really are very kind ... So talented, you must -'

She starts to hum, quietly at first, but then it becomes more annoying and Charlie joins in for the fun of it, pulls out his tongue at me, sidles up to her, when he was supposed to stay with me. Why did she have to say all that, and in front of Claude, I hate her, now she's turned Charlie against me again.

When my sister loses interest she just goes, no questions asked, even if she's still here. I should leave right now, go up to my room, slam the door behind me, they're all welcome to each other, the whole bloody lot of them. But I need Claude again, don't I and it's all her fault. I often wonder if she ever drifted off when she was a nurse, didn't notice her patient dying right in front of her.

Without saying her goodbyes, she eats up and leaves, Charlie trailing behind her like a cat.

'Shall we go up to your room, Ma Cherie ... Your headache has gone now, mais oui.'

This is it, my last chance to make Charlie so jealous, he'll come back to me for good.

'Come on then, you can help me clear up later.'

I grab his hand, kiss him hard, inch my hand down the front of his trousers. He gasps, pushes into me, and as if by magic, Charlie opens the door. I can't see his reaction, but feel a quiet fury fill the room. As Claude pulls away and drags me towards the stairs, I catch sight of Charlie's face, a mirror image of my own, a mixture of dread and loathing etched into his delicate features.

On the stairs, Claude's already pulling at my clothes, we stumble upwards together in an awkward embrace. When we reach the landing, he tries to pull my top over my head, I grab the handle to my bedroom door as he reaches for the strap of my bra, clawing his other hand through my hair. I want to scream, but his tongue makes me gag, digs into my throat, until it's impossible to breathe. We stagger together, performing some outlandish dance on the landing. Then he comes at us like a spectre, invisible, but all consuming, and with one almighty push we begin to fall, a tangled mass of semi-naked limbs.

At the last moment, Charlie catches me, pulls me away from Claude's clutches. We watch as he gains momentum, his head pounding violently on each stone step. He lands heavily in an unnatural position at the bottom of the stairs. I close my eyes to block it out, and when I open them, she's standing over him, her head bowed as if in prayer. I wait. She doesn't touch him, feel for a pulse, phone an ambulance, she just stands there, as if she could stare at his mangled body forever. Then before I can stop him, Charlie slips away through the front door, leaving nothing but a snail trail of laughter behind him.

Chapter 61

Stuart

Simplicity soothes like a salve. The quest for meaning in the mundane. The act of laying one brick on top of another, making something solid, honest, real. The house in London was purchased in Sarah's name, so it was easy to walk away. Until recently I thought the same about my wife.

For the last few weeks, she's been squatting in my brain. None of this was her fault, she was unwell, lied to by her parents, the very people she should have been able to trust with her life.

We're building a school, a modern brick construction designed to replace the drafty prefabricated building dating back to the war years they use now. With a cool breeze caressing my skin, a wall growing steadily under my hands, I think back to all those long soulless years in the office. Why did I give in to their demands, fail to question their generosity, was I really so weak, so empty, that I allowed Sarah and her family to remould me into something unrecognisable.

When I think of Hesther now, it's Marnie's face I see. The forced smile when I left her in Grasse, fear lurking in the corner of her eyes. To block out the memories, I use the bricks like rosary beads, chant a short incantation as I lay each one. Much later, after the three mile walk home, I'll cook a simple supper and read a book. I tell myself it's enough. But it's not.

Friday, closing time at the site, a snake of children arrive to survey their fledgling school, hard plastic hats on soft young heads. As an excited stream of chatter fills the air, I pack away my tools, carefully wiping each one clean with a cloth. Two of the kids break free from the line, come over to watch me work.

'Thanks for building it Mister, it's like the arctic circle in our school. They say this'll have proper heating, a canteen with hot food, and everything … Can I look at your tools.'

They look about twelve years old, a girl and a boy.

'My brother wants to be an architect when we grow up. We're twins, but I'm the oldest, so I know more than him ... My brain's bigger, you see ... I think I want to be an architect as well, we do everything together, don't we Marlon?'

The boy looks fondly at his sister, pushes her in jest.

'Only because you never bleedin leave me alone.'

She laughs, pushes him back. The teacher calls out their names, the girl runs back to the safety of the pack without a backward glance. The boy speaks in a mock whisper.

'You have to keep them in their place ... Girls ... Don't you mister ... That's what me dad says ... But anyone can see me mum's the boss really.'

With that he skips away with a wave. Marnie's life flashes through my mind, her face when I got her that teddy bear, the brutality of life in the children's home which she speaks about without any hint of emotion. It could have been so different, with a family who loved her, a family who belonged to her.

On my way home, I call into the travel agents. Book a one way ticket to the south of France.

Chapter 62

Marnie

'He's dead ... You know that don't you.' Her voice is strangely calm, like she's asking me if I want a biscuit with my cup of tea. Why isn't she screaming, crying, putting a mirror to his mouth to see if he's breathing, like they do on cop shows. He's probably just pretending, trying to scare me. If she won't do it, it's up to me. 'No Marnie, don't touch him. It's too late now.'

Blood is forming a halo round his head, he looks like one of the fallen saints in the pictures on the walls of the chapel at the home.

'We need to do something ... Call an ambulance, it was an accident, he just tripped, I didn't mean to -'

'He's half undresssed. He deserved it, didn't he. Go and sort yourself out, get changed, wipe your face and comb your hair ... An ambulance will solve nothing now, I told you it's too late. The authorites here are such bloody bureaucrats ... Endless paperwork for every little thing ... You must choose more carefully next time, the wrong boyfriend can be tiresome to dispose of.'

I dig my nails hard into the wound on my arm, the pain helps me to think. There's a boy lying dead in our hallway. Charlie's gone, so they'll blame me for killing him, won't they.

'But we have to -'

'Marnie, go, do as I say ... And pack a bag ... We're going to the beach, a couple of days should be long enough.'

Is she crazy, this is no time to be taking a fucking holiday. She goes up to her room, so I check his pulse, feel nothing, but I'm not the professional, am I, she's a trained nurse, why couldn't she do it. His face is the colour of old blackboard chalk, his mouth gaping open like a goldfish. His trousers are open, you can see his underwear. You're supposed to cover the dead, aren't you, that's what they do on detective shows, Charlie says it's to let us know there's been a murder. Am I really a murderer now, that's what they'll say, what they'll call me in prison. In my room, I shove some clothes in a bag and rip the sheet off my bed. On our way out, I linger behind her, cover him neatly, so at least he's got his dignity, if nothing else. On the TV they always cover the face, but that seems wrong somehow, so I pull the sheet up to his chin, like I'm his mother tucking him in for the night. Unable to think of a quick prayer, I lay a flower on his chest.

She hums all the way there. At least twice, I consider grabbing the steering wheel, making her turn round. But what's done is done and a couple of days won't make any difference will it. It seems wrong to swim, to eat, but that's what she expects me to do, so I do it, then pace up and down the beach all night, while she writes, watching the light flicker through the window of the study.

I've never seen a dead person before, not in real life. She must've seen loads, that's why she didn't panic. He was a bore, a creep, but he didn't deserve to die, not like that anyway. Charlie will love being officially labelled a killer, but it won't be him in prison, will it. If she'd phoned the police, we could've explained, told them it was an accident, I could've got away with it, but now we've ran from from the scene of a crime, left a dead boy in our house, has she done it on purpose, wants to get rid of me forever and took her chance.

This is her fault more than it's mine. Hers and Charlies and Claudes. I'm the innocent party here, and as usual I'm the one they're going to punish. She'll be tapping away on her typewriter like nothing ever happened, Charlie will be larking around somewhere without a care in the world and Claude's dead so got away Scot-free with being a disgusting pervert. Sometimes I think she gets her stories and the real world the wrong way round. Thinks what she types is fact and what goes on around her is made up.

'Marnie there you are ... We're going home tomorrow, I really have to -'

'But we can't ... Go back there ... Not ever, they'll -'

Worry, worry, worry ... It's not good for you, darling. Do try to relax, make the most of our last day here ... Do you know I find it more delightful every time I come. You probably think you were in love with him, but believe me, you were not. The pain will pass much sooner than you think ... I promise you that ... And you will be stronger, more of yourself than you were before ... So you see pain is always worth it ... In the end.'

Is she for real. Does she honestly think I'm like this because I miss him, that I actually liked him, nevermind loved him. Has it not crossed her mind that I'm upset because I'm going to prison, probably for life and none of it was my fault.

'But the police ... The body, we can't just -'

'Enough ... You're trying my patience now. There's a lobster in the fridge, a bottle of good Champagne. We'll swim ... We'll feast ... Then it will be over, and that's the end of it.'

The salty water stings my wound, she never mentioned it, probably never bothered to notice. Maybe I should just float out to sea and drown. It isn't really my home we're going back to, not really. I live there, but my home is in Chelmney with Charlie, it was ours, we could do whatever we wanted, within reason. If Charlie had let me go home with Stuey, none of this would've happened.

She goes back to the study. I'm completely at her mercy, I can't stay here, can I, so I've no choice but to go home with her. If the police aren't waiting, I'm packing up and going straight back to Chelmney. Charlie might be waiting and hopefully they won't find me in England.

She boils the lobster, opens the Champagne, the icy bubbles help to dull the dread.

'I'm glad we came now, the change of scene helped with a sticky point in my story.'

We eat the lobster with a loaf of fresh bread, I don't even bother asking where the food came from, it's the least of my worries. I keep imagining his decomposing body, the smell when we get back, unless they've taken him away, made the house a crime scene so we can't get in. On balance, I think that would be the better option than having to see him again.

She never listens to music, never switches on the car radio, but today I can't stand the silence, so find a station with some lively pop music to distract me. She says nothing until we're ten minutes from home.

'I'm going away ... Tomorrow ... I'm not sure how long for ... And I've been thinking, you were right, about university, Oxford, you should go, I'll miss you ... Of course, but things change, don't they.'

Does she not understand that I'll be in prison, you can do a degree in prison, but it's nowhere near the same as doing it at Oxford, is it, and what exactly will I do with a bloody degree when I'm locked up for life. When we reach Grasse, I feel sick with nerves, surely everyone will know by now. We should've gone abroad, Brazil or somewhere like that, they don't care if you're a murderer there, do they, you can live on the beach, drink cocktails for the rest of your life, mix with the criminal fraternity, where you don't feel like the odd one out, just because you killed someone by accident once. She doesn't even seem the slightest bit worried, like she's wiped the whole thing from her mind, like the piles of screwed up pages in her study.

The house looks just as we left it. There's no crime scene tape, no police cars parked outside. They haven't found him, what on earth are we going to do now. The first thing that hits me is the smell. She always keeps it clean, but it smells like the shop in Aix where I hid from Stuey; expensive soap, lavender, a mix of exotic perfumes. The hall floor has been scrubbed clean, fresh flowers are expertly arranged in the vases. It's just like it never happened, like she really has erased the whole thing with a swipe of her pen.

I kneel down on the spot where his head was, there's not a spot of blood to be seen. She acts like we're just back from a shopping trip, goes through to the kitchen, boils the kettle for tea. Every inch of the house is as spotless as an operating theatre. The supper pots have all been washed and put away in their rightful places. In my room, the sheets have been changed, the bed perfectly made, all my clothes that were strewn across the floor are washed, ironed and hanging neatly in my wardrobe. We sit together and drink tea, as if we really have just been on a relaxing trip to the seaside.

'What happened ... Who did all of this ... Claude, where's -'

'While I'm away I've asked Henri to keep an eye on you, he will be -'

'You can't leave me, not after what happened, what will I say, what about the police.'

'You will simply go about your normal business. This is nothing to do with the police, I have seen to that, but you don't need to thank me. I'll make sure the fridge is fully stocked, so you've nothing to worry about.'

Does she honestly think my main concern right now is the contents of the bloody fridge.'

'Tell me where you're going, you owe me that at least. If the police come, they'll want to know, won't they, they won't believe I don't know where my own sister is. They'll think you're hiding somewhere.'

'They're not coming, Marnie … I'm off upstairs to pack, I've a long journey ahead of me tomorrow.'

'Let me come with you, please, I could -'

She leaves me mid sentence. Is she going away so I take all of the blame. If she is she won't get away with it, I'll tell them it was an accident and she made me go without reporting it, without calling an ambulance, if I'm going down, she's coming with me.

Next morning she's gone. There's an envelope on the doormat with my name on it. The card is thick, expensive looking with a quaint bridge over a pretty stream on the front. A scene that looks more English than French.

'Dearest Marnie. Please accept my most sincere apology. He was my son, and as such I take my share of the blame. I fear he was more like his father than I cared to see. I can never thank you enough for not involving the police. The funeral will be a discreet affair in line with his crime. I can only hope and pray this offers you a crumb of comfort. My very best wishes, now and forever, Madame Dupont.'

At that moment Charlie slips in through the door, grinning like the Cheshire cat. He got away with murder, and he knows it. He'll be insufferable now.

Chapter 63

Stuart

It feels like another world, up here in the sky with a plane load of people who fly for fun, for business, to visit loved ones. I fall into none of those categories. Even I don't really know what I'm doing here. The man next to me wrestles with a broadsheet, the unwieldy pages invading my space. About an hour into the flight I feel an almighty need to escape the confines of this tin can floating precariously through space. My breath starts to come in short gasps, sweat drenches my shirt. He carefully folds his paper, asks me if he can help, probably alarmed by the prospect of a delay, due to the old cliché of a middle-aged man having a heart attack mid flight. I tell him I'm fine, order a large brandy from the flight attendant, down it, then order another.

The driveway's empty. I knock, there's no answer. As I turn to leave, she's walking up the street towards me, looks like she's wearing something made out of an old pair of curtains, someone far more young and vulnerable than that fiesty girl in a black leather jacket at Chelmney station. She sees me, charges like a bull, flings herself into my arms like a toddler. I can feel her bones, she's lost too much weight. When she finally allows me to pull away, I look into dull, bloodshot eyes. She's broken, it pains me to the core to see her like this.

'Marnie … Whatever's the matter … You look dreadful, where's Hesther, why isn't she looking after you … I've come to talk to her, about Sarah.'

She takes my hand, leads me into the house. It's a mess, bags of rubbish stacked high in the hallway, the kitchen sink crammed with dirty dishes, clothes strewn across the couch in the livingroom. Hesther's not here, and by the state of the place hasn't been for quite some time.

'Thank God you came … It's been awful Stuey, really awful, something really bad happened, then she just went away and left me … She's been gone for over two weeks this time. I was going to hitch a lift, back to Chelmney, but it seemed like too much trouble, so I just stayed here.'

'Is she with him … Henri.'

'No he's here, in Grasse … He comes round sometimes, to check on me, but I don't let him in, he's a creep, I hate him … Take me home, please Stuey … I hate it here, I should've gone with you last time, but I couldn't could I, but nevermind none of that matters now, let's just get in the car and -'

'I need to see Sarah … There's stuff I need to tell her, important stuff, and it concerns you.'

'Look I might as well tell you now … The bad thing that happened. His name was Claude, he was my boyfriend … I mean I didn't like him or anything, it just -'

'Oh Marnie, you still make me laugh, only you could end up with a boyfriend you don't like. You've lost weight, but you could still have your pick of boys, why end up with -'

'He's dead … Claude, and I think it was my fault … Please don't hate me Stuey.'

'That's terrible, but however he died, I'm pretty damn sure it wasn't your fault.'

This wasn't what I expected to find. She obviously needs looking after, so I open a tin of soup and cut thick slices of bread. She eats half her soup, picks at the bread.

'He fell … Down the stairs, he was trying to. Well never mind, I suppose it was an accident, in a way, but we left him … She … Hesther said we should go away … To the beach … And when we got back he was gone, his body I mean.'

'So the police classed it as an accident, they -'

'No Stuey, there were no police … I think it was Henri … He just sort of … Well I know it sounds mad, but he sort of fixes things for her, when they go wrong. I think he owns the house at the beach, but I don't think she likes him any more than I liked Claude, she just uses him, that's why she let him kiss her like that … She was pregnant, lost the baby, I bet it was Henri's, she used him to -' She forces a big lump of bread into her mouth, chews slowly. 'I need to show you something, come on.'

In the study there's a pile of screwed up paper on the floor next to the desk. The typewriter is missing, but there's a crib, a beautifully carved wooden crib, complete with blanket in the corner of the room.

'It just appeared one day, when she came back from one of her trips ... Long after the pregnancy thing Claude told me about.'

A forceful knock at the door startles us both.

'Bonjour ... Stuart, I presume.' He's so handsome he doesn't look real, more like one of those waxwork dummies they used to have on Chelmney promenade years ago. 'I have heard all about you, your charming little teenage romance. Marnie had one too, but it did not turn out so good, hey, Ma Cherie.' He reaches out lightly touches her face, I could kill him here and now with my bare hands, but that's not going to help Sarah, and I force myself to remember that's what I'm here for. He's smug as a hyena, all false charm and polish. 'Hesther would be amused to see you, if she was here, of course.'

'Look it's Henri isn't it. I need to speak to Hesther ... Do you know where she is.'

'Ah, our dear Hesther is a law to herself, is she not. An artist in the truest sense of the word.'

'That may be so, but she has responsibilities ... Now. Marnie has been through a tough time by all accounts, recently. If you don't know where Hesther is, you can leave me to look after her ... Marnie, I mean, from now on ... I intend to wait here, until Hesther returns.'

His eyes turn dangerously dark. Marnie was right about him, he's most definitely a man who would invoke fear in anyone with anything to lose.

'As you wish, but she will not be happy, she left her young sister here in my capable hands.'

He leaves without any further discussion, but something tells me this is far from over.

'Do you see what I mean, it's like she's put some sort of bloody spell on them, can do whatever she likes, and no one says a word against her ... You've read her stuff, it's meaningless crap, and I know you think so too, so don't say you don't.'

She's right, I remember all the hours I spent listening to her read from her notebook on the beach, or in the park. Her sweet voice was nectar to my ears, but to be honest I never understood a word, she could've been reading from the phone book, and I'd still have been a willing listener. I was under her spell, adrift on love, or what I thought was love, but now I see it, there's something missing in her, something she needs other people's reverence to fill. Marnie doesn't give her that, so she needs someone else. Is that why she goes away, to see someone who can provide the adoration she craves.

'It was a few months after me met … I was terrified it was going to end, never really understood how it even began. She'd just spent the weekend in London with her father … Your father … Some swanky hotel … The sort of place I was never likely to set foot in. She said she'd hated every minute, so I allowed myself to believe she was having a better time with me, hanging about the streets of Chelmney … It makes sense now, I think I was part of her made up world, one of her strange characters. She used to tell me about the London people, the parties, the circles her father … I mean your father mixed in. At the time it felt like she was unburdening herself, but now I can see it, she was letting me know how different we were, that it wasn't real, us … Anyway that time, she brought me back a present, handed me a small velvet box … You'll never guess what it was, Marnie … A pair of bloody cufflinks, inscribed with the name of some club in London, her father was a member, I think. At the time I nearly fainted with joy … Convinced myself she was telling me that one day I'd own a shirt, have enough money to go to London, take her to London, successful enough to be a member of a club.'

'It wasn't that though was it Stuey, you can see that now. She was tormenting you, reminding you she was better than you, in a different class altogether, that you were lucky to be with her … I think she feels the same about me, even though we're sisters, she's better than me, and she wants me to know it … I hate it here, living with her … She never tells me anything … Not anything I want to know anyway … The longer I live with her, the less I know, that's not normal, and don't say it is … Anyway, I've given up on family, don't care if Sarah's my mother or not … It's not all it's cracked up to be, is it.'

There's another knock at the door, is he back already, ready for a fight. I can feel my hackles rising just thinking about his smug face. A key turns in the lock, Hesther must be home. A woman walks into the kitchen, a woman in a green uniform, she looks like a nurse, it's clear Marnie doesn't know her any more than I do.

'Marnie ... Your sister, Hesther sent me to look after you while she's away ... She thought it would help, she did not intend to be away for so long.' She looks at me, anger burning in her eyes. 'You can leave now Sir. You are not required here.' She places a small leather bag on the table, nods in the direction of the door. 'Marnie will be taken care of, you can count on that, I'm trained in such matters.'

I remain firmly rooted to my seat. Marnie reaches for my hand, clutches it hard, the only thing I can offer her is the most reassuring smile I can muster up at such short notice.

Chapter 64

Sarah

She likes to say it's just like the old days. The two of us. I can't remember what fresh air tastes like. She says it tastes of popcorn and lemondrops. I watch the snow. She says snow isn't cold anymore, not like when it used to nip at our fingers and toes. Mummy would run them under warm water, to thaw us out, she said. Then she'd make hot chocolate, sprinkle it with pink marshmallows, my favourite colour, or at least I think it was.

The thing inside me moves. It makes me eat things, fudge, strawberry ice cream, onions on toast. She brings the things to feed it, sometimes shares, says she can feel it move inside her as well.

She told me a story, said she'd made it up just for me. She was barren as a forest after a fire, a doctor told her that. But what do doctors know. Then she met a man. She says they fell in love, but she knows nothing about love, and I should know. An American, a botanist travelling through Europe for research on a book he was writing. They were together for a month. Then he floated off like a petal. He was a spirit, not a real man, so he impregnated her with a spirit baby. The baby couldn't come into the real world, so went straight up to the spirit world where flowers never die.

My baby is made from flesh and blood. It struggles, wants to come out, is desperate to see me, but it's too soon. She says it's ok to swap babies, like we used to swap marbles at school. Sometimes we fall asleep, when I wake I watch her while the one in green watches me. The ones in green are always watching, that's what they're here for.

The pain comes from nowhere. Pain I remember from a long time ago. I watch the sun rise over the mountains, a peach melba globe, turning the snow into a bed of rose petals. When they come I hide the pain.

'She's overdue ... It should be any day now ... I hope you're ready Hesther.'

'What shall we do today Sarry ... It's a beautiful day, we could go out.'

She's lying. She's always lying. A firebolt of agony courses through my body.

'She doesn't look well, we should call the doctor.'

'She's fine, aren't you Sarry ... Who needs doctors ... I worked at a hospital, remember.'

This isn't a hospital, they think I don't know, but I'm glad. Last time a doctor killed my daughter, cut her out of me like a piece of meat. This time she'll come to me when she's ready, and not a second before. Last time my parents didn't want her enough, but now she's all mine, I want to feel the pain, it means she's real, she's alive. Hesther wants me to feel the pain as well, but she always did, didn't she.

'But what if something goes wrong, you were only a -'

'Let's stay in, talk, like the old times ... Sometimes I wish I never met him, Stuart I mean. What about you, do you regret it ... I suppose not, we wouldn't be here now would we ... I wonder if the baby will look like him, I think he'll make a good father, despite all his faults. I was unsure at first, but I think a baby will suit him.'

She leaves me, goes into that dream world where she lives for most of the time. It takes all my concentration to handle the pain, so this time I'm glad she's gone. When my daughter comes out, we're going away, just the two of us, into the mountains where it's safe. The one in green watches me waddle to the bathroom. Before I can reach the door, it come, a gush between my legs, soaking my nightgown, making a puddle on the floor.

'Hesther.' She doesn't hear, just hums a funny tune. 'Hesther ... It's coming ... The baby's coming.'

'Oh, really, I thought it would be today ... It's his birthday isn't it, Stuart's ... Well you know that Sarry, don't you.'

It's no use pretending anymore, so I let out a scream. She covers her ears, so I do it again, much louder, it rings painfully in my ears. She comes, takes me in her arms, rocks me like I'm a child. She smells of lavender and love. This is it, this is where we're meant to be, we'll be safe here and she'll live with us forever. I cry, heavy tears of relief and when she lets me go, she's crying as well. The pain ebbs and flows, bringing clarity in its anger. I submit to the agony until it almost seems like pleasure, she becomes an angel, floating above me, wiping the sweat from my brow, talking softly in ancient tongues.

A needle removes me from the drama going on around me. The world dissolves into whispers drifting in the air.

'The head's coming ... It's a boy, a healthy little -'

My dream fragments into broken pieces, her daisy soft hair tickling my face, daddy saying we look like two perfect peas in a pod, her jumping up on his knee, his pen idle on his desk as he pushes us high into a velvet sky on the wooden swing he took a whole day to make.

I'm in bed, it's Chelmney, mummy's making breakfast downstairs. But there's something wrong, I feel sore between my legs, reach down and there's blood on the sheets. I lie still, try to breathe the pain away, and only then do I remember. She's come to me, she's here now, she must be with mummy in the kitchen. I want to hold her, smell her newborn skin, so I force myself out of bed to go to her.

This is not mummy's house, this is some sort of a nightmare. It looks like a hotel room, there's a fridge containing a bottle of Champagne and two glasses, the window is thrown open revealing a perfect Alpine scene and the freshest air you could ever breathe, there's a fluffy white robe hanging in the wardrobe and a pair of slippers. The bathroom is full of expensive toiletries and soft towels, there's a vase of fragrant lilies and a bowl of fruit on the dressing table. My throat quivers in horror, where are the things for my baby, the crib, the bottles, the clothes, the toys, this is not the right room for a baby, something's gone horribly wrong.

I put on the robe and slippers, open the door, run down the corridor, searching frantically for my daughter. The place is huge, room after room, most of the furniture covered in dust sheets. In one enormous room, there's a grand piano fronted by lines of chairs, as if expecting an audience at any moment.

Outside there's at least a foot of fresh snow, I take off my slipper, test it with my foot, it's just as cold as ever. She was here, she told me otherwise, she lied. She's got my baby. She lied to me about the snow, everything she ever said to me was a lie and now she's taken my daughter.

Back upstairs, I run a bath, pour in a whole bottle of lavender oil, relish the sting where my daughter came from. Then it becomes clear, why they're not here, why the place is deserted, they're waiting for me, somewhere else entirely, somewhere safe. That's why she told me the story, so I'd understand when the time came, that's why she left the flowers. Where the flowers never die, that's where they're waiting. My baby belongs with her baby, we all belong together, I was stupid to think otherwise.

The Champagne tastes good, she left painkillers, so I swallow them slowly, one by one with the icy cold bubbles. A celebration. An earthly reward, before I follow them. I sit next to the window, take gulps of mountain air, allow my mind to soar free as a bird over the snowy peaks. I wait, watch the blizzard obscure the mountain tops, night gobble up the remnants of the day.

This was all part of her plan. I never listened, never understood. The moon rises high over the tallest mountain, the stars flash in code. At first I can't understand them, but the more I see the clearer it becomes. She wants me to leave now, go to them. Sitting on the window ledge, I catch snowflakes on my tongue, just like we used to on those special winter days.

I hear her voice, faint, distant, from high up in the mountain tops, call her name and the stars answer, say I don't have long, she needs me now. Falling through the snow is blissful, just like daddy pushing me high on the swing on a soft autumn day. She always insisted on going first, even then, that's how I know she's waiting with the little ones. When I land it pulls me under, sweet as candyfloss, and she was right, it isn't cold, but as warm as mummy's arms. She walks towards me, my perfect daughter, wearing the little red coat I bought and hid under my bed for when she was older.

Then I hear her voice, clear as day.

'Sarah ... Sarah, where are you?' Then I hear a baby cry from the open window. 'Sarah ... He's perfect, I took him to get checked over, he ours now, we can take him home.'

I can't believe I fell for it, again. She's not in the mountains at all, she's in my room. It's too late now, so I reach for my daughter's hand, try to call out to Hesther, but snow fills my mouth, devours my words. When I open my eyes for the last time, it's Hesther wearing the little red coat, not my daughter, the one that used to hang on the peg in the school cloakroom next to mine. We're seven again, together again, I can finally let go of the rope I've been been clinging onto for such a long time.

Chapter 65

Marnie

Everyone at college was so bloody nice it almost made me puke, never even mentioned his name in front of me. I still expect the police to come, but as the days and weeks tick by, it seems you really can get away with murder, if you've got someone like Henri in your corner, that is. In the end it was Stuey who came instead. I can feel Charlie's here somewhere, but he hides himself away from me, like he's playing a game and only he knows the rules, so it's a game I'm never going to win.

The cheek of the woman walking into my house as if she owned the place, Hesther must've given her a key. She looks like some sort of nurse, I'm not ill, so why would she send a nurse.

'He's going nowhere, he's my friend, and you've no right just letting yourself in like that, this is my house as well as Hesther's, I live here too, so I say who stays and who goes.'

She looks angry, keeps fiddling with her bag, Stuey's going nowhere, she can fuck right off if she thinks he is.

'I'll say it again, I'm looking after Marnie now ... She's right we're old friends, and please tell Hesther, I'm going nowhere until I've seen her ... Something's going on here, and I demand to see my wife.'

'All right, I will leave, but Hesther will not be happy, I was instructed to give something to Marnie ... To help her.'

She goes before I think to ask her for the key. Will she send any other weirdos to look after me, I dread to think what would've happened if Stuey wasn't here.

'Look Marnie ... We need to talk ... I've got stuff to tell you. That was strange, wasn't it, but don't worry, I'm going nowhere, not until I've seen Hesther, found out where Sarah is, then I think you should come with me to see her, your -'

'She really is my mother, isn't she ... She's crazy, but you

Stuey, well it means you're my step dad ... And I'm pleased, I trust you, you're the only one I trust.'

He's put on weight, looks much better than when I last saw him, his hair's grown, and he's tanned, like he spends his time outdoors.

'I don't live in London anymore, I moved up north ... Work on a building site, I -'

'But your lovely house ... Your wedding picture, the thing is, she'll get better one day, Sarah, and you can -'

'No it's over ... The thing is Marnie, relationships that aren't built on solid foundations fall down in the end ... You can rebuild them, but they'll never be the same, so it's pointless even trying. Look there's no easy way to tell you this, so I'll just come out with it ... Sarah's parents told her you died, when you were born ... She doesn't know you exist, that's why she said she wasn't your mother.'

'But what sort of people would do -'

'Let me finish, there's more ... You had ... I mean have a twin, a boy ...He was adopted, they didn't know it was twins, so that's why you were sent to the home.'

He's right here, under the table, that's where he was hiding all the time. He pokes out his head and winks at me. He might have been adopted but he's with me now, has been for ages, Stuey just doesn't know it yet.

He moves into her room, which seems a bit weird, but he has to sleep somewhere. Charlie likes playing tricks on him, hiding his reading glasses, pouring salt instead of sugar in his tea, he doesn't trust him, can't see we need him for protection against people like Henri and the nurse woman. He cleans the house, cooks us meals, does the washing, meets me from college, if I ask him to. Henri doesn't come to the house, but I see him sometimes in town, watching me, so I try not to go out without Stuey, it's safer that way.

Then one evening as I'm clearing my books from the kitchen table, and Stuey's stirring the pasta sauce, she walks in the door, says nothing, simply fills the kettle as if she's never been away. But instead of going to her like he usually does, Charlie hisses like a snake, comes to me, links my arm through his, and whispers something truly monstrous in my ear.

Chapter 66

Stuart

Despite her appearance, she's still a child. She has no concept of housework, cooking healthy meals, keeping on top of the laundry. So I take over, keep the house for us both, something I do very badly in my own flat, but here I'm needed, and the parent I was unaware was in me takes over. Sleeping in Hesther's bed feels wrong, but I need the rest in order to function, and she brought this on herself by going away and leaving a vulnerable child to cope alone.

I used to think the mystery surrounding her was enchanting, part of her charm, but now I look back on days of wonder overshadowed by dread, hope and despair. My inner turmoil, so readily dampened down by one of her special smiles.

It was two weeks of hell. We'd arranged to meet at our usual spot by the library, the first day of the school holidays. I waited all day. The following day I tried our usual places, the park, the beach, our bench, paced up and down at the end of her street. This routine followed for the next fortnight. I couldn't eat or sleep, even plucked up the courage to go to her house, but the gates were locked and there was no sign of life. My imagination was fit to bursting with disaster; a fatal car crash, a terrible fall, a mad axe wielding murderer. Or far far worse, some boy, rich, handsome, tanned, an arm draped artfully round her bare shoulders.

Two weeks to the day she appeared at the park, looked so vital, so alive, her hair in soft waves, lightened by the sun, a deep tan gracing her supple skin, she was positively glowing with health and happiness. She kissed me in a joyful, restless manner, and with each second of her lips on mine the red raw anger, frustration, terror in my heart faded to a dull grey, and everything came back to life again.

She said she forgot to tell me her father had booked a villa in

Tuscany for his family and a few close friends. The prospect of it was so tiresome, it had simply slipped her mind. While I was out of my mind with worry, she was merrily romping her way through Italian high society, lounging by a private pool, eating in the finest restaurants, exploring the Tuscan countryside from the comfort of a chauffeur driven limousine. I managed to convince myself there was nothing to forgive, it had all been just a big misunderstanding.

We fall into some sort of uneasy routine. She goes to college, I keep house, the problem being my small pot of savings is rapidly diminishing. The crib is the great enigma in the house, the thing we both avoid mentioning. Then one early evening, just as we're about to eat Hesther returns without warning. For a couple of minutes it's as if she can't see us, she boils the kettle, pulls out a solitary mug, makes herself a cup of tea. Then she finally acknowledges our presence.

'Stuart ... What a surprise.' She doesn't look in the least bit surprised. 'And Marnie, have you missed me?' She waits for an answer that fails to come. A soft mewling sound comes from the hallway. Marnie's face turns pale as the moon, her features form a picture of shock and something far deeper. 'It's really not a good time for me to have a visitor, Stuart, I really -'

'I need to see my wife ... Sarah, I've got important things to talk to her about ... Just tell me where she is and I'll go.' Marnie looks pleadingly at me.' And I'm taking Marnie ... You were right, Sarah is her mother.'

The cry gets louder, there's a baby in the hallway, and she's acting like it doesn't exist.

'I told you I'd take care of Sarah, you really shouldn't have bothere to -'

'A baby ... Is that what you've been doing, buying a baby ... The crib ... You left Marnie all this time to -'

Marnie crashes into the hallway, returns clutching a Moses basket, the mewl turns into a howl of discontent. She pulls back the cover, it looks brand new, far to young to be away from its mother.

'We're sisters and you never told me ... Who is it ... Where did it come from ... You treat me like I'm a bloody stranger, unless it suits you ... The nurse woman ... Henri ... Why.' Her eyes are alight with pent up anger. The baby seems to sense three sets of eyes on it, the simmering atmosphere in the room, starts to wail in an alarming manner, its tiny pink face wrinkled as a prune. 'Well do something then.' She's shouting, which upsets the baby even more. 'You brought it here, you're the fucking nurse, make it stop, I can't stand it.'

Marnie covers her ears. Hesther picks it up, holds it to her chest, rocks it, but it won't stop crying.

'The crib, you knew you were bringing home a baby ... But you didn't think to discuss it with Marnie ... What is it with the secrets ... Why can't you tell me where Sarah is.' The blood rushes from my head. I do a mental calculation. 'It's Sarah's ... That's Sarah's baby ... I knew she wouldn't tell her parents, if it wasn't true.' I'm shouting now, to make myself heard over the high pitched wailing, how can something so small make so much noise. 'Where is she, why have you got it ... Look at it, it's too young, it should be with its mother.'

I remember Mary's face when she told me about the last time Sarah gave birth. So cold, no sign of any regret or guilt, as if she truly believed she'd acted in her daughter's best interests. I have to return this baby to her, together with Marnie and her brother. Then I can walk away, knowing I did my best, in the end.

'Why don't you sit down, I'll tell you everything ... About Sarah ... The baby.'

'You won't though, will you ... You never tell me fucking anything. Will you shut it up, it's doing my head in ... And what about the other baby ... The one you lost, Claude told me ... I bet it was Henri's, he likes young girls, did you know that, Stuey's my family now, and if that thing is Sarah's it's more mine than yours, so it's coming with me.'

Clearly out of her depth, Hesther willingly hands the little bundle over to Marnie. She rocks it far too hard, its head wobbles like jelly.

'Marnie, give it to me, you have to support the head.'

If I'd never met Marnie, this would be my responsibility now, whoever the real father is. It calms in my arms, until at last there's silence.

'He's a perfect baby boy. I was right, you do suit babies

Stuart, I've decided, I want you to stay ... We can bring him up together.'

She comes over, bends down and kisses me on the mouth. I feel nothing but revulsion.

'Did you not hear me ... Me, Stuey, the baby and Sarah are the family, not you ... You should just -'

'I tried to help her. I really did ... The best doctors, the latest treatments ... But it turns out it was too late, you and her parents left it too long ... She's dead Stuart ... She didn't want the baby, but because of her state of mind, they wouldn't let her have an abortion, then when he came, she simply killed herself, to be rid of him forever. Tragic really, but maybe it was meant to be like this, can't you see, you and me, and now a baby. A family. It was always us, you know that as well as I do, Sarah was simply an incidental.'

'Dead, but she can't be ... She wouldn't -'

'Our own child, remember once we spoke about it, in that field near the park, you said that -'

'He's not mine Hesther ... I can't have kids ... A vasectomy ... Years ago, she must have had an affair or something.'

'If he's not yours Stuey, and he's certainly not yours Hesther, and his mother is dead, then he's mine, isn't he. He's my baby brother, and I should be the one to keep him.'

She tries to take him from me, she's too rough so he wakes, starts to wimper again.

'You can hold him, but be gentle, support his head.' A gurgling sound emerges from somewhere deep in his throat. This is wrong, it's perfectly apparent not one of us has the first clue how to care for a baby. 'Give him to Hesther, you were a nurse, you must know how to -'

'Oh, Stuart ... Can you really imagine me mopping up bodily effluent for a living. I did spend a few months, on and off at a hospital ... Conducting research, for one of my books. Sarah always wanted to be me, did you know that ... So when she came to Nice, I told her I was a nurse ... And she surprised us all by being quite good at it, didn't she, which was fortunate, because she couldn't write for toffee ... Such a funny girl, had no friends, until I took her under my wing. Did you know the full extent of her depravity ... I doubt it, who would have told you. My mother tried to keep it from me, but she was capable of very little by then. The police found two dead kittens in her room, she used the blood to draw diagrams of how she intended to kill me ... Of course I blame her parents, kept her caged like a bird. Birds go mad, did you know that, when they aren't allowed to fly.'

'But you already had the crib ... How could you possibly have known she was going to take her own life ... You were with her, weren't you ... That's why you never told me where you were, why you kept going away ... You wanted the baby, for yourself, because you lost the other one ... You're the crazy one you -'

It's quiet now, too quiet. I try the gentle approach.

'Put him in the basket Marnie, so he can sleep ... Where are the other things he needs Hesther, bottles, milk, nappies, clothes.'

'Oh Stuart, you always were such a fusspot. I'll go into town, pick a few things up tomorrow. He has your nose, can't you see that, vasectomies don't always work, do they ... I saw the crib in a sweet little antique shop, got it as a surprise for Sarah. I was going to help her with him, until she was well enough to take him back to England.'

Marnie puts him in the Moses basket, I tuck the cover around his tiny body, his breathing seems laboured, his chest rising and falling in an erratic manner. Marnie starts to twitch, looks like she's trying to brush something off her shoulder.

'You need to go now, we need to feed him, change him .... I saw a big supermarket just out of town, get everything he needs, I'll look after him while you're gone ... But I want to know, where Sarah was all this time, where she died, and you need to tell Mary, you owe her that, at least.'

'Marnie can look after him ... You come with me Stuart, we can talk about the future, about our life together, we should get married, as soon as -'

'Look at her, she can hardly look after herself, nevermind a bloody baby. I'm staying here ... You should have been more prepared, you had no right to -'

She looks at me, just like she used to when we were fifteen years old. A beatific smile settles on her flawless face.

'She got what she wanted in the end ... Didn't she, Sarah. She wanted me all to herself, and now that's what I'm going to do, give up my life for her, devote every second to her family, treat it as my own ... You can see we're doing the right thing, can't you Stuart.'

Chapter 67

Marnie

She leaves, shopping basket in hand, as if she's popping out for groceries. Stuey doesn't trust me with it, anyone can see that. Charlie is just about as mad as I've ever seen him, keeps shouting he's my brother, that thing is an alien that doesn't belong anywhere near us.

'Pack a bag Marnie, I'm not convinced Sarah's dead, we're going to find her. I'm going to force the truth out of Hesther, and then we're off, taking the baby with us.'

Charlie dances round me as I pack. We go downstairs and he pokes his tongue out at Stuey.

'Look you watch him, just for a couple of minutes while I get my things, if he wakes up call me.'

Charlie walks over to the crib, where Hesther put him, before she went out. He stares down at it, a dreamy look in his eyes. It senses he's there, starts to cry. What's the point of babies, if all they do is cry. If he could just shut it up, everything will be alright. At first it lies peacefully in his arms, its cries turn to soft wimpers, but then he starts to jig it about. Even I can see he's being too rough. It starts making weird noises, wriggles like an overgrown caterpillar. I try to take it from him, but he pushes me away. I want to call Stuey, but he puts his hand over my mouth to stop me, jigs it even harder. Just as Stuey comes in with his bag, I manage to wrestle it from Charlie's arms.

'Marnie ... No ... What did I tell you, that's not how you hold him, give him to me.'

He holds out his arms, but Charlie gets there first, pushes me hard, forcing me to stumble. Stuey catches it before I fall, but its head is hanging at a funny angle. My knee makes a loud cracking sound, then a flame of pain engulfs me. He puts it on the table, pumps at its tiny chest, and the last words I hear before the world fades away are.

'Marnie … For the love of God … What have you done.'

Charlie lets out a bloodcurdling trail of laughter, as once again he makes his escape.

Chapter 68

Stuart

She wraps him in the pale blue blanket. Gently, as if she still has the capacity to hurt him. He looks so perfect, his face feels like cool marble. I try not to look at Marnie lying unconscious on the floor. She needs an ambulance, but we're in no position to call one. She takes my sweaty palm into the cool softness of her own. I expected her to fly into a rage, cry, sling accusations, call the authorities. Instead she was quite serene about the whole thing, treated me like a child in shock from a cut knee.

I look into her eyes, wait for the tears, but they remain dry, a hint of a smile playing at the corner of her lips. I search for Sarah in his tiny face, but find no trace of her there.

'From the minute I saw him, I could see he wasn't for this world ... I was right wasn't I.'

'It was my fault, I shouldn't have left him alone with Marnie, I -'

'I had another child ... He went straight to heaven too, and do you know why. When we met, you were as innocent as a spring lamb ... The thing I loved about you, was that you believed I was too, treated me as an equal in childhood innocence ... And do you know what, sometimes, running on the beach, or lying in the grass, I almost believed it to be true.'

'But you were, we were just children, we hadn't -'

'You still believe in good, after all this time ... That's what innocence is, isn't it really. All children aren't innocent, sometimes it's ripped away from them, and however much they try, they can never get it back. Marnie is innocent, always will be, she believes good things will happen to her, and they probably will, for a while at least.'

She leaves me alone in a room with an injured girl and a dead baby. I can hear her muted voice on the telephone in the hall, but can't make out the words.

'Come on Stuart, we're going out.'

'Are you mad, we can't just -'

'Come on, she hands me my coat … Everything will be alright, I promise.'

She takes my hand, we walk like lovers, slowly, silently, until we reach the outskirts of town.

'It was Marnie, wasn't it … My sister has issues, but who wouldn't with a mother like Sarah … She's going to be cared for, for a while, at least. I can't have her back … I need my peace and quiet … You found, her didn't you, and you know what they say about people who find things … Now I'm going to tell you a secret.' I'm transported back to those long summer days in Chelmney, her mouth close to my ear, snippets of her life that were useless to anyone but me. 'When I came here, I vowed to stay until the day I died.' I take in the sun dancing on amber stone, flowers defying gravity to climb golden walls, flaxen spires towering in a clear blue sky. 'But now … It's time for me to move on … What I'm trying to tell you, is when you leave, never look back. It was looking back that made all of this happen, but I don't hold grudges … You need to move forwards now, you can see that can't you … Sarah took the easy way out, but it shouldn't be us left to clear up the ashes of her life.'

She drops my hand, stops to look at a painting in a shop window, I watch her dark hair blow in the breeze, tanned hand resting lightly on the glass, someone I thought I once knew. The house is silent, Marnie and the baby are gone, along with the crib and other baby things, every surface scrubbed clean, everything put away in its rightful place.

I don't knock. She's sitting at her desk, a single red rose in a crystal vase next to her typewriter, looking at a photograph, deep in reflection. I glance over her shoulder, it's her and Sarah, they look about ten or eleven, Ron standing between them, holding a small hand in each of his, face a picture of pride. The man I believed to be beyond reproach, the perfect father, husband, provider. She turns her chair, there's a tear running down her cheek.

'The doctors were right all along … I was never meant to have a child of my own.'

'Before I go, tell me where Marnie is … It was Henri, wasn't it ... All this ... I don't want him anywhere near her ever again, do you understand ... He has some sort of hold over you, or you over him ... Just keep her safe, that's all I ask, and I won't report any of this ... What went on here ... Just say yes or no, and tell me the truth, is Sarah really dead.'

She nods her head slowly, scribbles something on a piece of paper. We don't bother with goodbyes. The plane ticket eats up the remainder of my savings. I return to England with nothing to my name but a scrap of paper in my pocket.

Chapter 69

Marnie

Charlie killed a baby. My knee is mending nicely, but they say I've still got other issues, so they want me to stay a little longer. It's safe here. I like it. For the first time in my life, people actually want me to talk, almost force the words out of my mouth, but Charlie does the talking for me. He arrived a few days after I did. They say I'm full of anger. Charlie's always fucking angry, but they don't know that, do they. He refuses point blank to talk about our sister, but in the end he chose me over her, so I don't mind. He tells them about some of the fosterers, the home, the nuns. Some of his stories make them gasp, some make them laugh. Charlie always exaggerates, it's one of his things.

If I ever leave here, I'm not going back to her, Charlie would never agree to it. They're always watching, so he can't punish me here, not with the knife anyway. I don't think they know about the baby. Charlie's never going to tell them, so just like with the other baby, we make a silent pact not to talk about it. Some days I think I'll die here. It doesn't scare me, the dying thing, doesn't seem so bad, way easier than going back to the real world, I suppose.

Charlie's getting worse by the day, playing up, frustrated, bored, burning with anger. He's constantly whispering shit in my ear, won't give me have a minute's peace. They say I need to calm down, relax, think about my actions. Can't they see I'd be perfectly fucking calm, if it wasn't for Charlie. They give me pills, but he makes me pretend to swallow them, he can't torment me if I'm asleep, can he.

'It's you fault we're here … Looking for a mother who never even wanted us … Everything's your fault.' It's the middle of the night, he never lets me get more than a couple of hours sleep. 'Stupid dumb bitch, thought you could go to university, but ended up in a nut house like your mother ... Everyone hates you, your mother hated you so much, she'd rather die than see you again.' I try to push him away, but he's all over me like a plague of ants. 'You can't lock me away any more, I've got the key, so I'll always be with you, forever.' He's screaming at the top of his voice, if he doesn't shut up they'll hear him, and we'll be in for it again. 'I hate you, I hate you ... I'm going to tell them what you did ... Marnie killed a baby, Marnie killed a baby, Marnie killed a stupid ugly boy.' Why won't he stop, he knows we'll get into trouble. 'I only stay with you out of pity ... I wish I'd stayed with her, she's my real sister, not you.'

The scream escapes before I can stop it, the nurse comes, tries to put a needle in my arm, but he's strong, fights her off, manages to wrestle her to the floor. They fight like dogs, until finally she gets the better of him, plunges the needle deep into his chest. My heart feels like it's stopping, but it's not me who's dying, it's him. Charlie closes his eyes, and it's over.

Chapter 70

Stuart

Cold is the hardest thing to bear. Being warm wasn't something I ever considered. For many years, Sarah made sure there was very little I had to consider. A warm spring day in Rome comes to mind. We walked for miles, queued for a tour of the Colosseum, trailed a dour tour guide around St Peter's. Sarah rewarded her apathy with an over generous tip, the only tip I'd have given her was to try a smile every now and again.

Dusk was settling as we strolled back to our hotel. He was just a lad, no more than a teenager by appearance, tapped me on the shoulder and asked me for some loose change. Sarah's strict code of conduct was never to hand out money in the street, give in bulk to charity, a safer option, which to my knowledge neither of us ever actually did. There was something about him that touched me, so without thinking, I handed him a couple of notes from my wallet. His eyes bore into mine, like he could see deep inside my soul. He must have regognised the distaste in Sarah's face, I can still remember his words 'Signora, tonight I eat, tonight I am warm, tonight I pray well for your kindness.'

I waited for the rebuke, but it never came. Back at the hotel, we dined on silky artichoke hearts, follwod by melt in the mouth porchetta, all washed down with a bottle of Chianti. After brandies on the terrace, we retired to our room, made love to the sound of car horns and the flow of the river. When we got home, I made a mental note to set up a regular donation to a homeless charity. Two days later, a blond head on the tube wiped away all of my good intentions.

My preferred place to sleep is not always available. Nothing on the streets is guaranteed. It's a strictly first come, first served basis. I returned to the city, it's easier for people like me here. No one sees you, they walk past you like you're a ghost. That provides a safety blanket of sorts, apathy is a homeless person's best friend. One night I slept in the doorway of a restaurant where me and Sarah once dined. I found some scraps in the bin round the back, she would have been pleased to know the quality of the food hasn't diminished one jot.

The route of escape from the streets is fiercley debated. Do you start with a home, a job, go down the charity route, beg for mercy from a distant relative. I got a few days cash work on a building site after begging for the money to buy clothing and boots. Begging is both ridiculously easy and the hardest thing in the world, lounging around on a blanket, while some poor fool flings a few coins at you as they're rushing back to the office. Unfortunately due to a lack of storage facilites, one morning I woke up and my hard won possessions were gone.

Tonight's deluxe accommodation is the doorway of a deli on a quiet side street. As I make a bed out of cardboard and a filthy blanket, the curtain twitches in a window across the street. Some people out here, despise the term homeless, claim that a corner of the corporation car park is just as valid a dwelling place as a five bed town house in Berkley Square. Some of them even believe it. As I close my eyes, the cold creeps through the layers, intent on reaching my aching bones.

'Wake up, you can't sleep here … This is no place to spend a night like this.' He's old, seventyish, dressed in a suit and tie. 'You need to move on, find somewhere else.'

'I'm not doing any harm … No drink or drugs, I'll be gone early morning … Just let me get my head down for a bit, please.'

'Get up.'

'You can't tell me what to -'

'Come with me, I'll make you a hot drink.'

He looks pretty normal, but you hear stories, psychopaths who prey on the vulnerable, cautionary tales, the grisly fate of those who've been taken in by an offer of help from a stranger. A dire warning for those who still dare to trust, to think that someone might really care.

The sitting room is charmingly oldfashioned, a real fire in the grate. He brings me a mug of steaming tea and a plate of expensive looking biscuits.

'No drink or drugs, hey … So why are you here … It's

obviously your choice to live like this, then.'

'It's not that easy … You wouldn't … I mean, I don't have -'

'I never said it was easy, did I. Did you hear me say it was easy.' His voice sounds like he smokes forty a day, but there's no hint of cigarette smoke in the air. 'It is a choice, for someone like you, at least, the question is why did you make that choice.'

'But I had no -'

'You're punishing aren't you … Either yourself or someone else … Be honest with me, you like it don't you, thrive on it … Like a martyr to the cause … Grief, is it … Loss … It makes you feel superior to someone like me, a bona fide victim … But we're all victims in some way, it's how we choose to handle it that counts.'

I should be angry, none of us choose to live like this, who would. What does he know with his nice house, food in the fridge, money in the bank. But deep down, I know he's right. I gave up on life, because it seemed like the easy option, like a get out clause, something which would let me off the hook of the past. Out here I only have to think about myself, food, warmth, the odd wash. It's simple. It's damn right selfish.

'Look, thanks for the tea, I'll find somewhere else to sleep tonight, you won't see me again.'

'But you've found somewhere … Haven't you … Right there, where you're sitting … I think you're ready now, you just didn't want to face up to it … If you can't do it for yourself, you must dig deep and find someone else to do it for. There's a blanket over there, I dare say you'll be gone in the morning.'

I bask in the dying embers of the fire. I made a silent promise in France. Was I really so willing to give up on it so easily. Tonight for the first time in months, I sleep with both eyes closed.

Chapter 71

Marnie

They want to discharge me. I told them, I refuse to go with her, or Henri. I'd rather stay here for the rest of my life. They've explained a lot of things. I was right. None of it was my fault. All the bad things that happened were down to Charlie. It's kind of weird now he's dead. I feel guilty sometimes, for not missing him. They made me dredge up all this shit, from what they said was the basement of my memory, it helped to solve the riddle of why Charlie was like he was. So in the end neither of us were to blame, I suppose.

    It's much easier to concentrate without him. They gave me books to study, said they thought I was smart enough for university. My mind feels like it's had a massive spring clean which made room for the thoughts to flow freely, for the facts to sink in. Today I studied poetry and a certain passage stood out.

    'And though it in the center sit,
Yet when the other far doth roam,
It leans, and harkens after it,
And grows erect, as that comes home.'

    Poets are funny, it's hard to get what they're trying to tell you most of the time, but I can see now why I liked it, it reminded me of Charlie. However much I tried to leave him behind, he always knew how to find me, it was in his nature, so was meant to be. It blows my mind to think that John Donne, a dead old poet understood more about life than all the doctors and nurses put together. I wonder if that's why people buy her books, because even though the words don't really make sense, they can remind you of something deep inside, something that other people want you to forget.

    Now he's gone, the scars have almost gone too. They say I was trying to mask the pain, but they didn't know him, did they, he was the fucking pain.

'Marnie ... You're leaving us tomorrow.' She smiles, a bit to brightly for my liking, can't wait to get rid of me, the bitch. 'We've got you some things together, clothes and the suchlike, your sister sent some money.'

'Am I leaving alone, I'm not going with anybody, I refuse to -'

'We've spoken about this, haven't we ... Your knee is better, but the trauma you've experienced means you still need a degree of supervision.'

'So who is it, who's coming for me.'

'They haven't told me, but your sister has authorised it, so you don't need to worry.'

I wake early. It's Henri, I'm sure of it. My plan is to leave with him, then make my escape, my sister has put some money in an account for me. As I brush my hair in the mirror, a shiny, new version of myself stares back.

'We're all going to miss you.' I want to believe her, but of course I don't. 'He's waiting in the discharge lounge, can't wait to see you. A real gentleman, says you're like a daughter to him.'

It's Henri for sure, taken them in with his false charm, a wolf in a well cut suit. He's sitting in the corner, it's not Henri, but a thin man in sweat pants and an odd looking jumper, as I cross the room, there's something familiar about the way he's slumped in the chair, fiddling with his hair.

'Stuey ... I didn't recognise you, what on earth have you got on, you look awful, so bloody skinny and what have you done to your hair.' He laughs, displaying a hole where one of his front teeth used to be. 'What are you doing here, I think she's sent Henri to collect me, I don't want to -'

'Marnie, let me look at you ... You look amazing, they've been looking after you, that's plain to see ... Henri's not coming ... It's me ... I want you to come home with me, Hesther said it's ok, she wanted -'

The relief is so intense, I have to sit down.

'You mean home to England, but where will we, I mean where will I -'

'It's a surprise.' He looks ten years older than when we first met, like a substandard version of an older brother. 'They say you're a little delicate, need looking after.' He smells sort of fusty, like the clothes I used to buy from the charity shop in Chelmney. It's quite clear he's the one who needs looking after, not me.

As we drive he tells me about ending up on the streets, seeking help, finding a job, getting a small council house, where we're both going to live. We don't mention her or the baby, and that suits me fine. They got me a passport, at the hospital, so we sit together on the ferry, sipping hot chocolates until I fall asleep with my head on his shoulder.

It's dark when we arrive, he still won't tell me where we're going, but just being back in England is enough, even if he dropped me here at the side of the road, it would be fine.

'I've enrolled you at a local college, so you can finish your last year properly.'

'Is it Chelmney ... The house, is it in -'

'I don't think either of us would want to go back there, would we.'

The first time I see the sign, I know.

'When I applied for a council house they asked me if I had any connection with a certain part of the country. I told them my step daughter would be starting at Oxford university in a years time. I thought you might like to get to know the place, before you start your degree.'

I can't believe what he said, this is the best day of my life, for the first time ever, I'm actually somebody's daughter.

Chapter 72

Stuart

She amazes me on a daily basis. Her total dedication to her education. Oxford cast its sweet spell over both of us. The smell of youth in the air, dramatic architecture, tinkling of bicycle bells, the gentle flow of the river. The place is designed for personal improvement, so we both spend our days striving to be better, more worthy people.

When I collected her from the hospital, it was like a deep calm had settled somewhere deep inside her. I thought she'd be disappointed to find out it was me she was going home with, but she seemed relieved, happy even. We take care of each other now. I soon found out I needed her every bit as much as she needed me.

When she started university, I expected her to move into halls, immerse herself in the student experience. To save her from the guilt of telling me, I took the lead, said it was the right thing to do. She cried like a baby, clung to me like a limpet for the rest of the evening.

So nearly four years on, we're still here in our little terrace, a bedroom each, a cosy sitting room and a small but functional kitchen and bathroom. At first it was a challenge, seeing so much of Hesther in her, searching for fragments of Sarah, but over time they both faded away, and now it's just Marnie. She calls me dad. I can't remember when it started, but it seems perfectly natural now, so I refer to her as my daughter.

It was surprisingly easy to find Joshua. I was somewhat fearful at first, that his presence in her life would upset our carefully crafted equilibrium. She demanded I went with her to meet him. His physical resemblance to Sarah knocked me sideways for a few moments, but from the first minute, it was clear to see his connection to Marnie was seamless, a bond deeper than blood, almost spiritual in its intensity. The jealousy came as a shock, I'd had her all to myself for so long, but thankfully it didn't last. Josh pulled me in with his wit and wisdom, it was obvious the family who purchased him from Ron and Mary had made an excellent job of bringing him up.

He was right here, under our very noses in Oxford, graduated a year ago with a first in human biology, works as a research assistant for one of the colleges. Marnie's pride when she's with him dances like diamonds in her eyes. To her, he's God, and I gratefully accept second place for her affections.

It's less than three weeks until her graduation ceremony. She graduated with a first in psychology, and when she opened her results letter, I thought I would die with pride and love. Not the brittle love of a school boy crush, love which would have disintigrated years ago, had it not been held in the aspic of time. This is real love, love that heals, forgives, seals our lives together forever. She threw her arms around my neck and we both cried. Then I took her and Josh out for steak dinners, and our joy was echoed in his eyes. She said it was the second best day of her life, I never plucked up the courage to ask her about the best day.

The time is fast approaching when she'll leave me. She's a capable young woman now, nothing like the vulnerable girl I brought back from France. She says I saved her, but she's wrong, it was her who saved me. She's my purpose in life, I work, prepare meals, clean the house, pay the bills. The question is, will I be strong enough to do it for myself, when she goes. We don't speak of the past anymore, she says her life started again on the day I rescued her.

A few weeks ago, Josh started dating a fellow research assistant called Pete. I was terrified she'd take it badly, but to my relief she was thrilled for her brother. We haven't met Pete, so she's invited them both to her ceremony, the one day she says she's been waiting for her whole life.

Chapter 73

Marnie

Some girls dream about their wedding. Some of the girls at the home used to keep scrapbooks, stupid pictures torn out of magazines, the pop star they were going to marry, the style of dress they wanted. It was tragic, really, if they'd put half as much effort into school work, they could have ended up like me, rather than with some deadbeat boy and a trail of babies chaining them to the kitchen sink.

I'm never getting married, never even getting a boyfriend. When dads walk their daughters down the aisle, they call it giving them away. My dad's never going to give me away, not in a million years, I wouldn't let him, even if he wanted to. Today I'm going to walk onto a stage, all by myself, with my dad and my brother watching. This is my day, but it's their's as well. It's the three of us now, so when something happens to one of us, it happens to us all. I deserve today, for all the hard work and determination I've put in, no bride can say that, can they.

Dad's making breakfast, my favourite, bacon and eggs with loads of toast. I feel a bit nervous, but there's nothing to be nervous about, is there, it's not like when you're getting married and the other person might not turn up. The doorbell rings, we're not expecting Joshy for ages. The bouquet is huge, tied with a red ribbon. The smell makes me nauseous, takes me back to somewhere I've been trying to forget. There's a tiny envelope buried in the flowers.

'Are they from Josh, he's such a thoughtful boy.'

As I read the card, my skin prickles with anger. Just like her to try and spoil my day. How does she know where we are, that I'm graduating today.

'No, Dad … Listen … Dearest Marnie, Beautiful blooms for my beautiful sister on her graduation day … I hope you think of me often, with love.'

Dad rips up the card, takes the flowers out back and throws them in the bin. Then we carry on as if they never came. I bought myself a new dress and shoes with heels. I never wear heels, been having nightmares about falling over on the stage. Dad's got a new suit. He looks better now, put on weight, goes to the barbers. Joshy'll look amazing, he always does. He's so stylish, always on at me to make more of an effort, but dad wouldn't mind if I wore a bin liner.

Joshy's parents live in Scotland, they're loaded, own a whole estate, not a council estate like the one we live on, but a country estate, with people who work for them and horses. He wants me to meet them, but I'm not so sure. I've told him some things about Sarah, but I didn't really know her much more than he did. They told him he was adopted when he was a kid, he's always asking me about the home, but I don't like talking about it, not to him, it seems wrong leaving out the parts about Charlie. Even though I've got Joshy now, sometimes I miss Charlie. Joshy has his own life, with Charlie it was different.

Dad starts to cry as I come down in my gown. The doorbell rings, Joshy hands me a bottle of real Champagne, he looks like a film star in his suit. Pete is stunning, dark skin smooth as ebony, looks like he lives in the gymn. He hold out a hand to me, I go to take it, but he changes his mind, takes me in his muscular arms for the biggest hug I've ever been given. If he wasn't my brother's boyfriend, I'd have a serious crush on him.

'Marnie, this is Pete ... Wow, you look amazing, graduating suits you ... You don't scrub up too badly either Stuart.'

I swear dad blushes, he always seems in awe when Joshy's around.

'Well Marnie.' His voice is like honey. 'You are every bit as beautiful as Joshua promised, and brains too, just like your brother.'

He talks like he went to Eton, like a newsreader off the telly. I hope Joshy hasn't told him about Brimfield and the home, he probably thinks I'm some kind of charity case. But I'm here, aren't I, graduating at Oxford, so I'm just as good as him no matter where I grew up. Dad's putting tea bags into the big pot, the one we only use for special occasions. Pete shakes his hand, says our kitchen's nice. It's tiny, decades old, and although dad does his best, could do with a bloody good clean.

'Look, the Champagne is chilled ... Let's swap tea for bubbles ... After all this is my sister's big day ... The culmination of years of slog ... And that's just Stuart.'

We laugh, although it's not really funny.

'We don't have any glasses, we don't usually entertain ... Do we Marnie -'

Dad looks embarrassed, I don't know why, it's not as if we're in the habit of drinking Champagne for breakfast, is it.

'We can use the cups ... It all goes down the same way, doesn't it ... I've never understood all the fuss ... Different glasses for different drinks, and all that.'

I'm pretty sure that whatever he says, Pete has never drunk Champagne out of a Mickey Mouse mug. It goes straight to my head. Joshy is driving, so he only takes a few sips. Dad and Pete finish the bottle. Some of the neighbours come out to offer their congratulations, dad look like he's going to burst with pride. I love it when he's happy, he deserves this day as much as I do, working as a builder to pay the bills, doing the housework to the best of his ability, cooking most of my meals. I've seen other students coming into lecture halls hung over, discussing last nights parties. For me none of that mattered, I was more than happy to spend my evenings with dad, and he was happy to spend his with me.

As we get into Joshy's car, I start to feel a bit panicky. I've been waiting so long for this, but now it's here something feels wrong, somehow.

'Are you alright Marnie.' Joshy always knows when there's something wrong with me, usually before I do. 'It's only natural to be nervous, I was ... And I didn't even have you with me, did I.'

But he had his rich parents with him, didn't he, parents who wanted him, brought him up on a fucking country estate. I've got dad, but it's not the same, he only ended up with me because of her.

He whispers from the grave, soft and sweet, in that way he knows I can't resist. I tell him to go away, leave me alone, like they told me at the hospital. I tell him he's dead, he's had his life, it's my turn now. The problem is, I don't really mean it, and he can tell. There's no one on earth who knows me as well as Charlie knows me.

Chapter 74

Stuart

I worry about her. I worry about us both. We cling together, like two survivors on a life raft. Finding Josh helped a bit, but Josh has friends, his own family, a job, and now a boyfriend. We only have each other, and it pains me to say, I'm largely to blame. I should've encouraged her more, to go out, make friends, join clubs, do the things that young women of her age should be doing. Today she'll get her degree, confirmation that she's a scholar, but that's not enough, it's just a piece of paper. She's missed out on student life, precious years she'll never get back. She would be here today without me, of that I'm sure. But the question is, would I be here without her.

It was the flowers. They unnerved us. We're trying, but this isn't the day we planned. Hesther delivered the past into our home, and we're drowning in it. As he calls out her name, I forget to breathe. She walks slowly, clinging on to every second of the experience. Almost at the stage, she stops, searches the audience for our faces. I can't help it but stand up and wave wildly at her, breaking all graduation ceremony etiquette. She sees me and it's enough, she can continue. As the man in the gown hands her the scroll, Josh flashes away next to me with his expensive camera. She looks so small, so alone, that I can hardly bare to watch. Before she begins her return journey, she stumbles slighty, then ups her pace and disappears into a dark sea of graduates.

The remainder of the ceremony drags by. I want to be with her, hold her, tell her again how proud I am. It's finally over. Now we have to locate her through the crowds. If I'd known it would be this packed, so many people, I'd have arranged a meeting place. The air's potent with youthful joy, elation, voices raised to fever pitch. The three of us fight our way through the throngs, searching for one familiar face amongst the masses.

Eventually the crowd starts to disperse, each group drifting away to celebrate at their chosen location. Josh is with me, but there's no sign of Pete. We've arranged for photos in the courtyard of her college, before a picnic by the river.

'We've lost Pete.'

'It's ok Stuart, he know about the photos, he'll probably just make his own way there. He must have got swept away in the crowd.'

She's sitting alone on the grass, there's no sign of Pete. Josh looks concerned.

'Marnie ... Thank God you're here, have you seen Pete, we lost him in the crowd, but I told him we were coming here before the picnic.'

'I'm sure he'll be fine ... Catch up with us later.'

She looks more like her old self, the nerves of this morning evaporated into the cloudless sky. All the thousands of students who've studied here over the years, and now my little girl has joined the hallowed ranks.

'You were amazing Sis, handled yourself like a pro. Now let's get some pictures ... I'm sure Pete won't be long, he knows Oxford like the back of his hand.'

She kicks off her shoes, and barefoot on the manicured lawn, flings her arms around my neck.

'It's perfect Dad ... Let's get one of the three of us, your camera has a timer, doesn't it Joshy.'

He takes shot after shot as she flings her cap in the air, poses like a model, pulls a series of silly faces to make us laugh, but keeps glancing at his Rolex, clearly worried by Pete's absence.

'He must have gone straight to the river ... Take a couple of me and Marnie, Stuart, then I think we should go.'

She refuses to take off her gown, even though it's sweltering, so we keep our jackets on and suffer together for the cause. On our way we call into the deli to collect the hamper I ordered weeks ago. She chose the spot for our picnic. We discovered it on our first week here, a sweep of mossy grass stretching down to the Cherwell, dotted with trees for shade, and an ancient jetty complete with rotting rowing boat at the water's edge. There's no sign of Pete, the place is deserted, I can just about make out a solitary figure on a bridge downstream.

'I should go back to the hall ... Perhaps he got confused ... About the exact spot.'

'He'll be fine Joshy ... He's probably just gone home ... It must have been a bit boring for him, I mean he doesn't really know me or anything, does he.'

Josh looks unsure, but he knows how much this means to her, so shakes out the blanket, pulls Marnie down with him, opens a bottle of Champagne from the hamper and pours an inch of golden foam into three crystal glasses.

'To my genius sister.'

As we chink glasses, a rowing boat glides past, skimming the water as if it's on ice. A solitary swan darts out of harm's way. This morning's flowers are forgotten, the sun is high in the early afternoon sky, days don't get much more perfect than this. Finally she throws off her gown, tears a chunk of bread from a soft white loaf, runs down to the water and offers it to the grateful swan. Me and Josh discard our jackets and roll up our shirt sleeves, desperate for some respite from the sun. The hamper cost a small fortune, but it's worth every penny. She sets it out carefully; a whole side of salmon with cucumber slices for scales, chunky slices of beef and ham, three fresh loaves, a punnet of juicy strawberries, bowl of green salad, selection of local cheeses, homemade scones with clotted cream, a bottle of Champagne and two decent bottles of wine.

'This is amazing Dad ... The ceremony was ok, but this is way better ... Just the three of us and all this food.'

'It's strange ... Pete ... He was looking forward to today as much as I was ... Or so he said ... I really like him ... I hope he doesn't think I abandoned him.'

'He'll be fine Joshy ... Let's just enjoy the rest of the day ... You can catch up with him tomorrow.'

The food is delicious, Josh is driving, so me and Marnie go overboard with the wine. We rarely drink, so soon get slightly under the influence. She tells Josh about our night in Aix, leaving out a few unwanted details. She's already told him how we met, I was scared he'd react badly, but he saw the funny side to our escapade. He glances at his watch, but we both understand today ends when Marnie says it does, and not a minute sooner.

The air grows cooler, we put on our jackets, and reluctantly she says it's time to go.

'Come back to ours Joshy ... We can eat the leftovers for supper.'

We begin the trek back to the car.

'I'd love to ... But I want to phone Pete ... I'm worried about him.'

Josh needs some help, Marnie can be extremely persuasive when she wants something, and she always wants to spend more time with her brother.

'It's been a long day, Marnie ... Perhaps Josh could bring Pete round for supper tomorrow, the food will keep, we can have another celebration.'

'Will you both stop going on about Pete ... Pete that, Pete the other ... He's a grown man, isn't he, I'm sure he can find his own way home ... Anyone would think this was his day, not mine.'

She's had too much wine, she's tired and emotional.

'Marnie, love ... Josh is only saying, he's sorry we lost Pete in the -'

'Pete, Pete, Pete ... Bloody amazing Pete ... You hardly know him Joshua ... Does he know about our mother, that she was insane ... No, I bet you've only told him about your brilliant parents, living on a country estate ... He probably can't bear to be near me ... Someone who grew up in a children's home ... Probably wants you all to himself.' I've never heard her like this, not since she was discharged from hospital. 'Why don't you take him to meet your parents, instead of me ... He's way more impressive ... You know they could've taken us both ... Your precious parents ... But no, they left me to rot, split us up, and I bet that's what Pete's going to do now ... Your fucking parents are as much to blame as our grandparents ... Your perfect parents fed me to the wolves, just like everyone else did ... Even my own sister hated me ... Of course if she ever met you, she'd think you were the best thing ever ... And perfect Pete of course ... And what did I end up with, being taken in by a man who was living in the gutter and only got a fucking council house because of me ... Just admit it Stuart, you never wanted me either, did you, you only took me in to get a house

... Everything was about Hesther ... It still is, isn't it, you only want me because I'm related to her, I look like her ... There was only one person who ever loved me, he's dead, and it's my fault.'

We fall silent, the air thick with dread. Does she really think that boy Claude loved her more than we do. It's the drink talking, I know that, but there must be some truth behind her words. We reach the car, Josh breaks the stalemate.

'Look, Marnie, it's been a long day ... You'll feel better in the morning ... Let's get you home and you can sleep it off.'

He pulls up I front of our house. This is the first time I've seen him lost for words, she's never so much as raised her voice in front of him before. A car pulls up a little way behind us, but no one gets out.

'It was my fault ... For ordering all that wine in the hamper ... I know you didn't mean it ... Say goodnight to Josh and I'll make you a mug of hot chocolate before bed.'

She stays rooted to her seat, bats wildly with her hands, as if she's trying to fight off a swarm of wasps.

'Why can't you leave me alone ... You've ruined everything ... Again ... I wanted you back, but you only ever want to punish me, I hate -'

She's blaming me, and she's right, I've ruined what should have been her brightest day.

'Marnie, love, I'm sorry ... I never meant to do anything but spoil you, give you the best day I could ... A perfect day ... I love you, in my heart you are my daughter, I know we don't have much, I can't give you what Josh's parents can give him, but I truly try to -'

My voice breaks up, the tears come out in force, she's not as strong as I thought she was, and it's my fault, for keeping her too close, for not encouraging her to fly.

Her voice lowers to a whisper.

'Not you Dad ... I didn't mean you ... You could never ruin anything, even if you tried ... It was my fault ... I couldn't let him go ... Not forever, and he knew it, so he came back. It's just the two of us now, like it used to be, he won't have it any other way. I love you Dad ... Joshy ... But it's over, you have to let me go ... Charlie won, he always wins, in the end, anyway.'

Epilogue

She watches them embrace. Three people that make up her world. The girl throws her cap high into the sky, as the boy positions the camera lense for the perfect shot. The man laughs, like he's the luckiest man in the world. She tries to keep still so they won't see her, but the three of them are lost in their own private world.

She moved to Rome. Thought the city would enrobe her in its ancient glory. Instead the pace of life annoyed her, a deep hole grew in her heart, until there was only one thing big enough to fill it. She used to think of people as characters, transient, peripheral to her own existence. She knows better now. The boy intrigues her, he looks a lot like someone she used to know.

Her father taught her from a tender age that feelings were for the weak and uninitiated. He made sure she was never going to be one of the ordinary people. She loved her father deeply, but could see he was a monster in a well cut suit.

Her last book failed to sell. The critics said it was out of kilter with current sensibilities, so she's working on a new story, one that's opening up right here, in front of her very eyes. This one will be her masterpiece, the one she'll be remembered forever for.

From the old stone bridge, she watches as the girl and boy play fight. She's not near enough to make out their faces, but she knows the contours of the man's better than she knows her own. They need her. She's the linchpin, the glue that holds them together.

She never went to university. Never had a day like this. Her father hid her away, said she was in danger, but she knew full well the only danger was him. To compensate for life, she made up her own set of people, people she could manipulate, people who could not exist without her, people she could wipe off the page with a flourish of her pen.

They stay all afternoon, basking in the sun, sitting close together, eating, laughing, drinking. When they leave, she goes home to a small flat in town. The kettle boiled, she sits at her desk, taps the keys, slowly at first, building up to a dramatic crescendo.

This morning there were four instead of three. She watched the girl bask in her moment of glory. The hall was full, crowds of people trying to make their exit, all at the same time. The dark skinned boy stopped to greet a friend, and the other two drifted away on the sea of humanity. He smiled at her, before she uttered a word. She said she was Marnie's long lost aunt, here to surprise her, and what could he say, the evidence was right there in front of him. They left together, heading to the college courtyard, taking a shortcut along the river bank. He said he was Joshua's boyfriend, pleased to meet another member of his family.

She smiled, complimented him, quickly gained his trust. He confided in her, said he was glad to get it off his chest. Himself and Joshua had been offered a two year research post in America. Joshua was unsure, because of Marnie, his twin, the sister he'd only just met, but Pete was trying to persuade him, said Marnie could visit, it was only two years of their lives.

It was quick. She keeps it with her at all times now, wrapped in a silk scarf at the bottom of her bag. Henri explained the benefits of a silencer, many moons ago. She was right, she rolls his name around her tongue, Joshua. She tried with Stuart, and with Marnie, but it didn't work out, was too much hard work. With Joshua, it will be different, through Joshua her friend is going to come back to her.

She pours a large glass of wine, she drinks more than she used to, but blames her mother entirely. She dreams of him that night. They're lying on his bed, entwined like knotted rope, his mother downstairs with a bottle of Sherry for company. At that time she used to play to a crowd of one. The girl who was never far behind, used to sit outside her bedroom window, guard over her until she fell asleep, under the tree on which they carved their names and made a pledge never to part. The girl broke her promise, a long time ago. Joshua is hers, Joshua will never leave her. She just has to find a way of extracting him from Marnie. She didn't appreciate Henri enough, he really was the most useful of friends.

www.ingramcontent.com/pod-product-compliance
Lightning Source LLC
Chambersburg PA
CBHW070652120526
44590CB00013BA/923